Human Resource
Strategy

Advanced Topics in Organizational Behavior

The **Advanced Topics in Organizational Behavior** series examines current and emerging issues in the field of organizational behavior. Written by researchers who are widely acknowledged subject area experts, the books provide an authoritative, up-to-date review of the conceptual, research, and practical implications of the major issues in organizational behavior.

Human Resource Strategy

Formulation, Implementation, and Impact

Peter Bamberger
Ilan Meshoulam

Sage Publications, Inc.
International Educational and Professional Publisher
Thousand Oaks ■ London ■ New Delhi

For information:

 Sage Publications, Inc.
2455 Teller Road
Thousand Oaks, California 91320
E-mail: order@sagepub.com

Sage Publications Ltd.
6 Bonhill Street
London EC2A 4PU
United Kingdom

Sage Publications India Pvt. Ltd.
M-32 Market
Greater Kailash I
New Delhi 110 048 India

Printed in the United States of America

Library of Congress Cataloging-in-Publication Data

Bamberger, Peter.
    Human resource strategy: Formulation, implementation, and impact / by
Peter Bamberger and Ilan Meshoulam.
        p. cm.— (Advanced topics in organizational behavior)
    Includes bibliographical references and index.
        ISBN 0-7619-1424-2 (cloth: alk. paper)—ISBN 0-7619-1425-0 (pbk: alk. paper)
1. Personnel management. I. Meshoulam, Ilan. II. Title. III. Series.
    HF5549 .B258 2000
    658.3—dc21   99-050419

This book is printed on acid-free paper.

00 01 02 03 04 05 06 7 6 5 4 3 2

Acquisition Editor: Marquita Flemming
Editorial Assistant: MaryAnn Vail
Production Editor: Sanford Robinson
Editorial Assistant: Victoria Cheng
Typesetter: Rebecca D. Evans
Indexer: Molly Hall

Contents

To our families

Preface

The two of us began studying human resource strategy, albeit independently, over 15 years ago. At the time, one of us (Ilan Meshoulam) was an Israeli working as a senior HR executive in a major American high-tech firm, and the other (Peter Bamberger) was an American consultant working with high-tech start-ups in Israel. Both of us had "experienced" the link between HR practice and firm performance, and both of us were driven to contribute to the effort to further understand the nature of this relationship. Little did we know, at the time, that we were not alone. A small group of HR researchers, many coming from an HR planning orientation and others from an industrial relations tradition, were also beginning to examine the way in which HR could play a more central and strategic role in management.

Since that time, much has been written on the topic of human resource strategy and strategic human resource management. Our primary goal in writing this book was to summarize this body of research. However, given the state of the literature, we felt it necessary to try to go beyond a simple literature review. Consequently, we strove to provide a broad framework for understanding 15 years' worth of often-competing conceptual models and hard-to-reconcile empirical results. The framework that we offer has a definite sociological and industrial relations "flavor." As a result, we believe that our framework may offer a new way to examine the core issues studied by HR strategy researchers. In this sense, we believe that this book will most appeal to an academic audience.

Yet given Lewin's famous remark that "there's nothing as practical as a good theory," we believe that top-level executives engaged in setting business strategy—and not simply HR practitioners—will have much to gain from the framework and research presented here. Although our emphasis is on the results of quantitative empirical research, we draw from our own personal experience with a wide variety of firms (and consequently a diverse set of HR strategies) to provide down-to-earth illustrations of the concepts and issues examined. For practitioners, perhaps the greatest contribution of this book is that it will provide them with a framework for understanding the nature and role of HR strategy in their own organizations. Such an understanding is essential for managers who want to more closely align system-specific strategies with their underlying business strategy and who are interested in better harnessing their organization's human resources in the pursuit of their organization's mission.

As should be clear from the title of this book, *Human Resource Strategy: Formulation, Implementation, and Impact*, we attempt to review and expand on the HR strategy literature in all of its dimensions. Although the focus of the most recent literature has been on establishing the actual impact of HR strategy on the firm's "bottom line," our interest runs deeper. Of course, whereas there is no reason to examine HR strategy if it has little effect, once that effect has been established, it is critical to gain a deeper understanding of the dynamics underlying that effect. Thus, our framework is based on the assumption that one needs to explore how HR strategies are formulated and implemented in organizations and the way in which these strategies—either individually or as a group—can contribute to or detract from firm performance.

What should be clear by the end of our book is that the field of HR strategy is still quite "young" and that there remain many unanswered questions. Furthermore, the development of new organizational forms such as virtual organizations and venture-based alliances (e.g., that between Sun Microsystems and America Online) raise new questions with regard to the "fit" of traditional HR strategies and the nature of newly emerging configurations of HR policies and practices. It is our hope that the theoretical framework presented in this book, combined with a broad review of the research literature, will provide the foundation necessary for further scientific exploration.

The ideas presented in this book reflect the thinking of dozens of researchers and theorists in the fields of human resource management, industrial relations, organizational theory, psychology, and economics. Included among these are those theorists and investigators whose work we cite, as well as those of our colleagues and friends in the practitioner community who "live and breathe" HR strategy on a day-to-day basis. In addition, a number of individuals directly contributed to our own thinking with regard to HR strategy. These include Sam Bacharach, Lee Dyer, and Patrick Wright, all from Cornell's School of Industrial and Labor Relations. We also would like to thank Julian Barling and Kevin Kelloway, the series editors, for encouraging us to write this book, the reviewers for their helpful comments and suggestions, and the editorial staff at Sage for their help in the production process. Finally, it is to our parents, Ursula and Gerald Bamberger and David and Ida Meshoulam; our spouses, Ellen Sisselman Bamberger and Naomi Meshoulam; and our children, Zachary and Sarah Bamberger and Arnon, Judith, and Danna Meshoulam, that we dedicate this book.

1

Introduction

*Over the long run, the influence of human resource management profes-
sions in organizations rises and falls depending on how well they
anticipate and respond to changing external and internal forces
that shape employment relationships.* Kochan (1997, p. 1)

Origins of HR Strategy Research

The nature of human resource management (HRM) has shifted dramatically since its establishment as the discipline of personnel administration in the
first quarter of the 20th century. Emerging from the function of "welfare secre-
tary" at the turn of the century and encouraged by Frederick Taylor's disciples
in the 1920s, personnel management was grounded in the emerging paradigm
of industrial psychology and was viewed as a possible solution to such nagging
problems as worker inefficiency and worker unrest (Barley & Kunda, 1992).
Regarding the former, a core tenet of Taylorism was the notion that work becomes more productive and less arduous when individuals are placed in jobs
appropriate to their abilities and when they are paid fairly. How to match indi-

1

viduals and jobs and ensure that they are paid fairly was viewed by Taylor as a "technical problem" (Barley & Kunda, 1992, p. 371), one to be resolved by the emergent personnel function. For example, applying the scientific approach demanded by Taylor, personnel workers used new testing technologies to rationally select and place employees. Regarding worker unrest, personnel directors offered a new approach to employee relations grounded on the use of entitlements to solidify workers' allegiance to their employer. The personnel function became the locus of all activities having to do with employee relations and eventually contract administration.

The scope of these technical activities widened over the decades, with new functions and technologies added with every shift in managerial thought and discourse (Barley & Kunda, 1992). For example, during the height of the human relations movement (1930s–1950s), personnel directors widened their package of services to include management development (as a conflict avoidance mechanism) and collective bargaining, industrial due process, and labor-management collaboration (to structure and manage labor conflict). With the upsurge of operations research and systems rationalization in the 1960s and 1970s, personnel directors offered new technical services in the field of work redesign, job evaluation, personnel needs forecasting and planning, and performance appraisal systems design (e.g., management by objectives).

However, in the face of increased global competition and the demands for both cost-efficiency and quality in the 1980s, personnel management was at a crossroads. Since its establishment, the personnel function had based its legitimacy and influence on its ability to buffer an organization's core technology from uncertainties stemming from a heterogeneous workforce, an unstable labor market, and a militant union movement. Yet by the 1980s, managers had become less concerned with these technical sources of uncertainty and were paying greater attention to issues of quality, agility, and unique competencies as sources of competitive advantage. Indeed, by the early 1980s, the strategic management of human resources and the design of "strong" organizational cultures had become the focus of attention for a number of extremely influential management consultants and applied researchers (e.g., Deal & Kennedy, 1982; Ouchi, 1981; Peters & Waterman, 1982). These writers viewed the effective management of human resources as the key to ensuring quality and a critical source of competitive advantage. For example, one of Peters and Waterman's (1982) "Eight Attributes" was "productivity through people," which called for "treating the rank and file as the root source of quality and productivity gain" and "looking at human resources rather than capital investment as the fundamental source of efficiency improvement" (p. 14).

Not surprisingly, by the mid-1980s, an increasing number of HR researchers (e.g., Beer, Spector, Lawrence, Mills, & Walton, 1985; Dyer, 1983, 1985; Fombrun, Tichy, & Devanna, 1984) were calling for the personnel function to take on a more strategic or business role. Tyson (1987) called for the replacement of two traditional personnel models—in which the personnel director was the "clerk of works" (i.e., an administrative function responsible for the provision of pay, benefits, and employee welfare services) and/or the "contracts manager" (i.e., employee relations expert)—with a new, "architect" model. According to this architect model, personnel would return the responsibility for people management (e.g., appraisal, individual counseling) back to line managers and would instead focus on aligning the firm's human resource system with its business strategy. According to Wright and McMahan (1992), two important dimensions distinguish such a strategic approach to HRM from the more traditional practices of personnel management described above. First, "it entails the linking of human resource management practices with the strategic management process of the organization" (p. 298). That is, it calls for the consideration of HR issues as part of the business strategy formulation. Second, it places an emphasis on finding a synergy (or at least a certain degree of congruency) among various HR practices and ensuring that these practices are aligned with the needs of the business as a whole. Not surprisingly, this approach to HRM has been labeled *strategic human resource management* or *SHRM* (p. 298).

Conceptual Issues

Despite the increasing amount of attention paid to SHRM and HR strategy in recent years, researchers have failed to clarify the precise meaning of these two important concepts. Several scholars have noted that this lack of conceptual clarity has complicated both theory development and testing. One key definitional issue concerns the degree to which one or the other of these two terms relates to a process or an outcome. For example, Wright and McMahan (1992) defined SHRM as an outcome: "the pattern of planned HR deployments and activities intended to enable a firm to achieve its goals" (p. 298). Similarly, Snell, Youndt, and Wright (1996) viewed SHRM as "organizational systems designed to achieve sustainable competitive advantage through people" (p. 62).

Others (e.g., Truss & Gratton, 1994; Ulrich, 1997) disagreed. Ulrich (1997) described SHRM as "the process of linking HR practices to business strategy" (p. 189). According to Ulrich, this process involves the identification of those HR capabilities required to implement business strategy and the adoption of those HR practices and policies designed to secure those capabilities. For Ulrich, HR strategy is the outcome: that is, the agenda for the HR system, defining "the mission, vision and priorities of the HR function" (p. 190). In the sections below, we attempt to clear up some of the confusion with respect to these key constructs in the SHRM literature.

Business Strategy

Business strategy concerns the long-term direction and goals of a firm and the broad formula by which that firm attempts to acquire and deploy resources in order to secure and sustain competitive advantage (Faulkner & Johnson, 1992; Porter, 1980). Drawing from military science, management scholars (Mintzberg, 1990; Quinn, 1988) have come to define business strategy in terms of the set of organizational goals that business leaders attempt to achieve (i.e., ends) and the policies (i.e., means) by which these leaders attempt to position the firm and its resources in relation to the firm's environment, competitors, and key stakeholders) in order to maximize the potential for goal attainment (Porter, 1980).

According to Chakravarthy and Doz (1992), there are two key subfields of business strategy research. The first, policy or "content" research, focuses on the link between a wide variety of organizational parameters (e.g., structure, positioning, technology) and performance and the way in which this relationship may be moderated by a variety of environmental contingencies. Much of the research in this subfield is grounded on the seminal work of Chandler (1962) and his basic proposition that environmental (e.g., technological) contingencies shape organizational strategies, which in turn determine organizational structure. In contrast, process research examines the formulation and implementation of these policies as well as their dynamics over time and their impact on the firm's "bottom line." Much of the process research literature is grounded on the work of Galbraith and Nathanson (1978), who argued that the key to implementation is the realignment of core organizational systems (e.g., finance, marketing, operations, HRM).

These issues of strategy formulation and the link between implementation and firm performance are themes that we will constantly encounter throughout this book. For example, as we will describe in Chapter 2, there continues to be a debate as to the role of human resource strategy in the formulation of business strategy. As we will discuss in Chapter 7, the link between HR strategy and business strategy may have critical implications for firm performance.

HR Strategy

Consistent with the strategy literature (Miles & Snow, 1978; Mintzberg, 1978), we conceptualize HR strategy as an outcome: the pattern of decisions regarding the policies and practices associated with the HR system. Implicit in this definition are two core assumptions (Bamberger & Fiegenbaum, 1996). First, we assume that the focus of attention needs to be on the HR *system*, not the HR *function*. The HR system is one of numerous organizational systems (e.g., finance system, marketing system), each of which play a role in the formulation of organizationwide strategies and each of which is composed of function-specific subsystems (Bamberger & Fiegenbaum, 1996). In the case of HR, these subsystems are focused on staffing and development, appraisal and rewards, and employee relations (i.e., work systems design and workforce governance). Although in many organizations the HR function has primary responsibility for the implementation of decisions having to do with each of these subsystems, other functional units, along with the human resource function, may play an important role in making the decisions in the first place, as well as in implementing them.

Second, we assume that it is impossible to understand the nature of HR strategy without taking both intraorganizational politics and environmental/institutional contingencies into account (Bamberger & Phillips, 1991). Consequently, we recognize that there is likely to be a difference between a firm's "espoused" HR strategy and its "emergent" strategy. This assumption is based on the recognition that strategy at any level and regarding any organizational system is rarely if ever the outcome of a rational, explicit, and top-down process. Instead, it is a negotiated order (Strauss, Schatzman, Ehrlich, Bucher, & Sabshin, 1963), shaped by the political maneuvering of those interests and institutions likely to be affected by the outcomes of the strategic decision-making process.

Espoused HR strategy is therefore the pattern of HR-related decisions made but not necessarily implemented. It is often explicated as part of "corporate philosophy" or included as a central component of a managerial mission statement. For example, Analog Devices' (1993) corporate philosophy focuses first on its employees and only then on its customers, stockholders, and other stakeholders:

> Our corporate goals are thus best achieved in an environment that encourages
> and assists employees in the achievement of their personal goals while helping
> Analog Devices achieving its goals. We therefore seek to offer our employees
> a challenging and stable work environment where they can earn above average
> compensation for above average performance and contribution to the com-
> pany. Our policy is to share Analog Devices' success with the people who
> made it possible.

In contrast, the emergent HR strategy is the pattern of HR-related decisions that, although perhaps never made explicit, have in fact been applied: that is, the gestalt of negotiated people-related policies and practices in use. Whereas the analysis of espoused HR strategy focuses on the prospective claims of management with respect to desired ends and means, the analysis of emergent HR strategy requires a retrospective orientation and the induction of ends and means on the basis of those policies and practices actually in use.

Strategic Human Resource Management

We view SHRM as a competency-based approach to the management of personnel focused on the development of durable, imperfectly imitable, and nontradable people resources. Developing resources with such characteristics is the key to sustainable competitive advantage (Barney, 1991), particularly because people are the key "competence carriers" of organizations (Prahalad & Hamel, 1990, p. 87). As an approach to the process of people management in organizations, SHRM is not unrelated to HR strategy. Indeed, the formulation and enactment of an HR strategy designed to "link HR policies and practices with the strategic goals and objectives of the firm" (Truss & Gratton, 1994, p. 663) is a key element of SHRM. Thus, if SHRM is the process by which organizations seek to link the human, social, and intellectual capital of their members to the strategic needs of the firm, espoused HR strategy is the road map that organizational leaders use to secure that link, and emergent HR strategy is the road actually traveled.

The Role of HR Strategy in Strategic Management

That both HR practitioners and researchers have embraced this strategic approach to HRM is beyond dispute. Why the shift in orientation? From a rational choice perspective, it makes sense for any organizational function to shift its attention to those activities that are likely to provide the organization with the greatest possible return.

Rational Choice Theories

Indeed, a number of theories support such a perspective (Jackson & Schuler, 1995). For example, based on the assumption that employee behaviors are key to successful strategy implementation, *behavioral role theory* (Katz & Kahn, 1978) suggests that by aligning HR policies and practices with firm strategy, employees will be better able to "meet the expectations of role partners within the organization (i.e., supervisors, peers, subordinates), at organizational boundaries (e.g., customers), and beyond (i.e., family and society)" (Jackson & Schuler, 1995, p. 239).

Resource-based theory (Barney, 1991; Prahalad & Hamel, 1990) suggests that resources that are rare, inimitable, and nonsubstitutable provide sources of sustainable competitive advantage for the organization. Several researchers argue that, if strategically managed, a firm's "human resource deployments" have the potential to meet these conditions and thus provide the firm with an advantage in terms of its human, social, and intellectual capital (Nahapiet & Ghoshal, 1998; Wright & McMahan, 1992).

Similarly, *human capital theory* (Becker, 1964) suggests that because the knowledge, skills, and abilities that people bring to organizations have economic value to organizations, they need to be managed in the same strategic manner that other economic assets (e.g., land, machinery) are managed. Students of human resource accounting (Cascio, 1991; Flamholtz & Lacey, 1981) draw from human capital theory to generate utility models of HRM.

Transaction cost theories (Williamson, 1981) suggest that the adoption of a strategic approach to HRM can minimize the costs involved in controlling internal organizational exchanges. These costs stem from the need to establish, monitor, and enforce a "myriad of implicit and explicit contracts between employers and employees" designed to protect the organization from member self-interest and opportunism (Jackson & Schuler, 1995, p. 242). In theory, the adoption of a strategic approach to HRM should allow a firm to adopt more streamlined governance systems (such as those characteristic of firms with highly developed internal labor markets) when the nature of the work process is such that employee loyalty and/or firm-specific knowledge, skills, and abilities are highly valued (Baron & Kreps, 1999). Such an approach should also facilitate the decision to maximize efficiencies by competing in the external labor market when such firm-specific skills are not required.

Finally, on the basis of similar assumptions, *agency theory* (Eisenhardt, 1989) also suggests that a strategic approach to HRM is likely to provide significant returns to the firm. Given the inefficiencies inherent in monitoring and rewarding employees' (i.e., agents') compliance with the implicit and explicit contracts typical in employment contexts, agency theory proposes that through the strategic alignment of agent and principal (i.e., employer) interests, employment relations and systems can be streamlined. In recent years, the application of agency theory has been most apparent with regard to strategic compensation practices and, in particular, the widespread adoption of variable or performance-based pay practices.

Constituency-Based Theories

However, it is just as likely that HR practitioners and researchers have embraced SHRM out of a constituency-based interest. At least in the United States, as Wright, McMahan, McCormick, and Sherman (1998) noted, "The HR function has been neither traditionally viewed nor empirically demonstrated to contribute to firm performance, and has therefore been viewed as neither important nor effective" (p. 17). This is reflected in the level of compensation received by HR executives relative to executives in other staff functions. Moreover, it has created a vicious circle in many firms in which only those contributing to performance are invited to participate in strategic decision making and in which only those participating in strategic decision making are able to maximally contribute to firm performance. The adoption of a strategic approach to HRM may be viewed by some HR managers as an avenue by which to gain legitimacy and respect within the firm as a strategic partner. Similarly, for SHRM researchers, the empirical analysis of the link between HR practices and firm performance may provide an important means by which to secure greater respect for the field of HRM as a whole. Underlying such a constituency-based perspective are two established organizational theories.

The first of these, *institutional theory* (DiMaggio & Powell, 1983; Meyer & Rowan, 1977; Powell & DiMaggio, 1991), suggests that the adoption of any new organizational form or practice stems from an organizational interest in gaining legitimacy and acceptance from key stakeholders as a means to ensure continued survival. As suggested above, in many firms, the adoption of SHRM practices may stem from the coercive pressures exerted by the state (e.g., equal employment opportunity requirements) or the normative pressures exerted by the HR "profession" or the investment community. Mimetic pressures may have led many organizational leaders to follow managerial fads and adopt the SHRM practices of other firms as a way of coping with uncertainty. Indeed, as Abrahamson (1991) noted, imitation is a low-risk way of gaining acceptance and legitimacy.

The second theory, *resource dependence theory* (Pfeffer & Salancik, 1977), is grounded on the notion that organizations and organizational interests gain power over one another by controlling the resources that their constituents are dependent on. Because dependence is the basis of power (Bacharach & Lawler, 1980), those responsible for the human resource system may increase their level of influence in the organization by (a) enhancing the value of human resources to key organizational interests and (b) making other organizational interests dependent on them for ensuring the efficient and timely flow of human resources. A strategic approach to HRM may offer the potential to do both and may therefore offer particular appeal to those HR practitioners looking to gain greater influence in organizational affairs.

Issues of Concern to Students of HR Strategy

Drawing on this interest in SHRM over the past decade, students of HR strategy have focused their attention on three main issues. The first issue concerns the adoption of a strategic approach to HRM and the manner in which HR strategy is formulated. Of interest is not only how an HR strategy should best be formulated but also which organizations are most likely to adopt strategic innovations in HRM—for example, what organizational or environmental characteristics predict the adoption of strategic HR practices. The second issue concerns the content of HR strategy and, in particular, the policies and practices composing different HR strategies. Is it possible to identify unique strategic models? On what dimensions do these models vary, and how does this variance manifest itself in terms of specific HR policies and practices? Finally, SHRM researchers have perhaps paid the most attention to the consequences of HR strategy and particularly the degree to which different HR strategies have an impact on firm performance. Does HR strategy make a difference? Are there certain strategic or "best" practices that, when implemented, have a consistent positive impact on firm performance, or is a positive impact contingent on either the firm's overall strategic profile (external fit) or the "bundling" of these practices into an HR strategy that is internally consistent (internal fit)?

Our objective in this book is to review the research on all three of these issues. Our intent is not to examine each of HRM's core technologies (i.e., recruitment, selection, training) from a strategic perspective. Nor is it to provide a review of the latest research on specific HR practices. Rather, it is to examine whether and how human resources may serve to augment the strategic capability of the firm and how a firm's HR system can strengthen this link between human resources and firm performance. Thus, we take a macro view of HRM and focus our attention on the firm's overall HR system rather than the activities of its HR function. Our intent is not simply to summarize and evaluate the findings of HR strategy research for students of HR and HR practitioners. Rather, it is to provide some new insights into the link between human resources and the competitive activity of organizations, insights that should be meaningful to students of organizational theory, strategy, and HRM, as well as practitioners.

Plan of the Book

As should be clear from the discussion above, HR strategy is a fairly "young" field of research with far more questions than answers. Indeed, as we have noted above, a lack of consensus on basic conceptual issues has complicated the pursuit of systematic theory development, concept operationalization, and hence theory testing. Epistemologically, research reviews serve an important purpose when a subdiscipline reaches such a stage of development. With this purpose in mind, we have structured the book around the three central research issues described above.

We begin with a focus on the formulation and emergence of HR strategy in Chapter 2. Here we contrast a number of normative models of HR strategy formulation offered by HR practitioners with the descriptive models examined by HR researchers. In this chapter, we pay particular attention to the link between firmwide strategy formulation and implementation and HR strategy formulation and implementation, and we explore the role of organizational politics and external context in HR strategy formulation.

In Chapter 3, we go on to examine the various HR strategic models proposed in the literature. Although researchers have proposed a number of alternative strategic typologies, many of these are, at their core, quite similar. Nearly all differentiate among HR strategies on the basis of either the organizational approach to resource acquisition and retention (i.e., external vs. internal orientation) or the organizational approach to system control (i.e., focus on process vs. output). Viewing these two characteristics as orthogonal dimensions of HR strategy, we identify and describe four dominant or core HR strategies: (a) commitment strategy (i.e., internal, output oriented), (b) free-agent strategy (external, output oriented), (c) paternalistic strategy (internal, process oriented), and (d) secondary strategy (external, process oriented).

Viewing an organization's HR system as itself being composed of a number of interrelated, core subsystems "directed at attracting, developing and maintaining a firm's human resources" (Lado & Wilson, 1994, p. 701), in Chapters 4 through 6 we examine subsystem-specific strategies and the "bundles" of HR policies and practices associated with them. Our focus will be on three basic HR subsystems, namely staffing, compensation, and employee relations, and our discussion will be based on the four-part typology of HR strategies described in Chapter 3. Adopting a means-ends approach to our analysis, in each chapter we review the various strategic objectives that a firm might adopt for a subsystem, given its dominant HR strategy (i.e., commitment, free agent, paternalistic, or secondary). We then review the various policies and practices (i.e., means) that, in the context of each dominant strategy, are typically used to achieve subsystem ends.

Chapter 4 focuses on the people flow or staffing subsystem, its objectives of human resource composition and competence, and such HR practices as planning, recruitment and selection, career development and internal labor market structuring, and training and development. We then show how, according to the literature, both staffing ends and means are likely to vary across the four strategic models.

Using a similar analytical approach, in Chapter 5 we focus on the appraisal and rewards subsystem and its objectives of contribution and cost control. Among the practices and policy issues to be examined are job analysis and evaluation, performance appraisal, pay structure and mix, and the use of individual-and/or group-based pay for performance. Again, we examine differences in compensation ends and means across all four dominant strategic types and, drawing on Gerhart and Milkovich (1992), review a number of "best practices" in the realm of compensation.

In Chapter 6, we examine what we refer to as the "employee relations" subsystem. We view the establishment and reinforcement of the psychological contract between employer and employee as the primary objective of this subsystem, and such functions as job design, employee assistance, and dispute resolution as the primary means used to achieve this objective. After reviewing how the application of these functions varies across the four dominant HR strategies, we review the literature on a number of "best practices" in this realm, including team/cell-based work structures, employee participation and involvement, work-family programs, and alternative dispute resolution systems.

Finally, in Chapter 7, we review and evaluate the research on HR strategy's impact on firm performance. First, we evaluate the research exploring the magnitude of the impact of HR strategy on various dimensions of firm performance and discuss the problems inherent in measuring this impact. Second, we focus on the way in which HR strategy affects performance and on the possible moderators of strategy's influence. In the concluding section of this chapter, we discuss several of the key theoretical and operational challenges (e.g., construct measurement) facing researchers in this area, as well as the implications of this research with regard to the analysis and application of strategic HR logics.

2

The Formulation and Emergence of Human Resource Strategies

In the previous chapter, we suggested that a primary area of HR strategy research concerns the adoption of a strategic approach to human resource management (HRM) and the formulation of HR strategy. As we noted in that chapter, of interest is not only which organizations are most likely to adopt strategic innovations in HRM but also how HR strategies tend to be (and might best be) formulated. In this chapter, we will examine both issues. First, we will review studies explaining both the adoption of specific strategic practices (e.g., contingent pay) and the adoption of an overall strategic approach to HRM. By *strategic practices,* we are referring to those innovative HR programs, policies, and activities specifically adopted or designed to more closely align a firm's human resources with its overall strategic objectives. By a *strategic approach to HRM,* we are referring to a managerial logic requiring HR deployments and activities to be tightly aligned with strategic business or organizational objectives. Studies focusing on the adoption of strategic practices or a strategic approach to HR attempt to answer such questions as

- Are high-technology companies more likely than non-high-technology companies to adopt a strategic approach to HRM?
- Is the adoption of strategic HR practices a function of managerial ideology, organizational structure, institutional pressure, market forces, or some combination of each?
- What organizational or environmental characteristics predict the adoption of strategic HR practices?

We will then turn our attention to the normative and descriptive research regarding the formulation of HR strategy. The former attempts to identify ideal strategy formulation processes, and the latter focuses on identifying the processes that are in fact used by organizations when formulating HR strategy. As a whole, these studies address such questions as

- To what degree is the strategy formulation process affected by internal politics?
- To what degree is the strategy formulation process affected by conditions in the organizational environment?
- What is the nature of the relationship between overall firm strategy and HR strategy, and which one serves as an input to the other in the strategy formulation process?

One of the primary concerns in this section will be to contrast two different perspectives regarding the HR strategy formulation process: rational planning versus incrementalism. The chapter will conclude with a discussion of ways to resolve the differences between these two perspectives.

Predicting the Organizational Adoption of a Strategic Approach to HRM

As we saw in Chapter 1, the history of HRM is one of continuous innovation and adaptation. In each phase of its development over the past century, the field of HRM successfully developed and introduced new techniques, practices, and roles designed to allow it, as an institution, to respond to emergent sources of organizational uncertainty (Jacoby, 1985). Thus, for example, sophisticated

Table 2.1 Factors Potentially Associated With the Adoption
of a Strategic Approach to HR

Factor	*Examples*
Environmental	Unionization
	Competition
	Product life cycle
Organizational	Size
	Slack
	Complexity
Institutional	Legislative and regulatory requirements
	Professional norms
	Stakeholder expectations
Technological	Nature of production process
	Degree and type of interdependence

staffing planning methods were developed and introduced at a time (the 1950s) when systems optimization was viewed as a key source of competitive advantage and when institutional shifts in the realm of industrial relations placed new constraints on the ability of managers to respond to changes in market conditions by simply adjusting HR deployments. However, questions remain as to when such HR innovations are introduced and by which organizations.

Drawing on organizational innovation theory (Bamberger, 1991; Demanpour, 1991; Zaltman, Duncan, & Holbeck, 1973), a number of HR researchers have attempted to identify those factors associated with the adoption of a strategic approach to HR management, or at least the adoption of particular strategic HR practices. For example, in a relatively early study examining this issue, Kossek (1987) suggested a number of broad factors (discussed below) likely to account for much of the variance in the adoption of strategic HR practices across organizations. Johns (1993) suggested many of the same but also identified several additional sets of factors. Johns concluded his review of these factors by noting that the technical merit of strategic HR practices is neither necessary nor sufficient for them to be adopted in an organization. As he noted, political and institutional constraints tend to "cloud technical merit as the driving force" in the adoption of such practices (p. 576). Next, we review several of these factors, which are also included in Table 2.1.

Environmental Factors

The first factor listed by Kossek (1987) has to do with external environmental and market (both labor and product) forces. For example, there may be some reason to believe that the extent of unionization is associated with the adoption of strategic HR practices. One study (Goodmeasure, 1985), based on data collected from members of the American Management Association, concluded that strategic HR practices "flourish in either of two conditions: (1) no unionization, or (2) total unionization. . . . The middle ground—a mixture of unionized and nonunionized workers—may be less fertile for workplace innovation" (p. 10). However, Jackson, Schuler, and Rivero (1989) reported that strategic HR practices (e.g., use of productivity-based bonuses, emphasis on employee training and development) are more prevalent in firms with at least some union presence than in firms with no union presence at all. Others argue that the extent of unionization is predictive only of the realm in which strategic HR practices are adopted. For example, Kanter (1984) found that unionized firms were among the earliest to adopt strategic practices in the realm of culture management (e.g., quality-of-work-life interventions) and that nonunionized, high-tech firms were among the first to adopt strategic practices in the realm of staffing. Finally, on the basis of her review of the literature, Kossek (1987) concluded that given the strategic role of labor stability versus unrest in the past, historically, unions predicted the adoption of HR practices that were, at the time, strategic. Nonunion firms were often quick to adopt HR practices that were deemed strategic at the time as a way of maintaining their nonunion status or avoiding labor unrest.

However, Kossek suggested that with the decline of organized labor, the extent of unionization is likely to be a less significant predictor of strategic HRM than in the past. More significant environmental predictors are likely to be those related to threats stemming from the organization's market or economic context. For example, drawing on the experience of U.S. firms in the 1980s, Kossek suggested that the more an organization is exposed to global competition in its product markets, the greater the probability that it will adopt strategic HR practices originating abroad. Johns (1993) came to a similar conclusion, noting that "crisis often makes the relative advantages of innovation salient" and that the adoption of such strategic practices as knowledge-based pay and self-managed work groups "probably reflect economic turbulence rather than recent technical refinement" (p. 580). Empirical support for such a notion has been found by Lawler, Mohrman, and Ledford (1992). Their findings suggest that among Fortune 1000 firms, the implementation of employee involvement practices such as job enrichment and team building was associated with managerial perceptions of shorter product life cycles and increased foreign competition.

Organizational Factors

A second set of factors—structural organizational characteristics such as size, slack, and complexity—are also posited to be predictive of the adoption of strategic HR practices. A number of studies suggest that the presence of slack resources tends to be predictive of the level of financial support available to back the adoption and maintenance of strategic HR practices (Ferris, Schellenberg, & Zammuto, 1984) and consequently of the level of overall HRM innovation (Foulkes, 1980). For example, organizations with slack resources are more likely to employ HR specialists (as opposed to generalists) who may be more aware of the latest innovations in strategic HRM (Fennel, 1984).

Other studies focus on size as a predictor of the adoption of a strategic approach to HR management. In one such study, Jackson et al. (1989) found that a strategic approach to HRM may be more prevalent in smaller organizations. They found that formalized performance appraisals, an emphasis on training and development, and the use of contingent pay were less prevalent in large organizations than in smaller ones. However, the bulk of the research suggests the opposite relationship, with larger firms in a particular industry or organizational field tending to be among the first to adopt a strategic approach to HRM and smaller firms tending to copy them. Bernardin and Klatt (1986) found that larger firms tended to use more state-of-the-art performance appraisal methods than smaller ones. Dobbin, Edeman, Meyer, Scott, and Swidler (1988) found that larger firms tended to be the early adopters of due process and affirmative action programs. More recently, in their Fortune 1000 survey, Lawler et al. (1992) found a positive correlation between organizational size and the adoption of employee involvement practices such as employee stock options, gain sharing, and survey feedback. Kossek (1987) claimed that this may be due to the tendency of HR staff in smaller firms to perform diverse job functions and "to have less time to keep abreast of the latest techniques" (p. 81). Johns (1993) explained that this tendency may stem from two characteristics of larger organizations: (a) Such organizations have complex structures requiring more administrative fine tuning than smaller structures; and (b) such organizations are more visible and thus susceptible to legislative and political pressure to adopt certain HR practices (p. 581).

In addition to their research on organizational size and strategic HR practices, Jackson et al. (1989) examined the impact of horizontal differentiation (as one dimension of organizational complexity) on the adoption of strategic HR practices. Arguing that two alternative ways to departmentalize organizations are by function and by product, they found that although structure predicts the adoption of specific strategic practices, it does not appear to be related to the overall approach taken to HRM. Thus, contingent pay (i.e., bonuses based on productivity) was more prevalent in product-based organizations, whereas greater emphasis was placed on employee training and development in functional organizations.

Institutional Factors

Drawing on institutional theory (DiMaggio & Powell, 1983), Kossek (1987) claimed that the adoption of strategic HR practices is also partially a function of organizational legitimization needs: that is, that the rate of program adoption will be influenced by the need of organizations and their key decision makers to appear more legitimate in their environment. Consequently, a certain level of program adoption is likely to be accounted for by such coercive pressures as state and federal equal employment opportunity requirements. Indeed, Walton (1985) discovered that one of the key factors explaining the variance in the rate of diffusion of strategic HR practices in eight countries was the institutional/legal context. Organizations that fail to adopt the strategic practices required to meet minimal legal requirements may suffer a loss of legitimacy and find their survival threatened. In contrast, organizations may avoid the adoption of strategic practices if they have a questionable legal status or pose a risk to organizational legitimacy. Nike's decision to place constraints on its outsourcing practices in Southeast Asia is one example of such an inverse institutional effect.

The search for legitimacy is also likely to drive organizations to copy the strategic HR practices of those with whom they have network relations. Even in those cases in which the adoption of a particular strategic HR practice may offer no direct utility, that practice may be copied if, for example, it is viewed as a means by which to maintain positive investor relations. Kossek (1987) found that such imitation is most likely to occur with respect to strategic practices that are more easily "packaged" (i.e., easily communicated and divisible, thus allowing for incremental adoption) and marketed by consultants. Finally, strategic HR practices may be adopted on the basis of normative pressures associated with the professionalization and institutionalization of HRM. Over time, as strategic HR practices become institutionalized and recognized as "professional standards," those responsible for the HR system are more likely to develop a personal interest to adopt these practices in order to retain their own level of individual legitimacy with their professional colleagues.

Technological Factors

Other researchers suggest that organizational technology has been and continues to be a powerful predictor of the adoption of strategic HRM. In organizational theory, *technology* refers to the way in which labor inputs are transformed into outputs: that is, the way in which tasks are organized and coordinated (and not merely what kinds of machines, if any, are used). In general, theory suggests that the adoption of strategic HR practices is likely to be most prevalent in firms in which the technology (a) requires individual skills that are firm specific, (b) makes it difficult to monitor and control the transformation process, (c) demands a high degree of worker interdependence and cooperation, and (d) results in a high degree of role and task ambiguity (Baron & Kreps, 1999). Such technologies tend to be less prevalent in traditional, mass production manufacturing organizations (e.g., auto manufacturing) and much more prevalent in high-tech firms (e.g., biotechnology, software development). Support for such a perspective comes from a number of empirical studies. For example, Jackson et al. (1989) found that organizations using flexible specialization technologies were more likely than firms relying on mass production technologies to (a) have performance appraisal results contribute to the determination of compensation, (b) use client input in performance appraisal, and (c) offer productivity-based bonuses. Similarly, Arthur (1992) and MacDuffie (1995) found that technology is highly predictive of the adoption of strategic HR practices for firms in the steel industry and the automobile industry respectively. For example, MacDuffie (1995) found strategic training and compensation practices (e.g., contingent compensation) to be significantly greater in plants relying on flexible manufacturing technologies than in those using mass production technologies.

Political Interests and the Adoption
of a Strategic Approach to HRM

Finally, intraorganizational political factors also appear to explain the variance in the adoption of a strategic approach to HRM across firms. Johns (1993) argued that the long causal chains characteristic of the hypothesized (indirect) effects of strategic HR practices "provide plenty of linkages to be threatened by political constraints" (p. 578). Using executive pay practices as a case in point, Johns argued that although technical merit would suggest the use of longer term performance measures as the criteria on which to base executive bonuses, most firms in North America tend to base their executive compensation programs on such short-term criteria as earnings per share. Underlying this paradox, according to Johns, is the fact that decisions regarding executive pay are typically made by the board of directors in conjunction with other parties involved in dependence relationships with precisely those individuals likely to be affected by their decisions (Conyon & Peck, 1998).

Clearly, numerous factors underlie the cross-organizational variance in the adoption of strategic HR practices, and these factors themselves appear to be highly interrelated. For example, organizational size may predict the adoption of strategic HR practices as a function of its effects on organizational structure and institutional relations (i.e., visibility and threats to legitimacy). Nevertheless, these findings do point to one important conclusion, namely that the technical merit of particular strategic HR practices may in many cases have little to do with their adoption in a particular organization. This conclusion has potentially important implications for those attempting to understand the HR strategy formulation process. Specifically, it suggests that models of strategy formulation based on a rational planning perspective may offer less predictive utility than models assuming, for example, the existence of institutional and political constraints on strategy formulation. We explore this issue in more detail in the next section.

Rational Planning and Incremental
Approaches to Strategy Formulation

One of the central debates in the field of business strategy concerns the formulation of strategy. Dominating this debate are two main approaches: the rational planning approach and the incremental approach. According to the rational planning approach, strategy is (or at least should be) formulated on the basis of formal and rational decision-making processes. According to the incremental approach, the strategy formulation process is characterized by a high degree of informality, intra- and interorganizational politics, fragmentation, and, to a certain extent, even chance.

Although many practitioners still tend to advocate a formal and rational planning process, most have come to accept that given the bounded rationality of organizational decision makers (March & Simon, 1958), the most that can be done is to follow a more logical and systematic process of incrementalism (Quinn, 1978). Following this same mode of theoretical reconciliation, researchers have also begun to generate theories that attempt to narrow the gap between these two approaches. In this section, we distinguish between these two approaches by reviewing a number of descriptive and prescriptive studies. We then conclude with a discussion of one of the theories developed to bridge these two perspectives: strategic reference point theory. Our discussion follows the key points highlighted in Figure 2.1.

Models Based on the Rational Planning Approach to Strategy Formulation

Early studies of the HR strategy formulation process tended to be highly prescriptive. That is, their intent was to demonstrate, typically on the basis of organizational case accounts, the efficacy of one strategy formulation approach over another. Descriptive models of HR strategy formulation emerged out of this prescriptive research.

Many of the early, prescriptive models of HR strategy formulation were little more than extensions of basic planning models (e.g., Walker, 1980). Indeed, the key differences between personnel planning and HR strategy formulation as advocated in these studies concerned (a) the issues to be addressed in the planning process and (b) what might be referred to as the planning "horizon" (i.e., short term vs. long term). Personnel planning models advocate forecasting HR needs on the basis of 1- or 2-year business plans and then reconciling these needs with the results of some sort of internal supply analysis. Of primary concern are issues relating to the organization's required skill mix, intraorganizational personnel flows, and overall staffing levels. In contrast, these early prescriptive models of HR strategy formulation advocated taking into consideration the longer term needs of the organization (i.e., 3- to 5-year planning horizon) as well as a wider range of HR-related issues such as operational flexibility, employee

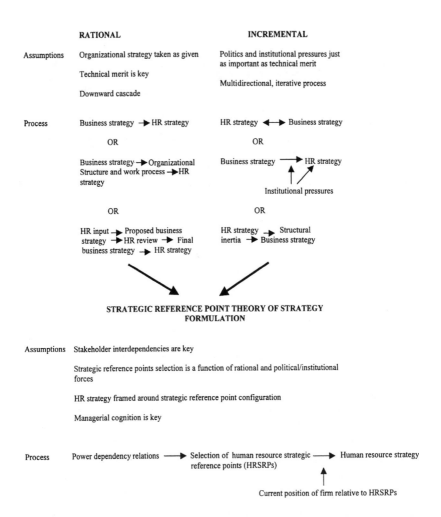

Figure 2.1. Alternative Theories of HR Strategy Formulation

competence and morale, and commitment. Nevertheless, these prescriptive models remain firmly grounded in the rational planning model and thus assume that there should be a one-way link between organizational or business strategy and HR strategy, with the latter based primarily if not entirely on the former. For example, a number of scholars (e.g., Kerr, 1982; Leontiades, 1983; Smith, 1982a, 1982b) admonished managers to make HR decisions that were consistent with organizational goals. Smith (1982a, 1982b) suggested that HR policies had to be tailored to reflect the future needs of the organization. Thus, in the same way that other functional units generated system-specific strategies (e.g., for finance or marketing) on the basis of corporate strategy, so would the HR function. Others (Gerstein & Reisman, 1983; Leontiades, 1982) suggested ways of matching personnel activities with organizational strategic plans.

More recently, Schuler (1992) proposed his "5-P model" of HR strategy formulation. It too is premised on the assumption that the HR strategy must be based on the organization's strategy. Strategy is viewed as a downward cascade, with the business-level strategy formulation process identifying and addressing business needs. External (e.g., economic, market, political, sociocultural/demographic) and internal (e.g., organizational culture, cash flow, technology) factors both determine these needs and shape the way in which they should be addressed. On the basis of an analysis of these needs, top-level management defines an overall, corporate-level mission, targets key mission-based objectives, and specifies broad programs and policies designed to help the organization achieve these objectives. These objectives, programs, and policies become the basis of HR strategy, or what Schuler described as the 5 P's: Philosophy, Policy, Programs, Practices, and Processes. Thus, this model also advocates a tight link between firm strategy and HR strategy and makes the latter strictly contingent on the former.

Early descriptive studies supported the application of such prescriptive models. For example, Dyer (1984) proposed that "organizational strategy is the major determinant of organizational human resource strategy" and cited a number of studies as providing support for this proposition (p. 161). One such study, LaBelle's (1983) exploratory analysis of HR strategy formulation processes in 11 Canadian companies, found that organizational strategy was the most frequently mentioned and most strongly emphasized determinant of organizational HR strategy. The study also found "clear differences" in organizational human resource strategy configurations across businesses that were pursuing different organizational strategies (Dyer, 1984, p. 161). Dyer also cited Wils' (1984) findings of the HR strategies pursued by 22 different strategic business units of a single corporation as further evidence that business strategy is the strongest predictor of HR strategy. Similarly, Ackermann (1986) applied Miles and Snow's (1978, 1984) typology of business strategies and claimed that because different HR strategies are appropriate for organizations adopting each of the main business strategies (defenders, prospectors, and analyzers), it is natural for HR strategy to be formulated on the basis of business strategy.

Finally, Schuler (1987) identified five dimensions by which HR strategies vary—planning, staffing, appraising, compensation, and training and development—and suggested that these subsystem strategies will vary across three main business strategies: a dynamic growth strategy, an extract profit strategy, and a turnaround strategy. Although the findings provide overall support for the idea that organizational strategy is a key determinant of HR subsystem strategy, they also reveal that these subsystem strategies are more heterogeneous within than across firms. Schuler concluded that, in general, organizational strategies are more predictive of HR practices at higher organizational (i.e., managerial) levels than at lower levels. Drawing on the same data, Jackson et al. (1989) found that innovation-driven organizational strategies were predictive of one set of HR subsystem strategies, whereas organizational strategies focusing on alternative means of achieving competitive advantage were predictive of a completely different set of HR subsystem strategies. For example, firms with an innovation-focused organizational strategy tended to place greater emphasis on employment security and on employee training and development than those with a non-innovation-focused strategy. Firm strategy may also have indirect effects on HR strategy by determining organizational structure (e.g., functional vs. product-based structure) and work processes (e.g., mass production vs. flexible manufacturing). As noted above, Jackson et al. found both of these factors to be predictive of different HR strategies. Despite somewhat mixed results, Jackson et al. concluded that "there is some evidence that organizations do adapt their personnel practices to fit their organization's competitive practices" (p. 775). A more recent study of the link between business strategy and HR strategy in the banking industry (Delery & Doty, 1996) suggests further support for this position.

Although most prescriptive models accept the premise that the HR strategy must be formulated on the basis of organizational strategy, by the mid-1980s several scholars began to advocate that organizational strategy take into account function-specific constraints. For example, Baird, Meshoulam, and DeGive (1983) suggested that although HR strategy must be formulated on the basis of requirements specified in the organizational strategy, the HR function must play a role in the formulation of organizational strategy for corporate strategic planning to be effective. They argued that the HR function has a critical role in helping to shape key elements of the organization's corporate mission, itself a key component of corporate strategy. Because this mission is defined as a function of environmental (i.e., technological, economic, demographic) and cultural (i.e., values, beliefs, philosophies) factors, and because the HR function is typically the organizational unit responsible for tracking shifts with respect to many of these factors, corporate-level mission formulation cannot be undertaken without some sort of HR input. Furthermore, because corporate strategy is also based on information stemming from the internal analyses and environmental scans conducted by functional units, the HR function has an additional role to play in corporate strategy formulation. That is, although the HR function has no *direct* influence on corporate strategy formulation, perhaps more than other functional units it has the ability to influence the information and hence premises on which corporate-level strategic decision making is based. Nevertheless, like those researchers cited above, Baird and colleagues have continued to advocate that HR strategy, like any function-specific strategy, should be based entirely on the corporate strategy.

More recently, Lundy and Cowling (1996) proposed an even more proactive and influential role for the HR function in the strategy formulation process (pp. 84-85). They argued that HR, like all other organizational functions, should shape business strategy by being granted not only an intelligence role but also a review role. Specifically, they recommended a process in which each functional area, including HR, would receive data concerning corporate or divisional opportunities and threats, as well as the strategic options being considered. Taking existing internal capabilities (i.e. structures, systems, processes) and external conditions (labor, economic, legislative) into account, the HR function would be asked to review and assess each of the various policy options. On the basis of each of these function-specific assessments of the various options, an overall business strategy would be selected. As with the earlier prescriptive models, Lundy and Cowling recommended that the business strategy still provide the foundation on which the HR strategy would be formulated. However, as is apparent from the process described, the business strategy adopted in this manner would be more likely to take into account the constraints and concerns of the HR system. With the business strategy formulated, "It is then possible to draw up details of implementation requirements and this forms the basis of individual, functional plans, that is, objectives to be reached" (p. 85). The researchers recommended that the functional plan for HR (i.e., HR strategy) be based on the results of the internal capability and external opportunities/constraints analyses and that it consist of (a) a statement of managerial philosophy to guide policy and program implementation, (b) "core effectiveness criteria" (i.e., objectives), and (c) a description of the HR activities to be implemented in order to achieve these objectives.

Using empirical data from the pharmaceutical industry, Bamberger and Phillips (1991) found support for certain elements of this rational model of HR strategy formulation while questioning other elements. For example, empirical support was found for the notion that the results of function-specific environmental scanning are often used as inputs into the formulation of organizational business strategy. Nevertheless, Bamberger and Phillips concluded that HR strategy is not necessarily grounded strictly on the organizational business strategy. Their data suggested that environmental factors such as uncertainty (Ellis, 1982), technology (Maier, 1982), and demographic changes (Fombrun, 1982) often *directly* affect the choices made by those responsible for the formulation of HR strategy. That is, although these environmental factors may have been used as inputs into, and considered in the formulation of, organizational business strategy, at least in the pharmaceutical companies studied, there was substantial evidence that HR strategists directly applied the results of their own environmental scanning and took such issues into consideration regardless of whether these were reflected in the organizational business strategy. More importantly, Bamberger and Phillips raised questions about the basic efficacy of a rational planning perspective when applied to HR strategy formulation. They noted that other factors such as institutional pressures and intraorganizational politics are likely to moderate the way in which those responsible for the formulation of HR strategy make sense of both business strategy and environmental conditions and the way these inputs shape the actual pattern of HR decisions made. In this sense, their research is in many ways consistent with the incremental perspective of strategy formulation that we describe next.

Models Based on the Incremental
Perspective of Strategy Formulation

Although most HR practitioners assume that top management has the ability to formulate and implement appropriate strategies as complete wholes, many scholars are skeptical of this approach. Such scholars can be divided into two groups. The first group acknowledge that strategic content and processes are subject to a large degree of influence by organizational actors but claim that this conscious shaping tends to occur incrementally and interactively rather than all at once (Quinn, 1980). As suggested in the conclusions reached by Bamberger and Phillips (1991), these scholars also acknowledge that the process is subject to a wide range of institutional and political forces. Drawing on notions of bounded rationality (March & Simon, 1958), researchers in this first group focus on emergent rather than espoused strategy and examine the dynamic organizational processes producing the "consistencies in behavior" (Mintzberg & Waters, 1982) or "patterns of decisions" (Mintzberg, 1978) that are referred to as strategy. A core element of their argument is that new strategies are not always formulated or adopted on the basis of technical merit alone. Rather, in many cases, intraorganizational politics (Ferris & Judge, 1991) and the desire to imitate the practices and strategies of other organizations (Abrahamson, 1991) also influence the strategy formulation and implementation processes (Johns, 1993). The second group acknowledges a far smaller degree of conscious shaping by organizational actors, assuming not only bounded rationality on the part of those involved in the strategy formulation process but also a high degree of environmental determinism.

Interactive Approaches to HR Strategy Formulation

In one of the earliest descriptive studies of HR strategy formulation, Dyer (1983) concluded that organizational and HR strategy formulation processes are interactive and identified three modes by which organizations integrate the two processes. In all three cases, the HR function contributes to organizational strategy formulation and in the process also gets early insights into its own strategic requirements. All three processes require an assessment of plan feasibility, desirability, and cost from the HR perspective. A *parallel planning process* was described as one requiring that business unit planners report on the implications of their strategic options from an HR perspective, typically after the strategic decisions have already been made. In addition to forcing business-level planners to consider the HR feasibility, desirability, and costs of their plan, such a process also requires those responsible for the HR system to start developing their own strategies for dealing with the HR challenges expected as a result of the plan's adoption. An *inclusion planning process* is one in which HR considerations are taken into account before the adoption of any particular plan. Business managers are required to demonstrate that their strategic plans are feasible and desirable from an HR point of view. A process in which data are provided proactively to those responsible for the HR system characterizes the third, *participative* approach. Firms adopting this approach allow these individuals to review and advise the organizational strategy formulation process by giving them the power to challenge plans, if necessary, all the way to top management levels. That is, such a participative approach to HR strategy formulation is one that gives HR decision makers a voice in the business formulation process itself.

In their "reciprocal interdependence" model of HR strategy formulation, Lengnick-Hall and Lengnick-Hall (1988) also subscribed to this notion of a two-way interaction between business strategy formulation and HR strategy formulation. They concluded from a review of the strategy literature that in most cases "human resources are considered means, not part of generating or selecting strategic objectives" and that "traditional models focus on matching people to strategy, but not on matching strategy to people" (p. 456). They claimed that models based on the rational perspective of strategy formulation make three questionable assumptions. First, they assume that organizational strategy has already been determined. Second, they assume that HR strategy is inherently oriented toward the implementation of organizational strategy and consequently that the HR system has little to contribute to the identification of strategic ends or the formulation of organizational strategy. Finally, they assume that although the HR practices implemented may shift in response to changes in organizational strategy, the issues addressed by these practices remain stable.

Contesting these assumptions, Lengnick-Hall and Lengnick-Hall demonstrated that HR strategy is not determined solely by firm strategy but is also influenced by firm readiness to deal with challenges and obstacles (i.e., life cycle stage). They also argued that the effects are not unidirectional and that HR parameters contribute to the shaping and implementation of overall business strategy. They proposed a contingency approach in which HR strategy is generated to fit both organizational growth expectations and organizational readiness to meet these expectations. Four different strategic scenarios were identified depending on the level of growth expectations and organizational readiness, and in each scenario, the mode of interaction between HR strategy and organizational strategy was identified. Thus, for example, organizations having high growth expectations but a poor level of readiness were shown to have three options: Invest in human resources to improve implementation feasibility, change corporate objectives to reflect lack of readiness, or change strategic objectives to take advantage of current HR deployments (p. 462). In all three cases, HR strategy is just as likely to inform and influence organizational strategy as organizational strategy is to influence firm strategy. The researchers concluded that firms that engage in strategy formulation processes that systematically and reciprocally consider human resources and organizational strategy will perform better than firms that either manage the two strategy formulation processes competitively or formulate HR strategy as a means by which to solve competitive strategy issues. Although no study has directly tested these propositions, studies do indicate that, increasingly, firms are bringing human resource considerations into business strategy formulation processes. Some level of integration between HR strategy formulation and business strategy formulation has been achieved in 20% to 45% of medium-sized and large firms (Burack, 1986; Nkomo, 1986).

More recently, Taylor, Beechler, and Napier (1996) used resource dependence theory (Pfeffer & Salancik, 1977) to predict the nature of the cross-level interactions in strategy formulation. They argued that the degree of reciprocal interdependence is likely to depend on (a) corporate orientation in the design of system-specific strategies (highly centralist vs. decentralized or learning), (b) the nature of intersystem resource transactions and which systems are deemed by corporate elites to be critical to successful implementation of corporate strategy, and (c) the competence of system leaders. The role of HR strategy in contributing to business policy is likely to be greatest in those organizations in which (a) there is an orientation toward decentralizing system-specific strategies, (b) the HR system is viewed by corporate elites as providing a key basis of competitive advantage, and (c) those managing the HR system are viewed as highly competent. Such a resource dependence model is grounded on notions of exchange, bargaining, and political interest. Thus, predictions of the nature and outcomes of the HR strategy formulation process are possible only to the extent that we have a firm understanding of the power and dependence relations among all of those with an interest in the outcome.

Deterministic Approaches to HR Strategy Formulation

The descriptive theories discussed above propose that HR strategy is influenced both directly and indirectly (via firm strategy) by environmental considerations. However, these theories leave it to HR system decision makers to identify, interpret, analyze, and then act on these considerations. Another set of theories suggests that the managerial role in shaping HR strategy may be much more limited. For example, as discussed earlier, in their search for legitimacy and acceptance from common institutional stakeholders (e.g., government agencies, professional associations), organizations may adopt a common set of HR strategies regardless of overall firm strategy. This institutional perspective (DiMaggio & Powell, 1983; Meyer & Rowan, 1977) suggests that even those elements of HR strategy most aligned with the strategic interests of the firm may be discarded in favor of HR elements perceived to be critical to the assurance of basic organizational stability and survival. As Wright and McMahan (1992) noted, "Not everything that happens is necessarily intended and not all outcomes are the result of conscious decision processes" (p. 314).

Recent research on international HR strategy supports this notion that conformity to perceived stakeholder expectations for behavior may play a key role in shaping HR strategy. For example, Hannon, Huang, and Jaw (1995) found that institutional forces in the local environments of multinational firm subsidiaries often constrain the ability of the parent to "export" key elements of corporate HR strategy. Huselid, Jackson, and Schuler (1997) found that U.S. firms tend to achieve higher levels of technical HRM effectiveness than strategic HRM effectiveness. They claimed that this is because the expectations and regulatory activities of key external stakeholders such as government agencies (e.g., the Equal Employment Opportunity Commission) and professional organizations shape these activities and provide a common basis for both professional HR training and evaluation. Their argument suggests that by structuring the regulatory requirements for the HR system and shaping the professional capabilities of HR managers, such institutional pressures implicitly constrain the range of strategic options available to an HR system. Finally, in their analysis of the literature on "fit" in HR strategy, Wright and Snell (1998) questioned a key assumption of those supporting a contingency perspective, namely that HR practices are adaptable to shifts in firm strategy. They claimed that institutional forces limit the ability of organizations to make their HR systems adapt to changing competitive requirements.

Population ecologists also discount the role of management in formulating strategy. These researchers argue that organizational performance and survival are largely determined by the nature of the environment in which the organization exists (Hannan & Freeman, 1989). In line with this theory, such environmental characteristics as population density and environmental turbulence have been found to have much greater predictive utility in explaining the "selection" of organizations for survival than strategy. Although most scholars criticize population ecology for downplaying the importance of choice of strategic direction for an organization, several contend that there is nothing inherent in population ecology theory that "implies that management actions and decisions are not important" (Welbourne & Andrews, 1996, p. 895). Indeed, Welbourne and Andrews argued that to the degree that structural cohesion—"an employee generated synergy" providing the firm with a key source of structural inertia— is critical to firm survival, the initial design of a firm's HR system is an important determinant of firm performance and survival. As they noted, "Rather than alter human resource systems to match life-cycle or business strategy (as contingency theory suggests), organizations should design HR techniques to strengthen structural inertia early in the life cycle and in this way increase their survival chances" (p. 896). Their findings suggest that organizations placing an emphasis on building a strong, cohesive workforce right from the start will increase their survival chances. Nevertheless, in line with the deterministic tendencies of population ecology theory, their findings also suggest that "the die is cast" early on in the life cycle of an organization and that the range of *effective* HR strategies to implement is greatly limited once the firm has embarked on its course. Indeed, any shift in HR strategy may only weaken inertia and hence the probability of firm survival.

Reconciling the Two Approaches: Reference Point Theory

In an attempt to reconcile deterministic and political incremental models of HR strategy formulation with those models based on the rational planning perspective, Bamberger and Fiegenbaum (1996) used the concept of strategic reference points (SRPs) to describe the HR strategy formulation process. HR strategic reference points (HRSRPs) are defined by the researchers as the targets or benchmarks that organizational decision makers use to evaluate their options, make strategic decisions, and signal to key stakeholders their systemwide priorities. The authors argued that HR strategy is primarily contingent on the configuration of reference points or targets selected by system decision makers. The HRSRP configuration may be depicted graphically on a matrix incorporating three key dimensions: internal capabilities, external conditions, and time (see Figure 2.2). The internal dimension captures the degree to which targets emphasize HR processes (i.e., means) versus outcomes (i.e., ends). The external dimension captures the degree to which the interests of various constituent interests and institutions such as customers, competitors, or regulatory agencies are taken into account. Finally, the temporal dimension focuses on the degree to which targets emphasize historical as opposed to future/desired states. The

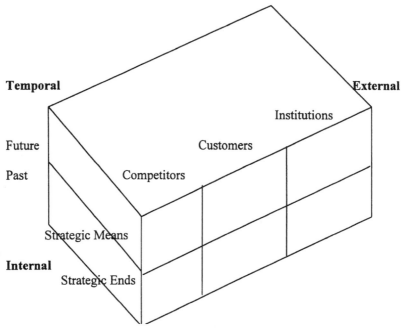

Figure 2.2. The Strategic Reference Point Matrix
SOURCE: Bamberger and Fiegenbaum 1996, p. 930. Reprinted by permission of *Academy of Management Review.*

theory proposed that managers frame HR strategy around this configuration of reference points.

Up to this point, SRP theory draws primarily on the rational planning perspective in that it views managers as having a high degree of control over the strategy formulation process. However, Bamberger and Fiegenbaum (1996) departed from the rational planning perspective in two ways. First, they proposed that highly deterministic resource- and power-based theories explain the nature of a system's SRP configuration. Second, they proposed that managerial interpretation and sense-making processes moderate the translation of the HRSRP configuration into HR strategy.

Drawing on organizational theory, the authors argued that resource- and power-based theories may be helpful in understanding the emergence of configurations at the system level. These include population ecology (Hannan & Freeman, 1989), institutional (DiMaggio & Powell, 1983), and resource dependence (Pfeffer & Salancik, 1978) theories. Zammuto (1988) suggested that despite their differences, all these theories lead to common themes with regard to organizational configurations because of the power- and resource-based contingencies on which they are all based. Furthermore, Ketchen, Thomas, and Snow (1993) found that configurations deductively derived from such theories offered greater predictive efficacy than inductively derived configurations. Extrapolating to the subsystem level, Bamberger and Fiegenbaum (1996) claimed that it is logical to assume that similar power- and resource-based contingencies may drive the clustering of system-level phenomena such as reference points into SRP configurations.

In this context, the ability of any organization or interest to dictate the nature of a given system's SRPs is likely to be contingent on the dependence relations between that organization or interest and the system over which it is attempting to exert influence. Although this assumption may not be consistent with the more conventional notion that system-level strategies are dictated entirely by constraints external to a given system, it is consistent with the reciprocal interdependence theory of strategy formulation discussed earlier. For example, on the basis of the assumption that power-related contingencies underlie the clustering of HRSRPs into specific SRP configurations, it is just as likely for a powerful organizational system to influence firm-level strategy as it is for top management to use firm-level strategy to constrain the emergence of a particular system-level SRP configuration

Bamberger and Fiegenbaum (1996) expanded on this underlying proposition (that the level of HR influence in the firm affects all three reference point dimensions and thus plays the key role in determining the nature of a firm's HRSRP configuration) by demonstrating how power-dependency relations influence the emergence of an HRSRP configuration. For example, drawing on earlier conceptual and empirical research (e.g., Dyer & Holder, 1988; Kossek, 1987), they proposed that in firms in which the HR function lacks influence, its ability to consider forward-looking HR programs and policies may be greatly limited. As they noted,

> When evaluating and selecting among reference points, managers in weaker functions will make greater use of historically oriented strategic reference points. These individuals feel the need to justify strategic choices on the basis of criteria that imply stability and (at most) only incremental change so that their potential for survival and advancement within the organization is not placed at risk. In contrast, managers in more influential functions will make greater use of future-oriented strategic reference points. It is important to these individuals to be able to justify their strategic choices on the basis of criteria that imply more overarching concerns and reflect their interest in

securing broader and more synoptic or comprehensive organizational change. (p. 940)

Similarly, Bamberger and Fiegenbaum (1996) proposed that in organizations in which the HR system is more influential, (a) the internal dimension of the SRP matrix will be dominated by an emphasis placed on outcome-oriented targets (i.e., ends) rather than process-oriented targets (i.e., means), and (b) the external orientation of the SRP configuration will be higher. With regard to the latter, they argued that although all HR systems are required by law to take certain institutional interests into consideration when identifying system targets, the extent to which additional external SRPs will be taken into consideration is a function of the power wielded by the HR system within the organization. For example, weak HR systems that are dependent on other organizational systems for resources and respect are obligated to pay close attention to the interests and concerns of those external stakeholders in framing HR policies and practices but tend to lack both the mandate and the resources to consider a broader range of external reference points.

Although eight basic SRP configurations were identified (see Table 2.2), Bamberger and Fiegenbaum (1996) argued that HR systems tend toward one of two primary SRP configurations: a "high-power" configuration (indicated by Cell 4) or a "low-power" configuration (indicated by Cell 5). For example, Jarrell's (1993) description of the role of HR in strategic planning at IBM and Amex suggests that HR strategy in these companies is driven by a high-power SRP configuration—one that is future oriented (5-year plans), outcome based (i.e., concerned with bottom-line, business outcomes), and externally driven (i.e., focused on the demands of a wide range of stakeholders in the firm's environment). In contrast, Bamberger, Bacharach, and Dyer (1989) showed that HR strategy in high-technology start-ups tends to be driven by a low-power SRP configuration focusing on the relative improvement in the efficiency of internal processes affecting primarily one internal customer (i.e., R&D) over past months or years.

In sum, although managers are posited to have a certain degree of control in framing the SRP configuration that serves as a core input into strategy formulation, Bamberger and Fiegenbaum (1996) posited that managerial control is often greatly bounded. Though incorporating and accounting for deterministic organizational theories, their theory placed a much stronger emphasis on the micropolitics of organizations (Bacharach, Bamberger, & Sonnenstuhl, 1996b) as a constraint on rational planning processes. Yet further *cognitive* constraints

Table 2.2 HR Strategic Reference Points Configuration Options
and Possible Tendencies

Managers' External Exposure	Loose/Outcome Control		Tight/Process (Behavioral) Control	
	Low Influence	High Influence	Low Influence	High Influence
Low	Cell 1	Cell 3	Cell 5	Cell 7
High	Cell 2	Cell 4	Cell 6	Cell 8

Cell Number	Internal Dimension		External Dimension		Temporal Dimension	
	Process/ Means Oriented	Outcome/ Ends Oriented	Low (Narrow) External	High (Broad) External	Past	Future
1		X	X		X	
2		X		X	X	
3		X	X			X
4*		X		X		X
5*	X		X		X	
6	X			X	X	
7	X		X			X
8	X			X		X

*High and low power configurations toward which HR systems may tend (assuming that the three determining factors remain stable over time).

on such processes were incorporated into their theory with respect to the way in which the HRSRP configuration was predicted to shape the pattern of HR policies and practices that we refer to as HR strategy.

Drawing on prospect theory (Kahneman & Tversky, 1979), Bamberger and Fiegenbaum (1996) argued that although the HRSRP configuration influences the nature of the HR policies and practices adopted, this effect is moderated by the firm's current position relative to its HR reference points. That is, the way in which the HRSRP configuration affects the nature of the strategic choices made by HR professionals is contingent on the degree to which these decision makers view the system as being above or below its strategic reference points.

Specifically, Bamberger and Fiegenbaum argued that the perceived position of the HR system relative to its SRPs will determine the conservative versus daring nature of the emergent HR strategy. In particular, on the basis of prospect theory (Kahneman & Tversky, 1979), they suggested that HR systems that are above their reference points will be more likely to respond to new issues and situations (e.g., the election of a new, more militant union leadership) as threats and will seek to minimize potential losses by adopting conservative and defensive policies and practices (e.g., retaining a traditional, confrontational approach to labor relations). In contrast, HR systems that are below their reference points will be more likely to view new issues and situations as opportunities and will seek to capitalize on them by adopting more daring policies and practices, radically departing from the norm or tradition. Using the example just cited, for an HR system well below its SRPs, a profound shift in union leadership might provide the impetus needed to encourage HR decision makers to question existing mental models (Senge, 1990) and adopt more innovative, joint labor-management programs (Kochan, Katz, & McKersie, 1986).

Thus, assuming that the skills of HR professionals are randomly distributed across firms, the application of prospect theory to HR strategy suggests that the HR system's position relative to its key reference points will influence the willingness of HR decision makers to challenge their own mental models and consider the adoption of more daring HR strategies. It does *not* suggest that HR decision makers, having identified their system as being above its SRPs, will suddenly discard or fail to build on proven strengths because the nature of some of these practices is still uncertain. Rather, it suggests that having identified the system as being above its SRPs, HR decision makers are likely to build incrementally on these strengths but to be reluctant to adopt programs that depart radically from proven methods. Indeed, when such HR systems confront new situations or issues to which they must respond, HR decision makers are more likely to opt for responses that are consistent with identified strengths and tested routines—that is, more conservative ones.

Summary

In this chapter, we reviewed a number of theories regarding adoption of a specific strategic approach to HRM and the way in which HR strategy is (or should best be) formulated. From our discussion, it should be clear that two distinct theoretical perspectives have dominated much of the research regarding both issues. The first, the rational planning perspective, suggests that strategic HR practices are adopted on the basis of technical merit. Because technical merit may vary from firm to firm (depending, e.g., on the nature of the work process or organizational structure), according to this perspective, such practices are likely to be adopted if they meet primarily technical and efficiency criteria. With regard to the strategy formulation process, this perspective suggests that HR strategy will, for the most part, be based on firm business strategy and will focus primarily on providing the means necessary for implementing that business strategy

In contrast, the second perspective, the incremental planning perspective, suggests that strategic HR practices are rarely adopted on the basis of technical merit alone. Instead, a wide range of external resource- and constituent-based forces determine which practices will be adopted and when. How these forces affect the adoption of such strategic practices is most apparent if we examine the HR strategy formulation process from the incremental planning perspective. According to this perspective, the strategy formulation process is both informal and politically charged. Furthermore, for those adopting this perspective, the link between HR strategy and firm business strategy is in many ways bidirectional, and the ability of HR managers to formulate system strategies strictly on the basis of internal technical and efficiency criteria is greatly bounded by institutional forces, political interests, and simple inertia.

Despite this debate over the adoption of strategic practices and the nature of strategy formulation, researchers have, for the most part, reached consensus on at least one key issue—the existence of strategic configurations. That is, on the basis of consistent research results across industries (Arthur, 1992; Delery & Doty, 1996; MacDuffie, 1995), most HR strategy researchers concur that HR practices tend to emerge in bundles or clusters and that these configurations tend to vary systematically across organizations. However, there is far less consensus with regard to such questions as how many configurations exist, how they differ, and which factors predict the emergence of these bundles of HR strategies across organizations. We explore these remaining issues in the next chapter.

3

Models of Human Resource Strategy

Having a better understanding of the forces driving the adoption of different HR strategies, we must next address the nature of these strategies. Specifically, in this chapter we will examine whether it is possible to speak of certain types of HR strategies and the degree to which these types of strategies systematically vary across organizations. The ability to effectively distinguish among HR strategies is critical for researchers hoping to generate and test theory regarding, for example, the impact of HR strategy on such outcomes as firm performance and the degree to which such effects may be contingent on overall firm business strategy.

Given that we have defined HR strategy as the pattern of decisions regarding the policies and practices associated with an HR system, on an operational level it should be possible to distinguish among HR strategies on the basis of the HR policies and practices in place. However, given the infinite number of combinations of HR policies and practices in existence, such an approach is likely to be rather unwieldy. Fortunately, as we noted in the previous chapter, many HR strategy researchers now concur that HR practices and policies appear to emerge in bundles or clusters and that these clusters of practices often tend to vary systematically across organizations as relatively stable configurations.

The analysis of the configuration of HR strategies in terms of typologies is appealing to HR researchers for a number of reasons. First, unlike taxonomies (which categorize phenomena into mutually exclusive and exhaustive sets with a series of discrete decision rules; Doty & Glick, 1994), typologies are grounded on less rigid conceptual schemes. These conceptual schemes, or, as Weber (1904) referred to them, "ideal types," are formed as "the one-sided accentuation of one or more points of view and by the synthesis of a great many diverse, more or less present and occasionally absent concrete individual phenomena" (p. 90). Ideal types do not exist in reality but rather provide a theoretical reference point against which observable phenomenon can be compared and assessed. In this sense, they "are intended to provide an abstract model, so that deviation from the extreme or ideal type can be noted or explained" (Blalock, 1969, p. 32). Without the identification of ideal types of HR strategies, it would be difficult (at best) to describe the differences in strategy across organizations and nearly impossible to generate falsifiable hypotheses. Thus, the development of empirically grounded typologies is a critical step in theory development, giving researchers the ability to identify relationships among the different typological dimensions, as well as to develop broader, more comprehensive, and more parsimonious theories.

Second, configurational analysis or analysis across identified types is well established in the field of management and organizational theory and has long been used as a basis for developing theory (Etzioni, 1961; Mintzberg, 1979; Porter, 1980, 1985). Indeed, Doty and Glick (1994) argued that configurational frameworks and typologies, when constructed properly, meet basic criteria similar to those for theories, namely that they are structured around specified and falsifiable relationships among a set of well-identified constructs or organizational characteristics. In this sense, as they noted, configurations are "conceptually derived interrelated sets of ideal types, each of which represent a unique combination of the organizational attributes that are believed to determine relevant outcomes" (p. 232). Meyer, Tsui, and Hinings (1993) added that because many organizational characteristics (e.g., practices, cultural artifacts, and membership composition) cluster into sets of configurations, this approach allows for multiple levels of analysis both within and across organizations.

Third, theoretically, individual HR practices should tend over time to support and reinforce one another. That is, there should be a tendency, over time, for internally inconsistent HR practices to be abandoned in favor of practices that are more aligned with the other practices already in place. Baird and Meshoulam (1988) referred to this tendency toward consistency among HR practices as "internal fit." Building on this notion, MacDuffie (1995) argued that the appropriate unit of analysis for studying HR strategy is not the individual HR practice but rather the "bundles of internally consistent HR practices" (p. 198). His findings in the automobile industry provide strong support for this argument, namely that HR practices tend to be "bundled" into distinct models or configurations, each having its own underlying logic.

Finally, the field of business strategy is, to a large extent, structured around the identification and application of typologies and strategic configurations. Two of the most well known typologies of strategy are those developed by Porter (1980, 1985) and Miles and Snow (1978, 1984), and these, in turn, have served as the basis for theory development in HR strategy as well.

Porter (1980, 1985) identified two main types of generic business strategies used by firms to achieve sustainable competitive advantage in a market. The first, a "cost leadership strategy," is based on the development of a lower cost structure designed to strengthen the market potential of a firm's products or services. The second, a "differentiation strategy," aims at allowing the firm to achieve competitive advantage by distinguishing itself from its competitors in ways that are valued by customers (e.g., quality, service, and timeliness). By thus positioning themselves relative to their competitors, firms can receive premium price for their products or services. Typically, the cost leadership strategy is associated with mass production methods and the differentiation strategy with "flexible" production methods (Piore & Sable, 1984). According to Porter (1980, 1985), firms with strategies close to one of the ideal types identified are likely to outperform those that adopt a heterogeneous collection of associated practices because the latter tend to be less able to align and focus the utilization of their resources.

Miles and Snow (1978, 1984) identified three ideal types of business strategies and argued that firms could be categorized accordingly as "defenders," "prospectors," and "analyzers." Defenders have a narrow and stable market for their product or service and focus on efficiency and the defense of market share as opposed to growth. Prospectors are searching for new business opportunities via new products, markets, or services. According to this strategy, resources are focused on generating and implementing innovations as well as on acquiring those competencies and synergies that cannot be developed internally. Analyzers operate simultaneously in both stable and dynamic product markets.

They are often leaders in the various markets in which they operate, and though they are not the initiators of change, they follow the changes more rapidly than do defenders.

A core assumption underlying much of strategic human resource management (SHRM) research is that each of these different overarching strategic types is associated with a different approach toward managing human capital: that is, with a different HR strategy (Delery & Doty 1996; Fombrun et al., 1984; Jackson & Schuler, 1995). Indeed, Delery and Doty (1996) suggested that if this basic premise is correct, "much of the variation in HR practices across organizations should be explained by organizational strategy" (p. 803). At the very least, these ideal types of organizational strategy provide us with a solid foundation on which to base our analysis of HR strategies.

Models of HR Strategy

Over the past decade, researchers have proposed a number of frameworks to differentiate among core or "ideal types" of HR strategies. Some of these models have been generated intuitively on the basis of theory, whereas others have been derived empirically. Though it may not be possible to reconcile all model differences, we will attempt to identify a number of common underlying elements across these models. We will conclude by proposing, on the basis of these common elements, a more integrative model of HR strategy.

Theory-Driven Models

Researchers have taken one of two approaches in attempting to develop typologies of HR strategy. The first approach is grounded in the nature of the employer-employee exchange and, more specifically, the labor market parameters underlying these exchanges. The second approach is grounded in the way the employer attempts to monitor and control employee role performance.

Resource-Based Models

HR strategy models grounded in the resource perspective rest on the implicit assumption that the set of employee behaviors, attitudes, and relationships underlying an organization's human resource system can be critical to the implementation of business strategy (Cappelli & Singh, 1992). As a whole, this set of behaviors, attitudes, and relationships *has the potential* to provide capabilities that are valuable, rare, nonsubstitutable, and imperfectly imitable and can thus serve as a source of competitive advantage for the firm. Underlying such models, however, is the recognition that the acquisition or development of such a set of behaviors, attitudes, and relationships can be costly and that a firm's competitive advantage may be secured more efficiently. Consequently, in the simplest terms, models grounded in this perspective distinguish among HR strategies according to the degree to which employers view their human resources in such a manner (i.e., as an asset as opposed to a variable cost).

However, resource-based models make a second basic assumption as well, namely that the degree to which a firm views its human resources as an asset (as opposed to a cost) influences the nature of the employer-employee exchange or "bargain." For example, to develop a unique set of employee behaviors, attitudes, and relationships and use employee knowledge about products, processes, customers, and suppliers as a source of sustainable competitive advantage (Kogut & Zander, 1992), employers viewing their human resources as an asset may be willing to exchange a guarantee of job security and organizational career development for an employee understanding that compensation will be governed more by internal equity norms than by the going market rate. This type of employment framework is commonly referred to as an internal labor market (ILM) (Cohen & Pfeffer, 1986; Doeringer & Piore, 1971). Employers viewing their labor costs as a drain on their income are likely to develop frameworks (i.e., highly unskilled, routine jobs) allowing them to exchange market-based compensation for employment at will (i.e., the ability to acquire and dispose of employees as market conditions demand). This type of employment framework is commonly referred to as an external labor market (ELM).

Adopting such a framework, Osterman (1987) identified four different HR strategies that he claimed are derivative of the firm's overall business strategy. The *craft strategy* is grounded on the assumption that participants in the labor market are skilled free agents with more loyalty to their occupation than to their employer. Mobility is an accepted fact, with staffing based almost entirely on an ELM, wages determined on the basis of market supply and demand, little guaranteed job security, and an assumption that the employer is "buying" rather than developing a set of employee attitudes and behaviors. Employers adopting such a strategy seek competitive advantage by reducing labor costs and ensuring a high degree of staffing flexibility, thus allowing them to avoid having to assume payroll costs when market demand is low. According to this classic ELM framework, employees forfeit job security in return for control over the work process and market-based compensation. The *secondary strategy* is also guided by an ELM philosophy. However, it assumes that jobs require only the most basic of skills, are poorly compensated, and offer no job security or internal career potential (e.g., janitorial positions, messengers). Staff turnover is encouraged as a means to keep labor costs down, with new staff recruited from a low-cost, secondary (and often contingent) labor market. Employees exchange flexibility, control over the labor process, and job security for market-based compensation.

As a kind of hybrid strategy, the *industrial strategy,* typically adopted in heavily unionized firms, is characterized by narrowly defined jobs with clearly defined job responsibilities and limited internal mobility based, for the most part, on seniority. Employees are viewed as a limited source of sustainable competitive advantage, and thus a partial ILM prevails. For example, wages are based on seniority and the actual job performed and are less influenced by ELM conditions, but employers offer only limited career development and retain some right to employment at will. Employees, in effect, exchange control over the work process and external equity in compensation for a limited degree of job security and a guaranteed wage. Finally, a *salaried strategy* is adopted in firms in which human resources are viewed as a key source of sustainable competitive advantage. It is characterized by a classic ILM: a strong commitment to job security, job descriptions that are open to revision by management, flexible job assignments, well-prescribed career paths with an emphasis on internal staffing, and a greater emphasis on meritocracy and salary differentiation. The exchange implicit in such relationships is one in which employers demand loyalty, flexibility in job assignments, and the forfeiture of external equity in compensation on the part of employees and in return offer job security, extensive development opportunities, and an organizational career.

As suggested by the description above, variation in HR strategy is manifested across one or more of four core dimensions, or what Osterman (1987) referred to as the "rules" governing the employment relationship. These are job classification and job definition rules (i.e., narrowly or broadly defined jobs and flexible or rigid definitions and classifications), career development rules (i.e., whether internal career development is possible and the criteria on which such development is contingent), job security rules (i.e., the degree to which the organization makes an explicit or implicit commitment to continued employment), and finally wage rules (i.e., the degree to which pay is strictly a function of the job classification or is contingent on other criteria such as performance, knowledge, or competencies). Osterman argued that each strategy has its own exchange-based, internal logic requiring an alignment among these employment rules. Thus, for example, firms that guarantee lifetime employment tend not to adopt rigid job descriptions. In this sense, HR strategy is manifested in terms of configurations of naturally aligned employment rules that are themselves a function of a firm's business strategy. Firms choose their employment rules on the basis of three overall strategic objectives: cost effectiveness, predictability, and flexibility. Clearly, each objective has its own trade-offs with respect to the others. Thus, for example, rules adopted with wage minimization objectives in mind may serve cost-effectiveness goals but may be deleterious with respect to predictability. Nevertheless, firms set their HR strategy on the basis of those goals most consistent with their overall business strategy and then implement those "rules" most likely to serve those objectives.

On the basis of Osterman's (1987) typology, we can already identify the three major components of a model of HR strategy that will reappear in one form or another in each of the typologies we will review: ends (Osterman's "goals"), means (Osterman's "rules"), and logics, the underlying philosophy that is used to (a) justify the ends and explicate their external fit with the overall business strategy and (b) ensure an internal alignment among the selected ends and means (Bacharach, Bamberger, & Sonnenstuhl, 1996b). This demand for internal consistency among the rules, policies, and practices composing the strategic means, as well as for at least some degree of external fit between the HR strategic means and the ends on the one hand and the firm business strategy on the other, is a core assumption underlying nearly all models of HR strategy (Baird & Meshoulam, 1988; Lado & Wilson, 1994). Still, Osterman's model may be criticized for not providing greater insight into which logic is appropriate for which competitive situation.

Two more recent models attempt to expand on Osterman's employment framework specifically by strengthening this critical link between firm strategy and the logic underlying the HR strategy. Delery and Doty (1996) proposed a typology of HR strategy based on the assumption that firms having a close fit between their HR practices and business strategy will perform better than those whose HR strategies are more poorly aligned. The authors suggested three ideal types of HR strategies: "market," "internal," and "middle of the road"—again governed by the degree to which human resources are viewed as an asset as opposed to a cost and by the nature of the employee-employer exchange. Instead of differing across four sets of employment rules (as in the case of Osterman's model), Delery and Doty's three strategic configurations differ across seven HR practices. For example, the market type of HR strategy is governed by an employer interest in reducing labor costs and is characterized by few internal career opportunities. Hiring is done almost exclusively from outside the organization, and there is little formal training, widespread use of profit sharing, limited employment security, and little opportunity for employee participation in organizational decision making. In contrast, the internal HR strategy is governed by an employer interest in using employee competencies and social capital as a source of sustained competitive advantage. It is characterized by an ILM, with most positions being staffed from within the organization; extensive employee training and a strong emphasis on socialization; performance appraisals focusing on behaviors rather than outcomes and geared towards employee development; limited use of incentive systems such as profit sharing; a great deal of employment security; a higher level of employee participation in decision making; and narrowly defined jobs positioned along a "taller" hierarchy. The middle-of-the-road strategy is defined as a hybrid of the two and is operationalized as the midpoint between the internal and market strategies along all seven HR practices.

Delery and Doty (1996) provided a strong theoretical grounding for their configurations, noting that on the basis of equifinality assumptions, these three ideal types of HR strategy incorporate practices that are internally consistent ("maximizing horizontal fit") and are, as a group, logically linked to alternative business strategies ("maximizing vertical fit") (p. 809). The alternative business strategies to which they are linked are those identified by Miles and Snow (1978). Specifically, the internal strategy's logic and practices are consistent with the defender business strategy and the HR objectives suggested by it, whereas the middle-of-the-road and market strategies' logics and practices are consistent with the analyzer and prospector business strategies respectively and the HR objectives specified by them. For example, to maximize efficiency, an HR objective for the defender business strategy is likely to be employee commitment (as a means to lower dysfunctional turnover and high replacement costs). As a group, the practices associated with the internal strategy are geared precisely toward such HR objectives and are thus well aligned with the defender strategy.

Like Delery and Doty (1996), Baron and Kreps (1999) offered a three-part model of HR strategy based on the nature of the employee-employer exchange relationship. However, unlike the previous two models, this model assumes that the successful implementation of *any* business strategy requires a unique and sustainable set of human resource competencies. Consequently, rather than distinguishing among HR strategies on the basis of the degree to which employees are viewed as a source of competitive advantage (versus as a cost), Baron and

Kreps differentiated among HR strategies according to the logic underlying the way in which firms seek to *efficiently* acquire, develop, and retain such assets. As a result, their model is even more firmly grounded in the notion of labor markets. The first type of HR strategy they identified is an ILM strategy. Similar to Osterman's "salary" strategy and Delery and Doty's "internal" strategy, the ILM approach is geared toward firms whose business strategies emphasize the following two HR goals: (a) the retention of firm-specific knowledge and (b) the minimization of recruitment and training costs. To achieve these objectives, firms implementing ILM HR strategies adopt sophisticated recruitment and screening mechanisms, place an emphasis on employee socialization, provide numerous opportunities for employee development, use incentives to encourage employee retention, avoid wage compression by emphasizing internal over external equity in compensation, and attempt to staff all but entry-level positions from within.

Similar to Osterman's (1987) craft or secondary strategy and Delery and Doty's (1996) market strategy, Baron and Kreps's second type of HR strategy, a "high-commitment" strategy, assumes that employees may be more committed to their line of work than to their employer and may thus have little interest in intraorganizational career opportunities. The underlying objective of this strategy is therefore to efficiently maximize employee outputs—that is, to use "HRM practices targeted at getting more out of employees by giving them more" (p. 2). Such HR practices include sophisticated recruitment and selection processes designed to identify superior job candidates, reward practices (individual and team) designed to encourage employee flexibility and a willingness to take on job assignments beyond those associated with normally assigned tasks, and a work culture placing an emphasis on employee involvement and discretion. In contrast to the ILM strategy, which is grounded on a tall hierarchy with organizational status based on one's bureaucratic position, the high-commitment strategy emphasizes egalitarianism. The ILM places an emphasis on internally developing employee competencies and preserving organization-specific knowledge by offering employment security and extensive career development potential. In contrast, the high-commitment strategy emphasizes the careful acquisition of such competencies. It takes some degree of turnover for granted but seeks to minimize its deleterious consequences by placing an emphasis on teamwork, a flat hierarchy, open communication and information, and results-based, deferred compensation.

Baron and Kreps's (1999) third model is in fact a hybrid. They argued that a high-commitment/ILM hybrid strategy is relatively rare in the West but is the strategy of choice in several Japanese firms (e.g., NEC, Toyota, Matsui). Such a hybrid may be an empirical anomaly in the West (although several U.S. auto makers such as Ford and Chrysler appear to be moving toward it) because it integrates the job security and internal staffing practices of the ILM strategy with the team-based work structure and results-oriented performance appraisal of the high-commitment model. An alternative hybrid suggested by the authors appears to be more apparent in an increasing number of American firms. This hybrid involves the application of a high-commitment model with respect to an organization's core tasks (i.e., the ones on which the success of the firm's competitive strategy is most contingent) and a kind of "secondary" model with respect to all other positions that is based on the outsourcing of all nonmainstream jobs (e.g., clerical, janitorial).

Despite their differences, the three typologies described above are similar in that they stem from a resource-based view of the firm (Barney, 1986, 1991) and view the employee-employer exchange relationship as providing the basic, defining logic linking strategic means to ends and ensuring that the means are not internally misaligned. Not only do all three of these theory-based models assume that the firm's competitive business strategy in effect "selects" the appropriate exchange relationship between employers and their employees, they also assume that the nature of this exchange relationship sets the basic framework governing the selection of HR goals and the practices to be used to achieve those goals. Specifically, the three models discussed above all assume that HR practices are selected to serve a set of HR objectives that are, at the very least, not inconsistent with the strategic goals of the firm as a whole. Moreover, the models assume that in addition to ensuring such "external fit," the logic implicit in the nature of the employee-employer exchange ensures that the practices and policies adopted to achieve these goals are internally consistent; that is, that there is a high degree of internal fit. Finally, because these models are based on two ideal types of employee-employer exchange (i.e., ILMs vs. ELMs), they tend to specify at least two ideal types of HR strategies along a continuum of logics consistent with, at one extreme a reliance on ILMs, and at the other, a reliance on ELMs. Hybrid HR strategies are adopted by those firms whose competitive strategy or occupational composition or both demand a logic taking both ILM and ELM relations into account.

Employee Control Models

A second group of researchers frame their models of HR strategy around the same three parameters—means, ends, and logics—but adopt an approach that is concerned more with employer control and employee role performance processes than with the nature of the employment relationship. As far as these researchers are concerned, a firm's competitive context places constraints on the way in which managers are able to efficiently monitor and control employee role performance. Thus, this second approach to modeling the types of HR strategy is based on the nature of organizational control and, more specifically, on the way in which the organization seeks to direct and monitor employee role performance.

Schuler and Jackson (1987b), in one of the earliest models of HR strategy proposed, argued that just as organizations differ in their strategies and characteristics (e.g., structure, size, age), so do the attitudes and behaviors of their members. The function of HR strategy is therefore to better align member attitudes and behaviors with firm strategy. Recognizing that HR practices can channel and influence employee role behaviors and help make these behaviors more predictable, these authors claimed that different clusters of HR practices are required to help the organization achieve its strategic objectives. Drawing on Porter's (1985) typology of competitive strategies, they claimed that for each strategy (e.g., differentiation, cost reduction) there is a corresponding set of ideal employee role dimensions (and consequently employee role performance objectives) that will be critical for strategy implementation. They identified 10 such role dimensions, including

- Short-term focus versus long-term focus
- Low concern for quality versus a high concern for quality
- Low risk-taking orientation versus a high risk-taking orientation

Role performance objectives supportive of the differentiation strategy, for example, are likely to include having employees with a high degree of creative behavior, a longer term orientation, a high concern for quality, a high tolerance for ambiguity, and a moderate to high degree of risk taking.

Jackson and Schuler (1995) argued that employers select HR practices designed to channel employee behavior such that individual role performance is consistent with these HR system objectives. That is, HR strategy, as they conceptualized it, is based on a set of employee role performance goals consistent with the firm's competitive strategy, as well as a bundle of HR policies and practices designed to channel and control employee attitudes and behaviors such that these goals may be achieved. The bundle of policies and practices vary from strategy to strategy along five dimensions: planning, staffing, appraising, compensation, and training and development. Thus, for example, depending on the competitive strategy and hence the HR objectives, an HR strategy may be composed of planning practices that are more or less formal, short- or long-term oriented, and more or less open to employee participation.

Although Jackson and Schuler failed to explicate the logic underlying each of their strategic types, two main control-based logics may be inferred on the basis of their discussion. The first is a logic of direct, process-based control in which the focus is on efficiency and cost containment (consistent with the nature of Porter's cost leadership strategy), whereas the second is a logic of indirect output-based control in which the focus is on actual results (consistent with Porter's differentiation strategy). Implicit in Jackson and Schuler's framework is that the logic underlying an HR strategy will tend to be consistent with the firm's overall competitive strategy. Thus, we are unlikely to find firms adopting a differentiation strategy with an HR strategy grounded in a process-based logic. Simply put, an HR strategy framed around a logic of process-based control is not likely to attract creative employees or help in the development of employee creativity, nor is it likely to encourage the long-term performance orientation on the part of employees that is desired by most firms adopting such a strategy.

This focus on employee control as a basis for distinguishing among HR strategies has its roots in the sociology of work. Control is defined by Edwards (1979) as "the ability of managers to obtain desired work behavior from workers" (p. 17). Thus, the control system is the crucial interface between labor and management in an organization. Over the years, changing technologies and increasingly competitive environments have forced administrators to adopt a diverse set of mechanisms by which to control labor (Edwards, 1979). Organizational theorists (Ouchi & Maguire, 1975; Thompson, 1967) view these mechanisms as being grounded in one of two alternative approaches, namely behavioral (or process) control and outcome control. Behavioral or process control is often highly cost-effective, but it entails the careful planning and direct monitoring of the processes used by workers to achieve a given set of ends. According to Thompson, because it is inherently means based, behavioral control is effective only when means-ends relations are completely understood (as in the case of an auto assembly line). When means-ends relations are uncertain (as is typically the case among firms adopting a differentiation strategy) but goals are agreed on by agents and principals, output controls (i.e., controls that focus on the ends themselves, such as margin or market share) may be effective. Because output controls are inherently more uncertain than process or behavioral controls, however, managers tend to adopt them only when they feel that they can reduce this uncertainty by predetermining the premises on which their subordinates make key decisions (Thompson, 1967). Consequently, organizations relying on output-based systems of governance tend to rely heavily on practices designed to shape the organizational norms and values underlying many of these decisions (Kunda, 1992)—practices that are themselves highly uncertain and both time consuming and costly to implement.

Dyer and Holder (1988) structured their typology of HR strategies around the notion of differing logics of control as well, again basing their typology on differing clusters of ends, means, and logics. Indeed, Dyer and Holder (1988) defined HR strategy as "decisions concerning major HR goals and the primary means in pursuit of these goals" (p. 1). Four key ends or goals were identified: contribution, composition, competence, and commitment. Contribution goals have to do with employee performance expectations (e.g., efficiency, creativity, flexibility, and innovativeness).Composition goals have to do with the makeup of the workforce, specifically its ethnic and gender mix, skill mix, and staff-line and supervisory ratios. Competence goals concern the level of employee knowledge, skills, and abilities: that is, the degree to which the workforce has the competencies necessary to implement the organization's strategic objectives. Finally, commitment goals have to do with the degree of employee attachment to the organization, from casual attachment to a total identification with the organization. Dyer and Holder claimed that organizations, to achieve these ends, select means from seven different realms of HR activity: training and development, performance management, employee relations, labor relations, government relations, reward management, and work system design.

Finally, three different types of logics determine how overall HR goals are configured across the four dimensions described above (i.e., contribution, composition, competence, and commitment) and which HR practices from across the seven realms of activity will be clustered to serve these goals. The link between logics, goals, and means is depicted in Table 3.1. According to Dyer and Holder's (1988) typology, an "inducement" logic is most likely to be adopted by firms engaged in a highly competitive business environment in which there is a strong focus on containing costs, maintaining low staff numbers, and ensuring that the process by which inputs are transformed into outputs is free from labor-based disruptions. Such organizations emphasize commitment goals (to minimize recruitment, selection, and development costs), narrowly define and routinize jobs (to reduce the level of uncertainty in the production process), and try to build a strong link between work effort and pay.

Table 3.1 Dyer and Holder's Typology of HR Strategies

	Logics		
Goals	*Investment*	*Inducement*	*Involvement*
Contribution	High initiative and creativity; high performance expectations; some flexibility	Some initiative and creativity; very high performance standards; modest flexibility	Very high initiative and creativity; very high performance expectations; high flexibility; self-managed
Composition	Comfortable head count (core and buffer); high skill mix; moderate staff	Lean head count (core and buffer); low skill mix; minimal staff	Comfortable head count; protected core; high skill mix; minimal staff
Competence	High	Adequate	Very high
Commitment	High; identification with company	High; instrumental	Very high; strong identification with work, team, and company
Practices			
Staffing	Careful selection; extensive career development; some flexibility; minimal layoffs	Careful selection; few career options; use of temps; minimal layoffs	Very careful selection; some career development; extreme flexibility; minimal (or no) layoffs
Development	Extensive; continuous learning	Minimal	Extensive; continuous learning
Rewards	Tall structure; competitive, fixed, job based, merit; many benefits	Flat structure; high, variable, piece rate; profit sharing; minimal benefits	Flat structure; high, partially variable, skill and competency based; gain sharing; flexible benefits
Work system	Broad jobs; employee initiative; some groups	Narrow jobs; employee paced; individualized	Enriched jobs; self-managed work teams
Supervision	Extensive, supportive	Minimal, directive	Minimal, facilitative
Employee relations	Much communication; high voice; high due process; high employee assistance	Some communication; some voice; egalitarian	Open and extensive communication; high voice; some due process; egalitarian, some employee assistance
Labor relations	Nonissue	Union avoidance or conflict	Union avoidance and/or cooperation
Government relations	Overcompliance	Compliance	Compliance

SOURCE: Dyer and Holder (1988, pp. 1-21).

In contrast, an "investment" logic is typically adopted by firms whose business strategy is framed around a tradition of product differentiation (i.e., brand recognition, quality, or functionality) rather than cost leadership. Such organizations rely on a kind of controlled adaptability and flexibility, resulting in an organization with a broad skill mix but with centralized decision making and a tall hierarchy. Jobs tend to be broadly defined, reward practices incorporate a mix of fixed and variable components to encourage creativity and initiative, and an emphasis is placed on employee development and commitment (to retain valuable in-house knowledge). Nevertheless, employee initiative is bounded by a relatively high level of direct, process-based supervision and a highly developed reporting system.

The third logic, "involvement" logic, is, according to Dyer and Holder (1988), characteristic of organizations with a hybrid business strategy focusing on both cost leadership and innovativeness. Such organizations typically adopt flat, decentralized structures to maximize cost effectiveness while still being able to respond rapidly to competitor actions and shifts in market demands. To meet innovation requirements, the cluster of HR practices associated with this strategy are characterized by an emphasis on staffing, job structuring, supervision, and rewards. Composition, commitment, and competence goals are attained by staffing the organization with a relatively high proportion of professionals with a very high level of technological know-how and by structuring jobs so as to provide maximum challenge, involvement, and autonomy. Contribution goals are attained by tightly linking rewards to results.

In an empirical test of the validity of this typology, Swiercz (1995) found support for the inducement and involvement logics but not for the investment logic. This finding suggests that strategic logics may cluster around the two extremes of organizational control, namely tight, process-based control (dominant in the inducement logic) and relatively loose, output-based control (characteristic of the involvement logic). In the same way that the hybrid employer-employee exchange model described by Baron and Kreps (1999) (combining elements of both internal and ELMs) was described as an empirical anomaly, so may be this hybrid control model. That is, in the same way that an employer-employee exchange approach to modeling HR strategy suggests two ideal types of strategies at opposite poles of a continuum (i.e., internal vs. external), so does the organizational control approach (i.e., process vs. output).

Indeed, Snell's (1992) examination of the link between strategic business contingencies and models of HR management control also suggests support for this notion of a process-versus-output continuum of HR strategies. Defining control as "any process that helps align the actions of individuals with the interests of their employing firm" (p. 293), Snell argued that HR practices, as the "principal methods used to regulate performance" (p. 293), in fact manifest control in organizations. According to his typology, HR practices tend to cluster around three main types of control: behavioral, output, and input. Like Dyer and Holder's (1988) inducement logic, HR practices grounded in the logic of behavioral control assume a high degree of task programmability (i.e., complete knowledge of cause-and-effect relations) and are based on carefully articulated operating procedures and the use of direct, in-process behavioral monitoring to identify and correct deviations as they occur. Snell argued that in contrast, HR practices grounded in output-based control are framed around the translation of intentions into targets rather than operating procedures. This logic (like Dyer and Holder's involvement logic) provides subordinates with discretion as to the means to be used to achieve desired ends. It assumes that the standards of desired performance are not only preset but also highly crystallized.

But what happens when cause-and-effect knowledge is incomplete and standards of performance are ambiguous? Snell claimed that under such conditions, firms tend to adopt HR systems based on input control: that is, they regulate performance by regulating the antecedent conditions of performance, such as training and selection (as in Dyer and Holder's investment-based model of HR strategy).

Snell (1992) used data from over 400 single-business-unit firms to show that environmental (i.e., product market variations) and technological factors (i.e., work flow integration) have an impact on both the knowledge of cause-and-effect relations and the clarity of performance standards and thus in turn determine the extent to which HR systems are grounded in behavior-output- or input-based logics of control. The findings suggest that

- "The constructs of input, behavior and output control provide a viable (and more parsimonious) framework for integrating human resource practices" (p. 318).
- The nature of administrative information (i.e., cause-and-effect relations and the clarity of performance standards) mediates the link between the strategic business context and HR strategy.
- Input-based control may provide the basis of a hybrid HR strategy in that although support was found for a mediated link between strategic context and both behavior- (i.e., process-) and output-based control, input-based practices such as training and selection remained fairly constant across strategic contexts.

Given the compelling evidence regarding both the exchange and control approaches, it is difficult to claim that one approach may be more valid than the other. Indeed, perhaps both approaches are correct and HR strategies in fact vary across two dimensions, one having to do with the strategy's underlying logic of the employer-employee exchange and the other having to do with the strategy's underlying logic of organizational control. Before we try to reconcile these two approaches and provide answers to such questions, it may be useful to explore some of the empirical findings with regard to the nature of HR strategy.

Data-Driven Models

Data-driven models of HR strategy focus on identifying the most common "bundles of practices" (i.e., means) as they exist in the field. Researchers may use a variety of statistical methods to identify these bundles, but the most widely used techniques are factor analysis and cluster analysis. Just as the HR theorists above were shown to link theoretical means to ends, these empirical researchers attempt to do the same. However, they do so empirically, identifying the statistical tendency of each bundle to cluster in firms with specific business strategies.

Arthur (1992, 1994) conducted one of the first empirical analyses of HR strategies in an attempt to test the proposition that differences in employee relations policies and practices are related to the differences in business strategy. Two sets of questionnaires were sent to a sample of 54 American steel mini-mills: one to HR managers concerning the nature of the plant's employee relations policies and the other to line managers regarding the importance of various competitive strategy characteristics, the number and type of products produced, and the total hourly cost of work. Data from line management were used to construct eight business strategy variables, and data from HR managers were used to construct ten employee relations variables. The cluster analysis, conducted on the basis of these two sets of variables, revealed the existence of two dominant HR strategies: a cost reduction strategy and an employee commitment strategy. These strategies were distinguished from one another on the basis of five realms of HR policy and practice: work organization, employee relations, staffing, training, and compensation.

Arthur (1994) concluded that the goal of the cost reduction strategy is to "improve efficiency by enforcing employee compliance with specified rules and procedures and basing employee rewards on some measurable criteria," whereas the goal of the commitment strategy is to develop a cadre of committed employees who "can be trusted to use their discretion to carry out job tasks in ways that are consistent with organizational goals" (p. 672). The study found that the commitment strategy's cluster of practices was characterized by higher levels of employee involvement in decision making, enhanced employee training in problem solving, a stronger emphasis on socialization-oriented development activities, selection methods aimed at maintaining a higher ratio of skilled to unskilled employees, and a higher average wage rate.

In this sense, Arthur's typology combines elements of both the resource and organizational control approaches. The cost reduction strategy is grounded in the assumption that "managers have a relatively complete knowledge of the transformation process (inputs to outputs) and a high ability to effectively set performance standards and measure employee outputs" (p. 672).[1] Under such conditions, employers may, in a highly cost-effective manner, directly monitor and reward employees on the basis of their meeting either process- or result-based standards. Labor costs are reduced because of generally lower levels of remuneration and a more limited need for the organization to invest in employee training and development.

However, when such conditions are absent (as is typical in the case of organizations adopting competitive strategies based on differentiation), the uncertainties inherent in the transformation process may be best controlled by adopting a commitment strategy. In addition to providing the organization with enhanced flexibility and agility, such a strategy may offer significant savings as a result of a reduced need for monitoring employee compliance with work rules. Nevertheless, the commitment strategy has significant costs associated with it due to the need to (a) recruit and select the best possible candidates to handle multiple, complex, dynamic, and often ambiguous job tasks; (b) develop a sophisticated program of employee socialization (to align the interests of these often externally recruited employees with the interests of the firm); (c) design work systems such that they provide highly skilled employees with the autonomy needed to deal with the uncertainties inherent in the transformation process; and (d) provide above-market, equity-based compensation to attract and retain highly valued human assets. These costs may be justified when, according to Arthur (1994), "the successful implementation of a business strategy requires a unique set of employee behaviors and attitudes" that cannot in any reliable fashion be "produced" on the basis of formalized work rules and task routines (p. 672). In this sense, Arthur's commitment strategy is labor market oriented and focuses on the structuring of the employer-employee exchange, whereas the cost reduction strategy is performance oriented and focuses on the structuring of behavioral rules and routines and the monitoring of employee compliance with such rules.

In a similar fashion, MacDuffie (1995) claimed that HR strategies are manifested in bundles of interrelated and internally consistent HR practices that may be empirically identified. Underlying each of these bundles, according to MacDuffie, is an "organizational logic" that ensures that the bundle of HR practices is "integrated with complementary bundles of practices from core business functions" (p. 198). MacDuffie predicted, on the basis of these logics, that organizations will use different combinations of HR practices and policies (means) to achieve three primary HR goals (ends): (a) ensuring that employees have the competencies (i.e., skill and knowledge) required to achieve firm business objectives, (b) ensuring that employees have the motivation and commitment needed to exploit these competencies, and (c) ensuring that the discretionary exploitation of these competencies is "appropriately channeled toward performance improvement" (p. 198). Among the practices and policies examined were the nature of organizational rewards (i.e., contingency-based compensation), recruitment and selection, and training, as well as the degree to which there was a reliance on work teams, job rotation, and employee involvement in decision making.

MacDuffie proposed that organizations doing business on the basis of a strategy requiring high-volume production (e.g., Porter's cost leadership) adopt an organizational logic of "buffering." This buffering logic places a premium on stable conditions and the ability to prevent any disruption of production. Specifically, such organizations have an inherent interest in adopting HR practices designed to "buffer" the production process from potential disruptions, such as hiring easily replaceable (i.e., unskilled) workers to perform narrowly defined jobs. Efficiency wages are used to ensure an adequate level of employee motivation, and close, direct supervision is used to ensure that employee effort is appropriately channeled. In contrast, organizations whose competitive strategy requires rapid market response and high-quality production (e.g., Porter's differentiation strategy) adopt a "flexibility" logic. This logic places a premium on quality control and continuous learning. These organizations, rather than adopting a technical "fix" for the problem of uncertainty, look to their human resource assets to absorb and learn from such contingencies. With such a focus on employee problem solving, this strategy requires HR practices (e.g., more comprehensive selection process, rewards that are partially contingent on performance, focus on employee skill development) designed to provide a workforce with the multiple skills and strong knowledge base required to absorb uncertainty and with "individual interests [that] are aligned with those of the employer" (p. 198).

Using an international sample of 62 international assembly car plants, MacDuffie's cluster analysis validated the existence of these two hypothesized HR strategies—labeled *mass production* and *flexible production*—but also found evidence of a third, intermediate or "transition" strategy. As predicted, relative to the mass production HR strategy, the flexible production HR strategy was characterized by significantly more extensive training and development activity, more widespread use of work teams, employee involvement and job rotation, a stronger reliance on contingent pay, and more limited status differentiation (i.e., flat hierarchies). The transition strategy was composed of a bundle of practices about halfway between the mass production and flexible strategies.

One limitation of a number of empirical studies designed to distinguish among particular HR strategies is that they are grounded in rather monolithic assumptions regarding the internally homogeneous nature of such strategies. That is, as Lepak and Snell (1999a, 1999b) noted, because they tend to focus on the extent to which particular practices are used across all employees of a firm, many of the studies noted above "ignore the possible existence of different employment practices for different employee groups within a firm" (p. 2). Lepak and Snell argued that it may be "inappropriate" to suggest that there is a common bundle of practices and policies for managing all of a firm's employees. Rather, like Becker and Gerhart (1996), they proposed that although in any given organization there tends to be a *dominant* HR strategy or HR system architecture, on a more operational level multiple bundles of HR practices unique to particular organizational subgroups are likely to develop.

A second limitation of both of the empirical studies discussed above concerns the nature of their respective samples. Both Arthur and MacDuffie based their analyses on a relatively small sample of organizations drawn from a single industry (i.e., steel and auto respectively). Despite the obvious similarity in their findings, until recently questions remained as to the generalizability of these findings to other organizations (particularly organizations competing in other types of industries). However, using a national probability sample of 548 for-profit and nonprofit organizations, Huselid and Becker (1997) found that HR practices indeed clustered into two core HR strategies paralleling those identified by Arthur and MacDuffie (i.e., the cost reduction or mass production vs. high-commitment or flexible production dichotomies respectively) and that this dichotomy was generalizable across a wide range of organizations.

In contrast to the theory-driven models discussed earlier, it should be clear that the empirical models presented above are not grounded in any single control or resource-based approach. Indeed, the models of HR generated from the field suggest the need to integrate these two approaches because, in practice, the nature of control and the basis of employee-employer exchange tend to co-vary. The clearest evidence of this is that organizations tend to adopt one of two dominant strategies, with some organizations adopting a middle, "transition" strategy. One is a control-based strategy placing an emphasis on both rule specification and compliance monitoring, as well as on ELMs and employment at will as a means to ensure efficient and undisrupted production. The other is a commitment-based strategy placing an emphasis on ILMs, aligned employee-employer interests, and the development of unique HR competencies as a means to ensure sustainable market responsiveness and organizational agility. In other words, although the theory-based models of HR strategy suggest two separate continua for distinguishing among HR strategies (a control-based continuum and a resource-based continuum), the empirical literature suggests the existence of a single continuum integrating the two. How might it be possible to reconcile the differences between the theory-based and empirical models?

An Integrative Approach

We propose that one way to reconcile these differences is by viewing the nature of resource acquisition and retention (external vs. internal) and the nature of organizational control (process vs. output) not as two alternative continua but rather as two distinct, orthogonal dimensions of HR strategy. From the discussion above, it appears that individually, neither of the two dichotomous approaches described above (i.e., resource and control models) provides a framework able to encompass the key variants of HR strategy in a comprehensive yet parsimonious manner. However, by viewing these two approaches as orthogonal dimensions of HR strategy, we propose what we believe to be a more comprehensive and parsimonious typology of HR strategy.

In the context of such a framework, the first dimension, "resource acquisition," concerns the "make-or-buy" aspect of HR strategy—that is, the degree to which the HR strategy is geared toward the internal development of employee competencies as opposed to the market-based acquisition of such competencies. The second dimension, "control," concerns the degree to which the HR strategy is geared toward monitoring employee behaviors and, in particular, employees' compliance with process-based standards as opposed to developing

	Internal	*External*
Output	1. Commitment	2. Free Agent
Process	3. Paternalistic	4. Secondary

Figure 3.1. A Typology of Dominant HR Strategies

an alignment of interests among employers and employees and ensuring that employees are motivated to fully exploit their competencies in order to serve these common interests.

As can be seen in Figure 3.1, by combining these two dimensions, we generate four ideal types of *dominant* HR strategies. As noted above, some degree of variance in the nature of particular HR practices for certain employee subgroups within a given organization is to be expected (Lepak & Snell, 1999a, 1999b). Nevertheless, for the *majority* of organizational members, these policies and practices will, at the very least, remain closely aligned with the key principles underlying the macro or dominant HR strategy. The cells on the diagonal (commitment and secondary) appear to be most similar to the two opposing dominant strategies described by Arthur and MacDuffie. That is, according to the findings of Arthur and MacDuffie, the inherent covariance of HR strategies along these two dimensions makes the strategies represented by Cells 1 and 4 likely to be the most prevalent in organizations. Those dominant strategies represented by the off-quadrant cells (i.e., Cells 2 and 3) are less likely to be prevalent because they are hybrids with inherent internal contradictions. As MacDuffie suggested, such strategies may be "transition strategies" adopted by firms in the process of moving from one dominant HR strategy to the other.

A similar four-type model of HR strategy recently received empirical support in a study of 153 different firms from 97 industries conducted by Lepak and Snell (1999a, 1999b). Specifically, the authors identified the following four strategic configurations of HR practices:

1. Commitment (similar to our commitment type)
2. Traditional (similar to our paternalistic type)
3. Compliance (similar to our secondary type)
4. Collaborative (similar to our free-agent type)

The likelihood that a firm's HR strategy would be characterized by one configuration over another was found to be strongly related to the strategic orientation or business strategy of the firm (i.e., the degree to which it was cost focused vs. innovation focused). However, the findings also suggest that although there may be four clearly delineated HR "architectures" or dominant HR strategies, at the more micro level within firms, the way in which these dominant strategies are applied may in some cases vary according to the nature of the particular workforces employed (i.e., workforces possessing unique firm-specific skills vs. those possessing low-valued and widely available skills).

As suggested by Arthur's (1992, 1994) findings, the commitment HR strategy (Cell 1) is most likely to be found in organizations in which management lacks a complete understanding of the process by which inputs are transformed into organizational outputs and/or lacks the ability to closely monitor or evaluate the efficacy of the employee behaviors instrumental to this transformation process. Under such conditions, employers must rely on employees to deal with the uncertainties inherent in the transformation process and can only evaluate the outputs of that process. Only by forging a commonality of interest can management increase the likelihood that employees will be motivated to (a) use their discretion to produce outputs consistent with organizational objectives (Organ, 1988) and (b) stay with their current employer (and thus not transfer valuable knowledge or social capital to competitors). To develop that commonality of interest, an employee-employer exchange based on the principles of an ILM (e.g., heavy emphasis on employee training and development, internal staffing, and internal equity) is typically used.

The other dominant strategy, the secondary HR strategy (Cell 4), is likely to be adopted by firms viewing a highly routinized, low-cost, and stable transformation process as the primary source of competitive advantage. As suggested by MacDuffie (1995), such firms use a technological "fix" to control the uncertainty in the transformation process and demand only that employees enact the specified behaviors required to facilitate undisrupted production. Implied by this definition is a focus on behavioral or process-based control in which "close monitoring by supervisors and efficiency wages ensure adequate work effort" (MacDuffie, 1995, p. 201). However, such systems of production are in many cases imitable, thus forcing the organization to look toward labor efficiencies as a complementary source of competitive advantage. Such efficiencies are provided by ensuring that (a) jobs remain simple enough to ensure a constant and stable supply from the ELM with minimal transaction and training costs and (b) labor costs remain variable (i.e., by maintaining a policy of employment at will and being able to rely on a contingent workforce). Increasingly, low-cost, high-volume producers have sought such efficiencies by shifting their production infrastructures to areas in which trade unions and government regulations pose less of a threat to such a strategy or by targeting their recruitment efforts at individuals (e.g., immigrants) unable to seek employment in the mainstream or "primary" labor market.

The free-agent strategy (Cell 2) parallels Osterman's "craft" employment system. As noted above, many employers find it more efficient to purchase the services of experts than to attempt to eliminate the uncertainty in a transformation process by routinizing that process. For example, rather than attempting to mass-produce buildings, contractors have long relied on independent craftspeople to provide highly specialized construction skills on an as-needed or employment-at-will basis. These individuals are employed for as long as the contractor needs them (typically, until the part of the construction process for which they are responsible has been completed) and are then returned to the market to seek alternative, temporary employment. However, because employers have relatively limited knowledge of the transformation process, these workers, while employed, are given extensive autonomy and are evaluated primarily in terms of the results of their efforts. Although Osterman (1987) referred to this as a craft system of employment, it has become quite prevalent among organizations requiring the services of highly skilled professionals, and it also serves as the HR strategy of choice among so-called "virtual organizations." Organizations adopting such a strategy often rely on the ELM to provide them with a stable supply of these highly skilled workers (often employed as independent contractors) simply because of the costs of relying on an ILM. Particularly when alternative, highly specialized skills are required, it is likely to be more efficient to acquire these competencies on an "as-needed" basis than to retain them on an "on-call" basis. Because they are employed to provide certain outputs or "deliverables" but engage in processes that are often well beyond the ability of the employer to comprehend, contingent pay (rather than in-house socialization or employee development) is often used to align their interests with those of their employer and to ensure that organizational objectives are met.

Finally, the paternalistic strategy (Cell 3) parallels Osterman's "industrial" employment system. As in the case of the secondary strategy, organizations adopting this strategy use a technological "fix" to control the uncertainty in the transformation process and demand only that employees enact the specified behaviors required to facilitate undisrupted production. However, unlike organizations adopting a secondary strategy, organizations adopting a paternalistic strategy use a limited ILM to guarantee that production remains undisturbed and to develop certain HR-based competencies (e.g., multitasking, team-based production) that might provide an additional source of competitive advantage. That is, in return for labor acquiescence to direct managerial process-based control and perhaps some degree of flexibility in staffing and task assignments, management provides to labor certain employment guarantees as well as a system of internal staffing, typically based on seniority. Furthermore, the use of an ILM approach to resource acquisition may provide such organizations with a limited learning capability that is typically unavailable to organizations adopting an HR strategy grounded in a logic of process control.

Although our discussion up to this point has highlighted some of the key differences between these strategies in terms of underlying logic, these strategies may also be distinguished from one another in terms of their respective ends and means.

Ends

Researchers have identified a wide variety of objectives that the HR system is intended to serve—objectives that are embedded in HR strategies (Bamberger & Fiegenbaum, 1996). Although each of the models reviewed above refers to the various ends or objectives on which different HR strategies might be grounded, it is our opinion that Dyer and Holder's (1988) framework offers one of the most comprehensive views of strategic ends. As will be recalled, they argued that the ends toward which HR strategies are directed vary in terms of four key dimensions: level of expected employee contribution (i.e., narrow, well-specified, and stable contribution criteria vs. broad, ambiguous, and dynamic contribution criteria), nature of workforce composition (i.e., supervisory ratio, skill mix), expected level of employee competence (i.e., level of workforce's knowledge and skill base), and expected level of employee commitment (degree to which individual interests of employees are aligned with those of management).

As comprehensive as their framework may be, to capture several of the other HR system objectives suggested by the other frameworks reviewed above, two additional dimensions might be added, namely agility and alignment. *Agility* refers to the degree to which the HR system needs to be responsive to shifts in the organization's external environment. For example, whereas the flexible production strategy identified by MacDuffie (1995) places a premium on the agility of the HR system, agility is a low-priority objective for the mass production strategy (because the entire strategy is grounded in a logic of stability and "buffering." Agility as an HR end is typically achieved through an emphasis on employee skill development (facilitating multitasking and problem solving), the development of an outsourcing capacity for noncritical tasks, and the use of contingency-based compensation.

Finally, *alignment* refers to the degree of fit among the various components of the HR system. Lado and Wilson (1994) claimed that HR strategies can be distinguished from one another according to the degree to which HR system attributes are synergistic. According to these researchers, HR strategies placing a premium on system synergy are more likely to be found in organizations in which the HR system is itself viewed as a potential source of sustained competitive advantage for the firm. When system attributes are tightly linked, the HR system becomes relatively immobile (i.e., not transferred across firms), causally ambiguous (thus making it more difficult for competitors to copy), or both. However, developing such synergy can be expensive, so firms relying on other sources of competitive advantage (e.g., economies of scale) are less likely to place an emphasis on this HR end (MacDuffie, 1995).

As can be seen in Table 3.2, the four main HR strategies identified according to our integrative model can be distinguished from one another in terms of the five key strategic ends. For example, whereas with the secondary strategy the expected employee contribution is relatively narrow, well specified, and stable, with the commitment strategy it is relatively broad, ambiguous, and dynamic. Whereas the commitment strategy's composition objectives include the acquisition and retention of a skilled workforce ready and willing to perform multiple tasks and able to work under very limited supervision, the secondary strategy's composition objectives include the acquisition of a relatively inexpensive and acquiescent workforce willing and ready to work under relatively tight supervision. Furthermore, the commitment strategy places its strongest emphasis on enhancing the degree to which the individual interests of employees are aligned with those of management. In contrast, the secondary strategy places little or no emphasis on employee commitment. Whereas the commitment strategy places a heavy premium on system agility and responsiveness, the secondary strategy places a premium on stability and the need to buffer the organization's core technology from change. Finally, with respect to alignment, as suggested by the findings of MacDuffie (1995), internal goal alignment is most critical for the commitment objective, whereas it is least central for his "transitional" strategy (in our case, the free-agent and paternalistic strategies).

Table 3.2 Typology of Dominant HR Strategies: Ends

Ends	Commitment	Free Agent	Paternalistic	Secondary
Contribution	Very high initiative and creativity; high performance expectations; self-managed	High initiative and creativity; high and relatively stable performance expectations; self-managed	Some initiative and creativity; moderate and stable performance expectations; tight control	Very low initiative and creativity; low performance and self-expectation; tight control
Composition	Comfortable head count (core and buffer); high skill mix; minimal staff	Lean head count (core and buffer); very high skill mix; minimal staff	Comfortable head count; (primarily core); moderate skill mix; moderate staff	Very lean head count; highly protected core; low skill mix; heavy staff; network based
Competence	High	Very high	Adequate	Adequate
Commitment	High; affective attachment to organization	Low; identification with work and occupation only	Moderate; instrumental and affective attachment	Limited; entirely instrumental attachment
Agility	Moderate	High	Limited	Very high
Alignment	High	Low	Low	High

Means

HR strategy researchers have generally adopted one of two approaches with regard to the analysis of the means (i.e., HR policies and practices) used to achieve strategic ends. One approach involves the examination of the specific and detailed policies and practices developed and implemented by the HR function (e.g., recruitment methods, selection criteria). The other involves the examination of the holistic processes embedded within the HR system that may or may not be the responsibility of the HR function. Wright and Snell (1991) advocated the latter approach for a number of reasons. First, they argued that if one adopts Mintzberg's (1987) definition of strategy as a pattern in the stream of decisions, a focus on function-specific practices only (rather than on organizational policies and practices having an impact on the HR system) may provide an incomplete view of the HR strategy as a whole. Although the HR function in many organizations has a key role in shaping the policies and practices underlying the HR system, policies and practices adopted by other functions may also influence the HR system and thus alter the emergent strategy. Consequently, a strategic analysis solely of the activities of the HR function is likely to make it more difficult for researchers to identify the conflicts and synergies among individual HR components of the overall HR strategy. Thus, Wright and Snell called for SHRM researchers to examine broad areas of HR activity that might be influenced by a variety of organizational functions other than the HR function.

Beer, Spector, Lawrence, Mills, and Walton (1984) were among the first researchers to propose such a holistic or system-based approach to examining the means by which HR goals may be achieved. They suggested that rather than examining each HR practice as an independent activity, researchers should examine the policies and practices affecting the HR system in terms of four major policy areas:

1. *Employee influence*: focuses on how much influence or authority over which policy areas should be allocated to whom
2. *Human resource flow*: focuses on the flow of people into and within the organization, including recruitment, internal mobility, termination, staffing, and performance evaluation
3. *Reward system*: focuses on intrinsic and extrinsic financial and nonfinancial rewards and the way in which such rewards tie into the behaviors and attitudes that the organization wishes to encourage
4. *Work system*: focuses on the design of and interrelationships among tasks and jobs, as well as competency utilization and skills development

Dyer and Holder (1988) concurred with this approach and proposed a similar framework for the analysis of HR means. Their framework includes six main policy areas:

1. *Development*: policies and practices having to do with the enhancement of employee knowledge, skills and abilities
2. *Rewards*: policies and practices relating to employee compensation and recognition
3. *Work system*: policies and practices having to do with the design of tasks, jobs, and the workplace as a whole
4. *Supervision and performance management*: policies and practices having to do with directing and evaluating the work of others
5. *Employee/labor relations*: policies and practices concerning discipline, dispute resolution, and union-management relations
6. *Government relations*: policies and practices regarding organizational compliance with government regulations

Although there is a great deal of overlap between these two frameworks for analyzing HR means at the system level, there are some obvious differences. For example, whereas Beer et al.'s (1984) framework pays little attention to policies and practices relating to union affairs, the framework proposed by Dyer and Holder (1988) neglects policies and practices influencing the flow of human resources into, within, and out of the organization. Furthermore, Dyer and Holder's framework, though not quite at the level of specific HR functions, is far more detailed than that of Beer et al. (1984). As noted by Wright and Snell (1991), one problem with function-specific frameworks for the analysis of HR means is that researchers are unable to identify the synergies and/or conflicts among the broader, underlying realms of activity.

In an effort to integrate these two approaches into a more parsimonious framework for analyzing HR means, we suggest that SHRM researchers study HR means in terms of HR subsystems. As in the case of the HR system as a whole, HR subsystems are likely to be most influenced by the policies and practices adopted and implemented by the HR function. However, as in the case of the HR system as a whole, the policies and practices adopted by other organizational functions are likely to also shape the nature of these subsystems. Furthermore, an analysis of HR means at the subsystem level focuses on broader realms of activity and is thus able to capture the synergies among unique but related policies and practices. An analysis of HR means at the subsystem level therefore offers researchers a mechanism to examine broad realms of HR-related activity without neglecting the impact of non-HR functions.

Drawing on the two frameworks discussed above (Beer et al., 1984; Dyer & Holder, 1988), in Table 3.3 we compare the means inherent in the four HR strategies identified earlier along three main HR subsystems:

1. *People flow subsystem,* including such HR activities as recruitment, selection, placement, employee mobility (internal and external), employee career development, training and development, and HR planning
2. *Appraisal and reward subsystem,* including such HR activities as performance appraisal, compensation, and benefits
3. *Employment relations subsystem,* including such HR activities as industrial and employee relations; work process, job, and task design; and culture management

In the following three chapters of this book, we use this three-part HR subsystem framework to further analyze some of the key differences between the four HR strategies identified earlier. Specifically, in each of the next three chap-

Table 3.3 Typology of Dominant HR Strategies: Means

Means	Commitment	Free Agent	Paternalistic	Secondary
People flow subsystem	Very careful selection; extensive career development and support; heavy reliance on internal staffing and promotion from within; extensive flexibility	Careful selection; extensive flexibility; limited career development and support; external staffing for most positions	Somewhat careful selection; moderate career development and support; moderate reliance on internal staffing but limited to certain types of jobs and within contractual framework; bounded job security; little flexibility	Very limited selection process; no career development and support; extensive flexibility; heavy reliance on temporary or contract-based employment
Appraisal and reward subsystem	Emphasis on internal and employee equity; performance-based pay at individual and group levels; heavy emphasis on benefits, deferred pay, and employee assistance; extensive use of 360-degree feedback	Emphasis on external equity; performance-based pay at individual level; skill-based pay; limited use of benefits; moderate use of alternative appraisal systems (e.g., 360-degree feedback, peer evaluation)	Emphasis on internal equity; limited use of profit sharing and group-based contingent pay; heavy emphasis on benefits; limited performance appraisal systems in place	Emphasis on external and employee equity; heavy use of contingent pay based on supervisor-based appraisal; extremely limited use of benefits and employee assistance
Employee relations subsystem	Broad, enriched, and self-managed jobs; self-managed teams; high, extensive use of multitasking; emphasis on organizational culture as a mechanism of organizational control; extensive internal communications; due process; some union presence	Enriched jobs; self-managed work teams; high degree of autonomy; minimal, facilitative supervision; emphasis on occupational culture as mechanism of control	Narrow jobs; some use of multitasking and team-based work; limited opportunities for employee involvement; process-based supervisory control; heavily unionized; highly developed grievance system with due process	Narrow jobs; limited opportunity for employee involvement; tight, process-based supervisory control; no opportunities for employee voicing; union avoidance

ters we will explore how, inherent in each of the four main HR strategies identified, a different set of integrated policies and practices is associated with either the people flow, appraisal and reward, or employment environment subsystems.

Summary

We began this chapter by asserting that HR strategies should be examined in terms of configurations or bundles of practices. We noted that such an approach is widespread in the field of strategy in general and that it offers a number of advantages to the field of HR strategy in particular. Adopting this type of configuration approach, SHRM researchers have proposed two main types of strategic frameworks: theory driven and data driven.

Theory-driven frameworks tend to be either resource based or control based. Resource-based typologies differentiate between HR strategies in terms of the degree to which the organization views its people as a key source of competitive advantage and in terms of the logic underlying the organization's efforts to acquire, develop, and retain its human assets. Control-based typologies differentiate between HR strategies in terms of the approach taken by the organization in its effort to deal with the uncertainties inherent in the work process (i.e., the process by which production inputs are turned into outputs).

Data-driven frameworks tend not to distinguish between these two perspectives. Instead, their empirical results suggest that HR strategies tend to vary along a continuum from an internally oriented commitment model to a process- and control-oriented mass production model. In some cases, these studies suggest the existence of a hybrid model of HR strategy that is somewhere in the middle of this continuum.

Finally, we argued that it may make the most sense to combine the two perspectives discussed in the theory-driven models and view them as orthogonal dimensions of HR strategy. Using this integrative approach, we identified four main types of HR strategy and began to show how they vary in terms of underlying logic, ends, and means. In Chapters 4, 5, and 6, we will expand on this analysis, attempting to show how the four types of HR strategy can be distinguished from one another with respect to three main HR subsystems.

Note

1. Whereas in his 1992 article, Arthur referred to this as a "cost reduction" strategy, in his 1994 article, he referred to it as a "control" strategy.

4

People Flow Subsystem

Our discussion in the previous chapter suggested that HR practices tend to cluster into discernable configurations or strategies. Furthermore, we noted that most contemporary strategic human resource management (SHRM) theories suggest that, in accordance with equifinality assumptions, these clusters tend to encompass practices that are both internally consistent and externally aligned (i.e., with business unit and/or corporate strategy). Reviewing a variety of theoretical and empirically derived frameworks, we argued that typologies of dominant HR strategies tend to be unidimensional, focusing either on the overall labor market orientation of the firm or on the approach taken to control the work process. Integrating both of these dimensions, we proposed that in fact four ideal types of dominant HR strategies might be identified: high commitment, paternalistic, free agent, and secondary.

In this chapter and the two following it, we explore how key HR subsystems, namely the people flow, appraisal and reward, and employee relations subsystems, tend to vary across each of these four types of strategies. In each chapter, after defining the parameters of the specific subsystem, we will identify some of the key strategic choices needing to be made, as well as the contingencies governing these choices. In each chapter, we will also examine the possible impact of these choices on key organizational outcomes (e.g., productivity, financial performance) and discuss how these choices tend to be made in more or less predictable patterns depending on the overall nature of the HR strategy.

Subsystem Domain and Significance

Dyer and Holder (1988) defined staffing as the set of practices designed to shape the characteristics of the organizational workforce: that is, the process of matching people with jobs. In this sense, the people flow or staffing subsystem encompasses those practices and processes that have a direct impact on the ability of the firm to meet its composition (e.g., running fat or lean), competence (e.g., stock of knowledge, skills, and abilities), and cost objectives. Others adopt an even broader definition of the staffing system. For example, Beer et al. (1985) described staffing as a process that governs "the flow of people into, through and out of the organization" (p. 9). As such, it encompasses a whole arena of interrelated organizational activities such as human resource planning, job analysis, recruitment, selection, entry and placement, mobility, evaluation, career planning and development, and termination. Similarly, Dreher and Kendall (1995) viewed the staffing system as encompassing all of the means by which the organization attempts to shape the composition of its workforce, including such functions as recruitment, screening, selection, promotion, and retention/separation management.

Most of these functions may sound quite technical, and it may be difficult, at least at first glance, to see how this HR subsystem might have strategic implications. Indeed, researchers have paid relatively little attention to the strategic implications of the people flow subsystem compared to the amount of attention paid to the strategic implications of organizational reward subsystems. However, when one thinks about it, such staffing and development practices can be put into effect only when a number of very basic decisions are made—decisions that can have profound, long-term, and hence strategic impact on any organization. These decisions concern, for example, the degree to which the firm is willing to be dependent on the external labor market (ELM) to supply it with its required human capital, the steps the firm is willing to take to protect its investments in human capital, and the extent to which the organization is willing to select candidates on the basis of some indication of "long-term potential" as opposed to proven achievements in the past.

Indeed, the potential strategic impact of the staffing subsystem has become increasingly recognized in recent years as human capital replaces other forms of capital as a primary source of sustained competitive advantage (Prahalad & Hamel, 1990) and as globalization presents firms with an increasing array of staffing options (Guthrie, Grimm, & Smith, 1991; Snow & Snell, 1993). In fact, Snow and Snell (1993) went as far as to suggest that because the workforce is essentially fixed, "It may be more prudent to assume that competitive strategy is a more adjustable element of the company" (p. 460). As a result, they argued, there is a growing realization that staffing strategy may in fact propel business strategy. That is, staffing practices not only may be derived from organization strategy but may contribute to its formulation.

Although relatively few studies have examined the precise impact of the people flow subsystem on organizational effectiveness, researchers have proposed a variety of models suggesting the need for this HR system to match the firm's business strategy. For example, Sonnenfeld and Peiperl (1988), defining a people flow or staffing system as "a collection of policies, priorities and actions that organizations use to manage the flow of their members into, through and out of the organization over time" (p. 588), suggested that two fundamental system properties—the degree to which supply flows are based on internal or external mobility and the nature of internal assignment flows—are likely to moderate the impact of business strategy on performance.

Furthermore, the initial research evidence suggests that this impact may be relatively powerful. For example, Terpstra and Rozell (1993) found a strong relationship between staffing system profile and firm financial performance. By *staffing system profile,* we mean the pattern of choices made with respect to a number of core staffing contingencies. Although we will discuss the particular contingencies examined by Terpstra and Rozell (1993) later on, let us first examine some of the key strategic choices that define the nature of organizational staffing systems.

Strategic Choices

Although the staffing system encompasses a wide variety of HR practices, most of the choices that need to be made with regard to these practices are, to a great extent, influenced by a single, basic choice, namely the so-called "make-

or-buy" decision (Miles & Snow, 1984). Thus, we begin our analysis of strategic choices by discussing this basic choice between an internal (i.e., make) as opposed to external (buy) labor market focus. We then discuss three other sets of choices having to do with (a) recruitment and screening, (b) selection, and (c) employee development and separation.

Basic Staffing Choice: Internal Versus External Orientation

Miles and Snow (1984) suggested that human capital, like any other form of capital investment, can either be made or bought. That is, as Lepak and Snell (1999a, 1999b) noted, "On the one hand, firms may internalize employment and build the employee skill base through training and development initiatives. On the other, firms may externalize employment by outsourcing certain functions to market-based agents" (p. 1). A tendency toward an internalized staffing system is consistent with the internal labor market (ILM) logic discussed in Chapter 3, whereas the reliance on a market-based staffing system is consistent with an ELM logic.

Internal Labor Markets and the "Make" Option

Although there remains a lack of consensus as to the precise nature of ILMs (Cappelli & Sherer, 1991), the term is used to describe the administrative (as opposed to market-based) labor-allocating systems that characterize employment relationships in many organizations (Baron & Kreps, 1999; Rousseau, 1995; Stark, 1986). In general, ILM-based staffing systems generally exhibit some combination of the following characteristics: limited and designated ports of entry (thus limiting job competition to other current employees), promotion from within along some predetermined career ladder on the basis of either seniority or merit (designed to encourage long-term attachment), skill and pay gradients reflecting firm-specific knowledge and on-the-job training (to encourage employee retention), the extensive specification of procedures governing employment relations (to ensure administrative equity), and job security (Baron & Kreps, 1999; Pinfield & Berner, 1994).

One example of an ILM firm is Missile Systems International (MSI Ltd.), a midsized, state-owned, international defense contractor employing approximately 4,000 full-time workers and specializing in the development and production of state-of-the-art missile systems.[1] MSI's primary customers are national defense departments, the largest of which (in MSI's home country) purchases MSI's products on a cost-plus basis. Furthermore, because MSI is a state-owned enterprise, in its local market, it operates largely in the context of regulated competition. Given these conditions, as well as the nature of the defense industry as a whole, there is little incentive to move away from traditionally slow and long product development cycles. MSI's internal organizational structure can best be described as a rigid and tall hierarchical bureaucracy. The company places a strong emphasis on loyalty, status symbols, formalized work relations and processes, and centralized decision making. Over 90% of MSI's workforce is unionized, with production workers, technicians, and engineers, as well as low- and middle-level managers, all represented by a variety of different unions. Management and the unions have traditionally worked together to ensure job security, and indeed, despite increasing cost pressure in the international market, MSI has managed to avoid significant layoffs. Furthermore, new employees are, with few exceptions, hired at the entry level only. MSI prides itself on staffing the majority of its positions from within. The company invests significant resources in organization-specific employee training and development as well as in employee career planning and management to ensure that it retains its human capital and thus its edge in competitive, state-of-the-art technologies. To reinforce its "clan culture," compensation systems are designed to reinforce an ideology of loyalty, so most pay increases are based strictly on seniority. Finally, the company attempts to strengthen its employees' attachment to the firm by providing "cradle-to-grave" social welfare services and benefits.

However, different firms tend to adopt different combinations of these practices for different sectors of their workforce. Indeed, relatively early on in the analysis of these types of employment frameworks, researchers noted that there may exist more than one kind of ILM. For example, Doeringer and Piore (1971) distinguished between a blue-collar ILM, which places a premium on on-the-job training and seniority as the primary criteria for advancement, and a managerial ILM, which assumes greater skill portability as well as a focus on merit as the primary criterion for mobility. Similarly, Pinfield and Berner (1994), after reviewing some dozen typologies of ILMs, identified what they believed to be three generic types of ILMs, all of which could conceivably exist within a single firm at the same time. The wage ILM tends to dominate in unionized frameworks (not necessarily blue collar) and places a heavy emphasis on seniority as the primary criterion for determining advancement. The two salaried ILMs, in contrast, use merit as the primary criterion for determining advancement and may be distinguished from one another in terms of the competition for advancement. Whereas those in the upper-tier ILM face job competition from only a relatively limited number of other managerial employees, those in the lower-tiered salaried ILM have more limited lines of progression and thus face more intense competition for advancement. Of the three types of ILMs, the lower-tiered salaried ILM is the least characteristic of a classic ILM framework.

According to Baron and Kreps (1999), the "make" option or adoption of an ILM-based staffing system may offer some organizations some important advantages. First, the ILM system promotes long-term employment by making it increasingly costly for employees to seek employment elsewhere once they have "paid their dues." Because rewards are based on firm-specific knowledge and experience, ILM employees tend to find it difficult to identify employment alternatives offering a similar return on their human capital investment (Baron & Kreps, 1999). For example, in recent years, many employees of the "Big Three" auto manufacturers have taken advantage of employer incentives to pursue advanced degrees. Thus, a substantial number of assembly-line workers in the auto industry now have bachelor's and master's degrees. Nevertheless, for the most part, these individuals remain in their old jobs on the assembly line. Given their seniority, even as newly trained professionals, it would be next to impossible for them to ever come close to matching their current compensation package or their future earnings (e.g., pension). Of course, the assumption underlying this is that those motivated to continue as employees will also be motivated to contribute. Fortunately, it appears that many of the characteristics of ILMs (particularly the potential for career advancement and above-market wages, as well as the ability to monitor long-term performance outcomes) are also, in general, associated with a motivation to contribute (Baron & Kreps, 1999; Freeman & Medoff, 1984; Kochan et al., 1986).

Second, because the system promotes long-term employee attachment, critical interpersonal networks as well as specific knowledge about the organization and its jobs may be accumulated and maintained over time. Not only may these networks and this job and organization-specific knowledge be costly to reproduce (in terms of recruitment, selection, and training costs), but they may in fact be *impossible* to reproduce given ambiguous cause-and-effect relations and idiosyncratic learning processes (Lepak & Snell, 1999a, 1999b; Pfeffer & Baron, 1988).

Third, the organization may be able to reduce its labor costs. Lower labor costs may stem from the ability to limit more costly external staffing expenditures to those relevant to entry-level positions only (Mahoney, 1992). Furthermore, given the low rate of turnover, firms with ILM-based staffing subsystems tend to have the ability to amortize human capital investments (i.e., training and development costs) over a longer period. In addition, particularly in unionized contexts, employers have managed to frame job security as a compensating differential justifying pay concessions on the part of employees. Finally, given the level of employee experience and commitment in such firms, there tends to be less of a need for direct monitoring and control, thus lowering supervisory costs.

Fourth, as Baron and Kreps (1999) noted, ILMs provide staffing efficiencies, particularly with regard to screening and selection. Whereas employers relying on external employment sources are forced to rely on data that may be of questionable reliability, ILM staffing systems tend to offer much more extensive and reliable screening data. Furthermore, as Gibbons and Katz (1991) suggested, this screening function may also discourage employees from leaving, because external employers tend to be suspicious when employees, particularly higher-level employees, leave the ILM organization and seek alternative employment.

External Labor Markets and the "Buy" Option

However, there is no doubt that firms opting for an ILM employment system can also incur some heavy costs. For example, particularly when merit is used as a basis for internal advancement, ILM-based staffing subsystems can create a highly competitive environment. In some firms, particularly those encouraging teamwork and cooperation, this can work against organizational interests. Second, given that they rely on administrative as opposed to market systems for allocating labor, over time, additional administrative elements (e.g., grievance adjudication mechanisms) may need to be added to solve newly arising problems and ensure internal equity. What this implies is the tendency of ILM systems to generate an ever-growing bureaucracy, which in turn suggests increased overhead as well as reduced organizational flexibility and agility. This lack of flexibility can be exacerbated by the need to structure the organization around jobs and rules. Third, with job security a core element of most ILM systems, labor becomes, in effect, a fixed cost. Although many firms have learned how to limit the downside of this (e.g., United Parcel Service's reliance on "part-time" drivers or GM's reassignment of highly skilled model makers to its engineering departments during lean times), the promise of job security can be costly to ILM firms. Fourth, as Baron and Kreps (1999) noted, ILMs can breed cultural inflexibility in that there is often an inbred resistance to change in general and to externally derived change in particular. Finally, given the nature of their promotion and compensation policies, firms relying on the "make" option may tend to discourage risk taking and breed mediocrity. As we noted above, firms selecting the "make" option are often able to pay less and thus secure lower direct labor costs by offering numerous side benefits such as job security. But the highest quality workers may, on an individual basis, discount the value of such side benefits (particularly if they feel that their own competencies afford them the most secure form of job security) and either avoid employment in such firms in the first place or, worse, allow the ILM firm to invest in the development of these competencies, only to "jump ship" when a better offer comes along.

Those organizations viewing the disadvantages of the "make" option as outweighing any of the possible advantages are likely to choose the "buy" option and develop an employment relationship governed by the terms of the external market. Firms choosing to "buy" their human resources and staff a majority of their positions from the outside are constrained only by the price of those resources on the market and the quality of the data they have on the potential productivity of the external candidates. That is, they will be forced to pay the market price and take into account the risks of making hiring decisions (often for top-level, executive positions) on the basis of limited and often imperfect selection information. On the other hand, assuming that candidates with the requisite skills are readily available on the external market at some reasonable price and that the firm has the ability to identify the best of these candidates, the firm may realize significant savings in terms of training and development and may also be better able to respond to external challenges in real time. The ability to respond more rapidly stems from the acquisition of human capital that has already internalized the required competencies. Although externally sourced staff may be less committed to the firm than staff who are "made" by the firm, given that the nature of their attachment is likely to be far more calculative than affective or normative in the first place, it may be possible to reduce the risk of turnover by simply "sweetening" the terms of the employment transaction. Although this suggests that high-quality labor may need to be employed at a market premium (thus inflating labor costs), these additional costs may be compensated for by ELM firms' avoidance of the overhead and administrative costs associated with ILM systems (Mahoney, 1992; Williamson, 1975) and their benefiting from increased labor variability (Davis-Blake & Uzzi, 1993; Pfeffer & Baron, 1988).

One example of an ELM firm that we are familiar with is RLA Textiles Inc., a publicly held but family managed multinational textile firm specializing in the production of both clothing and fabric for the clothing industry. The company employs over 2,000 workers (some 90% being low-skilled production workers) in its production plants in three different countries. Production processes in all of its plants are highly automated and computer controlled, with most employees handling a variety of highly simplified machine-tending and packaging tasks. The company recruits the bulk of its workforce in the open market, often on a daily basis and typically via contractors. For example, in one of the countries in which it operates, it is not unusual for a clan or neighborhood leader to offer the plant manager a certain number of family members to work for a given period of time, typically ranging from 1 week to several months. No formal contracts are signed with workers employed in the bulk of RLA's facilities, and employees in these facilities have no union representation. Pay is hourly and turnover is extremely high. According to RLA executives, these conditions meet the strategic needs of the company in that the textile industry is highly cyclical and is increasingly driven by the cost of production. Because labor accounts for a significant portion of overall production costs, RLA, like its competitors, seeks to retain a high degree of employment flexibility, allowing it to rapidly shift its production to those countries in which labor costs are lowest.

Contingencies Governing the Make-or-Buy Choice

So what determines the degree to which either of these two options is likely to yield a greater benefit to the firm? Although a number of researchers have proposed that the make-or-buy choice is governed by the nature of business strategy (e.g., Miles & Snow, 1984; Olian & Rynes, 1984), at a more rudimentary and theoretical level, several factors are likely to determine the extent to which a firm tends to rely more on making or buying the bulk of its required human resources. A number of researchers have attempted to identify these factors.

Baron and Kreps (1999), as part of their general discussion of ILMs, proposed that firms will tend toward the adoption of an ILM staffing framework and hence be more likely to make (as opposed to buy) required human resources when (a) the organizational work process is highly complex and firm specific, thus demanding firm-specific human capital; (b) the work process is relatively stable and the pace of technological change slow enough to allow for continuous human capital upgrading; (c) the labor market is just tight enough to provide a firm with an internal labor supply a cost advantage over those relying on external recruitment but not so tight as to encourage high-quality employees in whom the firm has invested to consider alternative employment; (d) the business strategy calls for steady, evolutionary growth based on employee synergies or customer service rather than opportunistic, rapid growth; and (e) the firm culture emphasizes stability and commitment over flexibility and innovation. Firms exhibiting more of these characteristics, they suggested, will be the most likely to adopt and benefit from an ILM-based staffing subsystem.

Osterman (1987) claimed that the choice between "make" or "buy" depends on the extent to which organizations value predictability as opposed to flexibility. By *predictability,* Osterman (1987) was referring to the ability of firms to "plan confidently upon the availability of a qualified labor supply at foreseeable prices" (p. 55). By adopting an ILM-based staffing system, organizations are more able to control the supply and price of labor. In addition, such systems allow the organization to exert greater implicit control over employee decision making due to the strong emphasis placed on socialization and the creation of "appropriate" decision premises (Simon, 1947). Particularly in organizations in which the (catastrophic) risk of a wrong decision far outweighs the potential benefits of a correct decision (e.g., nuclear power plants), such an advantage may be greatly valued. However, for many firms, the rigidity implied by predictability and such a compliance-based "clan culture" (Ouchi, 1980) can be costly, particularly if the organization depends on employee creativity and risk taking and if the organization is unable to deploy its labor in the most productive manner. Thus, firms relying on skills that are readily available in the ELM and that need to retain maximum flexibility in their staffing levels and deployments are likely to opt for "buying" their human capital.

However, Kerr and Jackofsky (1989) questioned many of the assumptions underlying Osterman's argument. They claimed that flexibility may in many ways be enhanced by ILM-based staffing processes. For example, they argued that organizational flexibility may be enhanced when the organization has a pool of readily available, versatile, and well-trained managers "on call" and ready to go. That is, ILM-based staffing systems, at least at the management level, provide the "managerial depth" (p. 160) that is often critical for organizational responsiveness.

Finally, Lepak and Snell (1999a, 1999b) based their predictions on three separate theories. According to *transaction cost theory* (Williamson, 1975), there are costs associated with managing human resource allocations on the basis of both market arrangements (i.e., transaction costs) and administrative arrangements (i.e., bureaucratic costs). Administrative arrangements can offer a more efficient means of staffing if the work process is such that the costs of such arrangements are offset by the ability of employers to more effectively monitor employee performance (as is the case when the work process is more complex and long linked). According to *human capital theory* (Becker, 1964), firms will opt for "making" their own human capital when the skills that they require are highly specialized and hard to come by on the external market and when it is possible to reduce the risk that these skills might be transferred to other firms. Finally, according to *resource-based theory* (Barney, 1991; Prahalad & Hamel, 1990), firms will select the "make" option and develop an ILM-type staffing system only when labor is viewed as a core competency (i.e., one that is rare, valuable, inimitable, and nontransferable) providing a key source of sustained competitive advantage. Otherwise, they will opt for the more flexible external acquisition option.

On the basis of these three theories, Lepak and Snell (1999a, 1999b) argued that although many firms adopt a "make" or "buy" policy on an organizationwide basis, some firms adopt a combination of the two, with the ILM-type staffing frameworks adopted for more "core" employee groups and ELM-type staffing frameworks adopted for less central groups of employees. Specifically, they claimed that two dimensions of human capital—value and uniqueness—will determine the extent to which firms adopt an internal as opposed to external staffing logic. By *value,* they were referring to the potential for human capital to contribute to the "competitive advantage or core compe- tence" of the firm" (p. 5). The greater the potential contribution, the greater the interest in avoiding the risks associated with the outsourcing of these competen- cies. By *uniqueness,* they were referring to firm specificity. The more unique or firm specific the desired competency, the less likely it is to be available on the external market in real time, thus necessitating the possible internal stockpiling of such skills. That is, as the authors noted, "As human capital becomes more idiosyncratic to a particular firm, externalization may prove infeasible, and/or incur excessive costs" (p. 6). On the other hand, generic competencies may be more efficiently secured in most cases on the external market (Teece, 1984).

Firms tending to rely on human capital that is both valuable and unique, ac- cording to Lepak & Snell's (1999a, 1999b) framework, are the most likely to "make" their own human capital and adopt ILM-based staffing frameworks. Employers adopting such a framework need not fear the loss of human capital to competitors as long as the value is generated from firm-specific competencies and skills (such as a knowledge of which forms to use in special situations or personal relations with a key stakeholder). Although Lepak and Snell (1999a, 1999b) assumed that such employers will automatically adopt staffing policies and practices consistent with Pinfield and Berner's (1994) "salaried ILM" framework, depending on the nature of organizational control processes, it is just as likely that practices consistent with their "wage ILM" framework will be adopted. That is, in organizations combining output-based systems of control with an internal employment orientation (i.e., high-commitment HR strategy), one or both of the salary ILM staffing frameworks are likely to be adopted. However, in organizations combining process control with an internal employment orientation (i.e., paternalistic HR strategy), a staffing framework consistent with Pinfield and Berner's (1994) "wage ILM" model is likely to be adopted. Firms relying on human capital that is either low in uniqueness or low in value (or both) will tend to either acquire or contract this labor from the external market, using a variety of employment frameworks and staffing mechanisms.

As can be inferred from the discussion above, whether a firm tends to make or buy its human capital for the bulk of its employee groups is likely to greatly influence other staffing options. We next explore some of the other strategic choices relating to the staffing subsystem.

Recruiting and Screening Choices

Rynes (1991) defined recruiting as encompassing "all organizational activities and decisions that affect either the number or types of individuals who are willing to apply for, or to accept, a vacancy" (p. 5). Recruiting and screening practices can have a strategic impact on the firm because they determine the nature of the pool from which new hires are chosen and thus can greatly influence the flow of human capital into the firm as well as the ability of the firm to retain these individuals (at least in the short run). These practices are relevant regardless of the labor market logic (internal or external) adopted by the firm because even firms adopting an ILM-based staffing system rely on recruiting and screening processes for their entry-level positions.

Although recruitment and screening practices vary along a wide range of dimensions (see Rynes, 1991, for a complete review of these dimensions), among the most critical choices that need to be made when considering the nature of organizational recruitment and screening are (a) the recruitment philosophy (selling vs. realism), (b) past versus future orientation, and (c) the breadth of the recruitment effort.

Recruitment Philosophy and Message

The literature on recruitment has been dominated by a debate over which of two types of recruitment messages yields the greatest long-term benefits: realistic messages or inflated, "sales-oriented," or "flypaper"-type messages. Various hypotheses regarding the consequences of one type of message over the other have been proposed and tested (see Rynes, 1991, for a review), but several aggregation and meta-analytic studies (e.g., Premack & Wanous, 1985; Reilly, Brown, Blood, & Malatesta, 1981) suggest substantial effect sizes in favor of realism. For example, Reilly et al. (1981) found that on average, the turnover rate for realistically recruited subjects was 5.7 percentage points lower than that for employees recruited through more conventional messages. Most interesting was the finding that although realism was found to have universally positive effects on turnover, the effect was greatest for more complex jobs. The differences in turnover rates between experimental and control groups was found to be 1.9% for jobs rated lower in complexity, whereas it was 9.5% for jobs rated higher in complexity. McEvoy and Cascio (1985) reported similar findings in their meta-analysis. What is missing in the literature, however, is an analysis of the impact of message realism on the quality of the candidate pool (Rynes, 1991). A realistic recruitment philosophy is likely to yield positive strategic effects only to the extent that it increases the rate of hiree retention without reducing the quality of those candidates available for hire. Thus, although it appears that the benefits of message realism may be universally positive, when jobs are relatively noncomplex (as is typically the case when organizations rely on process as opposed to output control), these benefits may be insufficient to balance the potential negative impact of realism on candidate quality. The implication is that message realism may be less likely to generate positive outcomes in organizations adopting process-based systems of control (i.e., heavy reliance on preprogrammed jobs) than in organizations relying on output-based systems of control).

Also missing in the literature is an analysis of the potential impact of an ILM- versus an ELM-based employment system. It is likely that in an ILM-based firm, message realism pertaining to the organization and careers within it is more critical than message realism pertaining to the job itself. Furthermore, the value of such message realism is likely to be greater in ILM-based firms due to the increased reliance on low employee turnover.

Breadth of the Recruitment Effort

When designing a recruitment program, employers need to determine the extent to which they want to target their efforts. Targeting recruitment efforts tend to generate a higher-quality, though smaller, pool of applicants, whereas a "wide-net" approach tends to generate larger applicant pools. Some employers purposely set qualification levels high and target their recruitment efforts toward specific subpopulations (e.g., Ivy League universities only), whereas other employers prefer to "cast a wide net" to enhance the efficiency of validated selection mechanisms (the efficiency of these mechanisms increases as the size of the applicant pool increases). At least one study (Mason & Belt, 1985) found that by raising qualification levels and targeting the recruitment message, employers were able to reduce the likelihood that unqualified individuals would apply. On the other hand, qualified (but perhaps less secure) candidates may also self-select not to apply or, worse, to apply elsewhere. In addition, overly rigorous specification may lead to subsequent employee underutilization and thus, in turn, to dissatisfaction and turnover (Rynes, 1991).

Underlying the questions of qualification setting and candidate targeting are issues of efficiency and risk. Clearly, to the extent that costs of candidate selection rise in direct proportion to the number of applicants considered for each position, high qualifications and candidate targeting are likely to enhance overall staffing efficiencies. Furthermore, to the extent that setting high qualifications and targeting candidates are essentially early screening processes, they may reduce the risk of hiring "false positives." On the other hand, only by casting a "wide net" can the organization be sure that its recruitment process does not increase the risk of "false negatives"—that is, increase the likelihood that potentially qualified candidates will be discouraged from applying. Firms with ILM-based staffing systems tend to have more to lose by hiring "false positives" because these individuals, once in the system, are more difficult to remove. Furthermore, if as we noted above, ILM firms (particularly those relying on output-based control systems) are more concerned with avoiding catastrophic errors than with capturing every business opportunity, there is more to gain by avoiding false positives than by missing out on false negatives. Consequently, such firms are likely to have higher hiring standards and to attempt to target their recruiting campaigns. On the other hand, firms relying on the ELM are likely to be more concerned with the risks of overlooking a potential "star" only to find such individuals subsequently recruited by a competitor. Firms with ILM-based staffing systems are likely to be less concerned with the loss of such potential "stars" because they rely less on identifying and acquiring such stars from the outside than on their own internal capability to develop such stars. Thus, as suggested by Baron and Kreps (1999), firms with ILM-based staffing systems—and especially those relying on output-based systems of control—tend toward adopting more cautious and targeted recruitment efforts. In contrast, it is likely that firms with ELM-based staffing systems will tend toward "casting a wider net" in their effort to attract job candidates, particularly if there is a process-based system of control in place to limit employee discretion and ensure careful and close performance monitoring.

Recruiting Methods

Firms can use a variety of methods to recruit job candidates, including newspaper advertising, employee referrals, and employment agencies ("headhunters"). Some methods are likely to be more effective (in terms of yielding lower posthire rates of turnover and absenteeism and higher levels of job performance) simply because they provide more information on which to base selection decisions (Schwab, 1982). Others are likely to be more effective because they perform important prescreening functions and thus influence the quality of the applicant pool (Rynes, 1991).

These theoretical explanations underlie much of the research in recruitment method effectiveness. Unfortunately, the findings in this line of research are far from consistent. Although findings are for the most part consistent with regard to the least effective recruitment methods (newspaper ads tend to be associated with higher rates of turnover and poorer employee performance; Schwab, 1982), there is little consistency as to which particular method performs best (Rynes, 1991). For example, some studies have found employee referrals and other informal recruitment sources to generate positive outcomes (Breaugh, 1981; Kirman, Farley, & Geisinger, 1989), whereas others suggest a potential negative effect (Caldwell & Spivey, 1983), particularly in companies with low morale or poor employment conditions. Similarly, although external employment agencies might, in general, enhance the quality of applicant information and perform an important prescreening function, as Olian and Rynes (1984) noted, particularly in organizations in which staffing needs and criteria are subject to rapid change, external agents' prescreening may become dysfunctional. Specifically, these agents may end up screening out desirable candidates that fail to meet the "old" criteria and end up forwarding only those candidates meeting the obsolescent employment requirements. Finally, the breadth of recruitment methods may vary across organizations, depending on the organizational need to maximize employee diversity. Organizations requiring a heterogeneous mix of employees may find that by relying on only one or two highly effective recruitment methods (e.g., employee referrals) they are unable to meet equal employment opportunity requirements and may even place limits on the ability of the organization to "learn" and innovate (Schwab, 1982; Senge, 1990).

What these studies therefore suggest is that choices regarding the adoption of recruitment methods are likely to be contingent on the firm's overall strategic configuration. Indeed, several studies (Miles & Snow, 1978; Olian & Rynes, 1984) suggest that compared to firms with defender strategies, prospector firms are more likely to structure their recruitment effort around a greater number of recruitment methods and, within the context of this mix, to rely more on informal recruitment methods (e.g., employer referrals) than on external agents. Similarly, the choice of recruitment methods may be associated with the degree to which the firm adopts an ILM- versus ELM-based staffing orientation and the extent to which the organization relies on process versus output control. As noted earlier, ILM firms tend to place a premium on the maintenance of a strong clan culture (Ouchi, 1980). Consequently, they are more likely to sacrifice a heterogeneous candidate pool for one that is more likely to reflect existing organizational norms and values. Thus, ILM firms may place greater emphasis on informal recruitment methods and may in fact rely solely on them. For example, in recent years, several GM business units have recruited strictly on the basis of employee family-based referrals. Firms relying on process-based systems of control tend to have highly routine and less flexible production technologies. Given the rather extensive constraints on employee discretion, such firms tend to perceive less risk in contracting out much of their recruitment function to external agents. Indeed, many traditional manufacturing firms rely on state employment agencies to perform their initial recruitment and screening function.

For example, RLA Textiles relies on both clan leaders and state employment agencies to provide casual labor when needed. In both cases, screening is minimal and is typically based on a number of simple physiological (i.e., health) and cognitive (i.e., basic literacy) criteria. In fact, however, the primary screening occurs on the job. Given the low costs of hiring and training, if after 1 or 2 days on the job it is apparent that a hiring error has occurred, the company simply dismisses the employee and turns to the contractor for a replacement (typically provided within a number of hours).

Selection Choices

Selection Criteria

By *selection criteria*, we are referring to those parameters according to which job candidates will be screened and evaluated. As Dreher and Kendall (1995) noted, "Choices about selection criteria often reflect the overall theme or guiding principles that surround a company's approach to employment mobility" (p. 449). That is, to a large extent, the choice of selection criteria tends to follow the core staffing decision discussed above, namely the degree to which the staffing subsystem is consistent with an internal or ELM logic. However, the choice is also likely to be influenced by the nature of organizational control processes.

Selection criteria choices are likely to vary along at least three main dimensions. First, they are likely to vary according to the degree to which criteria emphasize past achievement as opposed to future potential (Olian & Rynes, 1984). Clearly, organizations adopting more of an ILM-based approach to staffing will be more concerned with the candidate's development potential (i.e., basic aptitude) and ability to follow predetermined organizational career paths and will place less of an emphasis on the individuals' current skill or knowledge base (Dreher & Kendall, 1995). Indeed, because ILM-based firms internalize the transfer of skills and knowledge and in many cases prefer to transfer these skills as they apply specifically to the particular firm (thus reducing their external transferability), there is little economic reason to focus the selection process on the assessment of such preexisting competencies.

Second, they are likely to vary with regard to the extent to which they focus on individual disposition or attitudes (e.g., assertiveness, agreeableness, openness, positive or negative affectivity) (Barrick & Mount, 1991). Some organizations, particularly those relying on team-based task structures and output-based control, place a stronger emphasis on what is often referred to as the "cultural fit" of the candidate. From a game theory perspective, at least in the short run, such organizations are prime candidates for employee free riding. Although various monitoring and reward structures may be put in place to constrain such free riding (which we will discuss in the next chapter), as Axelrod (1984) noted, the maintenance of cooperative meta-norms is the most effective weapon against free riding. Consequently, such organizations have an interest in screening out any candidate who might pose a threat to these critical preexisting meta-norms. ILM-based organizations are also likely to place a premium on such criteria because one of the principles guiding such organizations (as we have already noted) is the maintenance of a clan culture and a culture of compliance. Individuals not likely to "buy into" such cultures can pose a potentially serious threat (Kunda, 1992).

Finally, as Snow and Snell (1993) noted, criteria are likely to vary in terms of the degree to which they are focused on certain role-based core competencies (applicable to a variety of current and potential "jobs") as opposed to being based on the characteristics of a single job. In fact, traditionally, selection criteria have been based on job analysis, a process by which the core tasks, duties, and responsibilities of a job may be identified. However, this approach assumes that "individuals, jobs and the match between them are stable over time" (Snow & Snell, 1993, p. 452). As long as change is predictable, job analysis can be broadened to take into account the nature of the job "as it will be" (Schneider & Konz, 1989, p. 51). However, change is not always predictable, so a number of researchers (Borman & Motowidlo, 1992; Gerstein & Reisman, 1983) suggest that in those organizations facing unpredictable change there is a tendency to structure criteria around strategic roles and the competencies required to fulfill these roles. In this case, selection criteria may be more likely to focus on synergistic competencies (i.e., ability to work in the context of a team and integrate multidisciplinary concepts and ideas) than on job-specific aptitudes. Snow and Snell's theory (1993) suggests that such role- or competency-based criteria may be difficult to incorporate into many ILM-oriented staffing subsystems because ILMs in many firms are job rather than role based. This is particularly likely to be the case in ILM firms relying on process-based control and highly preprogrammed work processes. Especially in these cases, such role-based selection criteria are likely to be inconsistent with the nature of the jobs needing to be staffed.

Selection Methods

In the same way that selection criteria are, to a large extent, influenced by the "make-or-buy" decision, the choice of selection methods is to a large extent a function of the chosen selection criteria. Simply put, certain criteria (e.g., potential) strongly suggest the adoption of certain selection methods or tools (e.g., aptitude tests) over others (e.g., achievement tests). Thus, in the same way that the utility of certain selection criteria might vary by HR strategy, so might the utility of certain selection methods. However, a number of studies suggest that many selection practices (e.g., validation) are in fact "best practices" and are likely to benefit most, if not all, organizations (Schuler & Jackson, 1987b). So is there any choice to be made here at all?

A recent study by Terpstra and Rozell (1993) provides at least some initial insight into a possible answer to this question. These researchers examined the prevalence of several innovative selection practices and methods (e.g., use of validation research, structured interviews, cognitive aptitude and ability tests, and biographical information blanks [BIBs] or weighted application blanks [WABs]) among a random sample of some 200 firms. They also sought to esti-mate the degree to which the use of such methods could influence the financial performance of the firm. As predicted, they found that the overall prevalence of these methods was relatively low (no practice was adopted by over 50% of the firms studied) and that method adoption varied by industry. They also found that, as suggested by Schuler and Jackson (1987b), firms engaging in more of these practices had both significantly higher annual profit and profit growth than organizations that engaged in fewer. The causal issue (i.e., profit leading to practice or practice leading to profit) aside, these results suggest that such HR activities have the potential to qualify as universally "best practices." However, Terpstra and Rozell's findings also suggest that the potential impact of these methods on firm financial performance is contingent on internal and external contingencies. Specifically, they found the relationship between practice use and performance to be greatest in the service industry and weakest in manufac-turing. They speculated that this is because in the service organizations, "Hu-man resources are the primary input and there may also be fewer constraints im-posed on employee performance (i.e., fewer pre-programmed work processes) in this industry than in others" (p. 43). Thus, their findings suggest that the adoption of more sophisticated selection methods may be more likely to offer greater benefits to organizations adopting HR strategies based on output (as op-posed to process) control. More generally, however, their findings indicate that although effective selection methods may benefit many organizations, "the rel-ative degree of benefit may vary as a function of critical contingency character-istics" (p. 45).

Breadth of Involvement in Selection Process

Who should be involved in making individual selection decisions? In many ILM-based staffing systems, internal selection decisions are made almost auto-matically on the basis of seniority criteria. In these cases, as long as basic ap-plicant criteria are met, the position goes to the individual with the greatest seniority. Individuals in the human resource function do not so much make the final decision as administer a highly preprogrammed selection process.

However, external selection decisions cannot be based on seniority criteria and therefore tend to demand that some individual, office, or group take responsibility for individual selection decisions. Certainly, to the extent that a single individual can make decisions, staffing processes might be more streamlined and efficient. Furthermore, to the extent that such decisions are made by a single staff function (such as HR), selection decisions may be more likely to be consistent and equitable. However, as Olian and Rynes (1984) noted, under certain conditions, such narrow, centralized decision-making processes might work against the long-term interests of certain types of firms. As they suggested, individual decision makers (particularly those in a staff function) are likely to be less able to assess the candidate's potential with respect to a highly complex and ambiguous (nonpreprogrammed) job than a team of decision makers already performing similar work (e.g., members of the project team that the hiree will work with). Their research suggests that both the level of job ambiguity (i.e., nature of organizational control) and the centrality of equity and compliance norms (i.e., ILM vs. ELM orientation) are likely to shape choices regarding the breadth of involvement in selection decisions. The breadth of involvement is thus likely to be the greatest in ELM firms with less preprogrammable jobs (i.e., firms adopting more of a free-agent HR strategy) and the least in ILM firms and firms with highly preprogrammable jobs (i.e., firms with more of a paternalistic HR strategy). ILM firms with nonprogrammable jobs (i.e., firms with high-commitment HR strategies) are likely to adopt a decentralized selection system that involves a relatively large number of organizational interests but is carefully regulated and monitored by a central staff function to ensure consistency and equity.

Other Staffing Choices

Norms Versus Competencies Versus Skills in Employee Development

From our discussion of the basic "make-or-buy" choice above, it should be clear that firms opting to "make" a larger proportion of their human capital stock are, by definition, going to place a stronger emphasis on employee development than those opting to "buy" this stock from the ELM. But how should these ILM-oriented firms invest their development resources? Should they focus more on training employees in basic skills, or should they attempt to develop firm-specific competencies and norms? Furthermore, assuming that even ELM-oriented firms are likely to engage in some degree of employee development, even for them the issue of how such firms should invest their training and development resources is relevant.

A number of studies suggest that labor market orientation is likely to be the driving force determining the focus of organizations' employee development activity. For example, Lepak and Snell (1999b) noted that firms tending to "make" their own human capital "invest significantly to develop unique (i.e., firm-specific) skills through extensive training initiatives" (p. 7). They argued that such firms often rely on career development and mentoring programs to supplement traditional training programs in order to ensure that the knowledge, skills, and competencies transferred to these employees are both idiosyncratic and highly imitable. Indeed, in ILM-type firms, competency development is likely to be far more experiential and to be based more on lateral mobility and long-term career patterns than on short-term workshops and training programs.

In contrast, firms relying on acquiring their human resources from the ELM are likely to select employees on the basis of their achievements and *current* human capital assets. Several studies (see Koch & McGrath, 1996; Snell & Dean, 1992) suggest that such firms tend to rely on more sophisticated selection techniques to recruit and select those individuals already possessing the desired skills, thus allowing those selected to begin performing immediately. Supplementary skill training may be not only unnecessary but also inefficient and risky. It may be inefficient because, in the absence of a staffing subsystem geared toward the enhancement of long-term commitment, the return on these human capital investments may not necessarily accrue to the firm making the investment. It may be risky in that proprietary knowledge may end up being disseminated to direct competitors (Matusik & Hill, 1998). Consequently, these firms are likely to focus on developing employee competencies and firm-specific norms that will ensure the successful integration of new hires. Such investments are likely to be particularly important to ELM-type firms, given the heterogeneous background of their staff. If staff lack a common set of organizational experiences, critical synergies may not emerge unless and until employees gain a clear understanding of critical firm-specific competencies and norms. Furthermore, because such competencies and norms tend to be both complex and idiosyncratic to the firm and its culture, dissemination risks are negligible (Matusik & Hill, 1998).

However, classic organizational theory (Edwards, 1979; Simon, 1947; Thompson, 1967) suggests that organizational control structure is also likely to influence the nature of firms' employee development activity. To the extent that the organization relies on output-based systems of control, it places much of the uncertainty in the transformation process in the hands of its workers. Simon (1948) noted that to limit the degree of risk inherent in such a control system, organizations attempt to provide the "premises" on which workers will make decisions when confronted by such uncertainty. Such premise framing is not necessary when organizations rely on process control. In these cases, workers are given little discretion to begin with. However, as soon as the nature of the control process provides employees with a significant degree of discretion—as is the case when firms structure the work process around nonpreprogrammed jobs—there is a tremendous incentive to channel employee thinking and thus reduce the risk of some catastrophic error. As Kunda (1992) noted, organizations relying on such systems tend to place a heavy emphasis on the development of appropriate employee norms. For example, although knowledge-based firms relying on output control allow workers to come and go as they wish, formal and informal development practices are used to generate a "feeling" that it is inappropriate to be the first one to leave in the evening (Perlow, 1998).

The discussion above therefore suggests that both control and labor market factors will influence both the pervasiveness and nature of employee development in organizations. Whereas firms with ILM- and process control-based HR strategies (i.e., high commitment) are likely to emphasize all three dimensions of development (i.e., skill, competency, and norms), firms with ELM- and output control-based strategies (secondary) are likely to deemphasize training altogether. Paternalistic firms are likely to place a premium on skill development, whereas firms with free-agent HR strategies are likely to emphasize competency and normative development.

Internal Mobility

How is human capital to be deployed within the organization? As we already discussed, firms with people flow subsystems grounded in an ILM-based (as opposed to an external) logic are more likely to look to the current workforce as the primary solution for staffing needs. Thus, all else being equal, opportunities for upward mobility are likely to be greater in ILM-based firms. Furthermore, particularly in ILM-based firms, human capital deployments are likely to be made on the basis of predetermined, vertically oriented (as opposed to lateral) career paths.

What criteria should be used to govern such movements? Merit-based criteria—some composite of ability, skill, knowledge, and future potential—tend to provide the employer with far more flexibility in determining how to maximize human resource deployments. Still, as already noted, many ILMs tend to rely on seniority as the primary mobility criterion to maintain employee loyalty and the clan culture, simplify decisions relating to human resource deployments, ensure that employees perceive a high level of procedural justice, and reduce the risks of disputes. Nevertheless, as Pinfield and Berner (1994) suggested, even in these types of firms, the more complex and nonpreprogrammed the nature of the work process (as is the case in most managerial jobs), the greater the likelihood that merit will be used as the primary criterion. Yet even in these cases, the precise merit criteria are likely to be different in ILM and ELM firms. A study of mobility patterns in 14 firms conducted by Kerr and Slocum (1987) suggests that in the ELM firm, the primary merit criteria are likely to be performance and readiness. In contrast, in the ILM firm, a longer term, developmental perspective is likely to be taken, and thus the primary criterion is likely to be potential.

In sum, the discussion above suggests that firms adopting HR strategies grounded in a logic of ILMs and process-based systems of control will be the most likely to rely on seniority or developmental merit as the primary criterion for mobility. In contrast, firms adopting HR strategies grounded in more of an ELM logic and relying on output-based systems of control will tend to place the greatest emphasis on current performance and readiness-based merit criteria.

Other choices that need to be made with regard to mobility have to do with (a) the pace of progression (i.e., should promotion occur rapidly, or should mobility be characterized by slow, evolutionary steps?) and (b) the openness of the promotion "contest" (i.e., should the mobility pattern be shaped around a tournament in which only those reaching level "b" are allowed to compete for promotion into level "c," or should candidates from all levels be considered?) (Forbes & Wertheim, 1995). In general, it appears that most American firms adopting merit-based criteria tend to shape their mobility patterns around a tournament model in which those advancing rapidly early on in their careers have the highest probability of reaching top executive positions (Cooper, Graham, & Dyke, 1993). According to Kerr and Slocum (1987), this tendency appears to be the greatest among firms with ILM-based HR strategies that nonetheless use merit as the primary mobility criteria.

Employee Separation Options

Organizations face numerous options with regard to how to influence employee separations. The primary choice faced, however, concerns the degree to which the employer is willing to use "reductions in force" as a means by which to meet cost targets and/or enhance or restore firm profitability. Once this basic decision is made, a second critical choice concerns the way in which such reductions are structured.

Regarding the stabilization versus reductions-in-force choice, as noted earlier, organizations adopting an ILM-based logic, and particularly those relying on hard-to-develop employees able to staff nonprogrammable jobs, tend to make employment stability a cornerstone of the HR strategy (Baron & Kreps, 1999). For such organizations, employee loyalty is key to the success of their overall business strategy. To the extent that employees might view the promise of job security as something less than "ironclad," they might be tempted to seek alternative and more secure employment when "times are good" (Armstrong, 1994; Richey, 1992).

Furthermore, as Gerhart and Trevor (1996) suggested, although short-term profitability may be enhanced or restored by employee separations, over the long term these can have a negative impact on profitability for a number of additional reasons. First, employees in whom the organization has invested may end up offering that human capital to a competitor. Second, such hard-to-develop human capital may be less available on the open market when the firm is ready to rehire, and the time necessary to internally *re*-develop these assets may place severe constraints on the organization at a critical time (Greer & Stedham, 1989). Third, a reduction in force may serve as a signal to potential high-quality but risk-averse candidates to look elsewhere for employment and may thus limit the firm's recruitment potential. Finally, the direct financial cost of such separations (particularly when the costs of restaffing are taken into account; Cascio, 1991) may greatly reduce the benefits of such reductions unless the organization undertakes large-scale restructuring to enhance long-term efficiencies (Whetten, Keiser, & Urban, 1995). Although these disadvantages need to be considered by all organizations, for obvious reasons, they are likely to be particularly relevant for ILM-based firms and firms with fewer preprogrammable jobs (i.e., HR systems based on output-based systems of control).

However, many organizations—including some ILM-based organizations—nevertheless view reductions in force as a critical means to control labor costs and/or ensure labor cost variability and hence strategic flexibility. Those organizations choosing to incorporate the potential for employee reductions as a core element of their staffing strategy need to make additional choices regarding the way in which such reductions are to be carried out. That is, choices need to be made as to whether such separations are going to be voluntary (e.g., attrition, early retirement incentives) or involuntary (e.g., layoffs or contractual terminations) (Dreher & Kendall, 1995). For the reasons suggested above, many ILM-based firms prefer the former. But because this effectively gives the choice to the employee, the firm runs the risk that those with the greatest potential (i.e., those most valued and thus least preferable to leave) will be the most likely to take the offer.

Assuming that such separations are going to be involuntary, are they going to be based on seniority, merit, or some other criterion? Most employers tend to prefer merit-based criteria, thus allowing the firm to "reduce" its "deadwood" (i.e., those offering the firm a relatively lower rate of return on every compensation dollar spent) and avoid losing those in possession of critical competencies. However, this can raise serious questions of equity and ethics, particularly if current performance or future potential cannot be assessed reliably or if such separations violate employee norms of procedural justice. Assuming that the most senior employees are also those offering the firm the greatest human capital, seniority-based criteria might therefore provide the greatest long-term efficiencies, particularly in ILM-based firms. However, particularly in ILM-based firms, those employees with the least seniority also tend to be the most poorly compensated, thus demanding that a relatively greater number of employees be dismissed to meet cost reduction requirements.

Furthermore, there is no guarantee that those with the greatest seniority are also the most productive. Thus, ILM-based firms often seek alternative separation criteria. For example, until recently (when the practice was deemed in violation of basic equal employment opportunity regulations), to ensure that flight attendants never reached higher seniority-based pay grades, female flight attendants were contractually dismissed as soon as they married. In this way, U.S. airlines were able to constrain labor costs and maintain some degree of labor variability, while still basing their staffing subsystem on an ILM logic.

Summary: HR Strategy and the Staffing Subsystem

The analysis presented above suggests that the profile of organizational staffing practices is likely to vary as a function of a firm's overall HR strategy. That is, depending on the nature of organizational control systems and the ILM-versus-ELM orientation of the firm, staffing practices may tend to cluster into four identifiable patterns, each associated with one of the four ideal types of HR strategies identified in the previous chapter. Table 4.1 presents each of these

Table 4.1 Staffing Subsystem Characteristics by HR Strategy Type

Choice	High Commitment	Paternalistic	Free Agent	Secondary
Basic				
ILM vs. ELM	Salaried ILM	Wage ILM	ELM	ELM
Recruitment				
Philosophy and message	Realism is critical; focus on organization and organizational career	Realism is moderately important; focus on organization and organizational career	Realism is important; focus on job rather than on organization	Realism is relatively unimportant; costs may outweigh benefits
Breadth	Narrow; very high standards	Narrow; moderately high standards	Wide net; moderately high standards	Wide net; minimal standards
Methods	Limited mix; informal; limited if any reliance on external agents	Limited mix; informal; some reliance on external agents	Extensive mix; formal and informal; moderate reliance on external agents	Extensive mix; mostly formal; heavy reliance on external agents
Criteria	Developmental potential; mix of job- and competency-based criteria; heavy emphasis on "cultural fit"	Developmental potential; job-oriented criteria; some emphasis on "cultural fit"	Current competencies; some emphasis on "cultural fit"	Current competencies and job-based KSAs; little or no emphasis on "cultural fit"
Methods	Greater reliance on sophisticated methods	Moderate reliance on sophisticated methods	Greater reliance on sophisticated methods	Limited reliance on sophisticated methods
Breadth of involvement	Moderately broad involvement; centralized regulation of decentralized decision-making process	Narrow involvement; centralized decision making	Very broad involvement; decentralized decision making	Moderately broad involvement; decentralized decision making
Development	Extensive; focus on skills, competencies, and norms	Extensive; focus on skills	Limited; focus on integrative competencies	Almost nonexistent
Internal mobility	Extensive; merit based; tournamentlike	Extensive; seniority based	Moderate; merit based	Limited
Separation	Heavy emphasis on stabilization	Moderate emphasis on stabilization; reductions (if necessary) based on seniority	Moderate emphasis on reductions when needed; reductions based on merit	Heavy emphasis on reductions; reductions based on merit

four patterns, showing how, across each of the choice parameters discussed in this chapter, staffing practices may tend to vary depending on the HR strategy in use.

As can be seen in Table 4.1, the staffing subsystem in firms adopting a high-commitment HR strategy tends to be based on the kind of salaried ILM framework described by Pinfield and Berner (1994). Recruitment processes are designed to reduce the risk of ultimately selecting "false positives" and to increase the likelihood that those hired actually stay with the organization. Selection processes are future oriented and place a heavy reliance on innovative selection technologies to maximize selection efficiency. Although the selection process provides multiple interests with the opportunity to influence the selection decision, the overall process is subject to centralized regulation to ensure internal consistency and enhance employee procedural justice perceptions. Finally, staffing systems in such organizations are geared toward employee retention and mobility and therefore place a heavy emphasis on employee development in the broadest sense.

For example, Intel relies on multiple individual and group interviews with potential supervisors, subordinates, and peers to assess not only the candidate's knowledge, skills, and abilities but, just as important, the degree to which the candidate will fit into the company's highly emphasized corporate culture. Jobs are designed to encourage employee retention by placing an emphasis on autonomy, challenge, and personal growth. Career structures are developed to facilitate individual development and professional advancement. Although hiring-related decision making is decentralized, these decision makers are required to follow highly specified and centrally controlled hiring processes and policies. Finally, Intel invests significant resources in employee and management development and attempts to closely link these development programs with individual career management.

Like organizations adopting high-commitment HR strategies, firms adopting paternalistic HR strategies (such as MSI Ltd., described earlier) are also oriented toward an ILM-based staffing system. However, in this case, the staffing system is likely to be more consistent with the wage- (rather than salary-) based ILM (Pinfield & Berner, 1994). As in the case of the commitment HR strategy, paternalistic recruitment processes also tend to be oriented toward minimizing the risk of hiring a "false positive." However, in this case, such processes are adopted not so much because of the catastrophic damage that such an employee could cause (process-based systems of control greatly reduce that risk) but rather because of the difficulty of removing this individual from his or her job.

As will be recalled, at MSI, every effort is made to ensure employees the highest degree of employment security. Given the more limited risks, organizations adopting the paternalistic HR strategy may outsource some of their recruitment function to external agents. As in the case of the high-commitment strategy, the paternalistic strategy places an emphasis on identifying candidates with future potential rather than those with currently needed skills or competencies. But because work processes in such organizations tend to be subject to greater process-based controls and because work roles tend to be framed by the demands of relatively stable jobs, criteria tend to be more job oriented and less demanding of sophisticated assessment methods. Furthermore, the extensive focus on standardized and consistent administrative processes requires a highly centralized decision-making process. Finally, given their ILM orientation, organizations adopting the paternalistic strategy place a heavy emphasis on employee development. However, in this case, formal development activities tend to be skill oriented, with mobility contingent more on seniority than on readiness or merit.

Organizations adopting the free-agent and secondary HR strategies develop their staffing systems around an ELM orientation. The preprogrammed nature of jobs in the case of the latter allows such organizations (e.g., RLA Textiles) to adopt quantity- rather than quality-oriented recruitment practices that do not necessarily transmit a realistic message and that can easily be contracted out to external agents. In contrast, given the lack of preprogrammed work processes in their organizations and at least a short-term interest in retaining skilled individuals once selected, firms adopting the free-agent HR strategy tend to adopt recruitment processes that are, for the most part, realistic and based on moderately high standards. Although some reliance on external agents may be necessary to secure a broad enough pool from which to make selections, given the dynamic nature of jobs in such organizations, too much of a reliance on such agents may have detrimental effects on the nature of the candidate pool.

Selection processes across both types of strategies tend to be far more oriented toward identifying past achievements and determining what the candidate can offer on an immediate basis to the firm. Typically, in these organizations as opposed to organizations adopting high-commitment and paternalistic HR strategies, little attention is paid to candidates' future potential. Nevertheless, the fluid nature of "jobs" in the case of many organizations adopting the free-agent strategy demands that such organizations assess current competencies (applicable to a variety of work roles) rather than just current job-based knowledge, skills, and abilities (as in the case of the secondary strategy). This, in turn, justifies the adoption of more sophisticated selection methods and the involvement of a wide variety of organizational interests in individual selection decisions.

Finally, the ELM basis of the staffing subsystems adopted by both free-agent and secondary firms places relatively limited emphasis on employee development, advancement, and retention. Nevertheless, firms adopting more of a free-agent HR strategy are bound by the less preprogrammed nature of their work processes to ensure that externally recruited employees gain those competencies necessary for teamwork and internal coordination. Furthermore, such work processes tend to increase the dependence of the firm on their workforce (and hence the relative value of the workforce to the firm) and expose the firm to greater risk when employees have the ability to easily move from one employer to the next. Consequently, for firms adopting the free-agent strategy there tends to be a greater interest in retaining current employees, at least as long as their current competencies are demanded and valued. Merit-based internal mobility may be used to retain those employees most highly valued. Furthermore, to the extent that employee reductions are used to maximize flexibility and responsiveness, such reductions are likely to be more limited and structured so as to balance the need for labor variability with the firm's human capital interests.

This is precisely the approach used by many of the larger law, accounting, and consulting firms around the world. These firms tend to employ recent graduates at the "entry level," often in the employment context of a temporary internship or "freelance" relationship. More permanent employment may be offered to a handful of these workers on the basis of a tournament model. That is, the incentive of eventually being offered a junior partnership is used by these firms as a way to encourage those most highly valued professionals to develop a greater sense of commitment to their employer. Similarly, although nearly all contractors in the construction industry tend to rely on free-agent skilled-trades workers (e.g., carpenters and electricians), the larger contractors also tend to offer more permanent employment to a small number of the most highly valued of their "freelancers" as a means to retain critical human capital, develop some degree of employee attachment, and ensure a tighter alignment of employer-employee interests.

Note

1. At the company's request, this corporate name used in this book is fictitious.

5

Appraisal and Reward Subsystem

As noted in Chapter 3, the appraisal and reward subsystem focuses on in-trinsic and extrinsic financial and nonfinancial returns to the employee and the way in which the organization attempts to use such returns to direct and encourage desired attitudes and behaviors. Numerous researchers have applied several different theories to explain the link between organizational appraisal and compensation practices and performance and the way in which a wide variety of contingency factors can moderate such a relationship. In this chapter, we first review several of these theories. We then examine some of the strategic considerations that managers need to consider when designing an appraisal and reward subsystem. In this discussion, we will highlight the results of the initial empirical research focusing on the link between specific compensation practices and firm performance and the possible contingencies governing such potential links. Taking these contingencies into consideration, several researchers have proposed that distinct compensation practices tend to cluster into internally consistent appraisal and reward subsystems. In the third part of this chapter, we therefore review several of these proposed subsystem frameworks and also discuss the extent to which different clusters of appraisal and reward practices might be associated with one or more of the four dominant HR strategies identified in Chapter 3 (i.e., commitment, free agent, paternalistic, and secondary).

Frameworks for Understanding the Compensation-Performance Link

Underlying the appraisal and reward subsystem in many organizations are likely to be a set of assumptions regarding the way in which rewards may be used to motivate employee participation, contribution, and retention. These assumptions regarding the ways in which assessment, pay, and recognition may be used to direct and control employee attitudes and behaviors are themselves grounded in a few seminal psychological and economic theories. Two such theories, expectancy theory (Vroom, 1964) and equity theory (Adams, 1963), provide the foundation for contemporary compensation strategy. More recently, reward strategies have begun to take into account the assumptions embedded in two additional theories, namely human capital theory (Becker, 1975) and agency theory (Eisenhardt, 1989; Fama & Jensen, 1983).

Expectancy and Equity Theories

Building on reinforcement theory (or the notion that a response is more likely to occur when it is followed by a reward), Vroom (1964) argued that it is not so much the prior reward experience per se that shapes motivation but rather the degree to which the individual perceives the existence of an instrumentality link between behaviors and rewards. That is, the more an individual perceives his or her personal effort to account for only a small proportion of the variability in output, the less effective an output-contingent reward is likely to be in motivating such effort. Furthermore, such expectancies are likely to motivate only if the expected value of the outcome or reward is personally meaningful. As we will discuss in more detail below, the contingencies embedded in expectancy theory provide the basis for determining when and how to adopt what is widely referred to as a *variable pay strategy,* or one based on the notion of pay for performance.

However, expectancy perceptions are unlikely to be the only factor determining the degree to which rewards can channel and encourage desired employee attitudes and behaviors. According to equity theory (Adams, 1963), norms of fairness are also likely to shape employee action. For example, if employees feel that their reward/contribution ratio is less than that of a similar set of employees in the same or another firm, they may adopt any one of a variety of actions (e.g., reduce effort, quit, strike) designed to restore equity or a sense of balance in these comparative ratios. The matter becomes more complex when we take into account that employees may select from among three different types of reference groups when making such comparisons: (a) other employees in different positions in the same organization (what is referred to as *internal equity*); (b) other employees in similar positions in other organizations competing in the same labor market (what is referred to as *external equity*); and (c) other employees in similar positions in the same organization (what is referred to as *employee equity*). From the employer's perspective, it may be next to impossible to ensure equity at all three levels. For example, to ensure external equity (and thus avoid turnover among highly valued employees who might perceive enhanced reward/contribution ratios outside of the firm), it may be necessary to "break" existing pay structures and thus violate internal equity norms. But when should one form of equity take precedence over another? Indeed, as we will see below, many of the choices and contingencies that need to be addressed in designing appraisal and reward strategies can be considered in relation to these three different forms of equity.

Human Capital Theory

The two theories just reviewed focus primarily on the impact of pay on motivation or effort. However, performance is not simply a function of effort. It is also a function of the knowledge, skills, and abilities that individuals can bring to bear when motivated to do so. Indeed, this is a core assumption of recent resource theories of the firm (Barney, 1991). In line with these arguments, human capital theory (Becker, 1975; Gerhart, 1990) assumes that higher earnings go to those who, by investing in themselves through education and experience, improve their knowledge, skills, and abilities (KSAs) and thus enhance their productive capacity. Because there are costs for doing so (i.e., time, tuition, opportunity costs), to the extent that an organization is willing to reward individuals for overcoming such barriers, the organization is likely to be successful in attracting and retaining individuals with these desired attributes. The theory therefore suggests two ways to enhance an organization's human capital base: (a) by widening the differentials between entry-level positions and KSA-rich executive positions in a pay structure and (b) by increasing the degree to which pay increases are contingent on human capital enhancement (i.e., knowledge- or skill-based pay). Firm competitiveness and performance is likely to be enhanced to the extent that the organization expands and creates synergies on the basis of its in-house, human capital base (Barney, 1991) and to the extent that it can leverage these KSAs to increase operational flexibility (Murray & Gerhart, 1998).

Agency Theory

Yet perhaps one of the most influential theories affecting organizational appraisal and reward subsystem strategies in recent years is agency theory (Eisenhardt, 1989; Fama & Jensen, 1983). Underlying this theory is the assumption that although the interests of employers (principals) and employees (agents) may be divergent, organizational reward systems can be used as an efficient means to enhance interest convergence. According to agency theory, employees are averse to effort and (all else equal) exert only as much effort as is required to ensure continued employment. Because the employer compensates the employee at the same rate regardless of the latter's effort level, this transfers all the risk of employment onto the employer, who (like the employee) is risk averse. To reduce that risk and ensure that the employee exerts the desired amount of effort to justify the agreed-on amount of pay, the employer (principal) must be able to monitor employee (agent) effort. However, such monitoring is not always cost-effective or even possible, particularly when work processes are complex and the means-ends linkages on which they are based are poorly understood and difficult to preprogram (as in such fields as teaching and medicine). In these situations, it may be to the principal's advantage to share some of the risk with agents by making a portion of the latter's reward contingent on the achievement of some outcome desired by the principal (e.g., profit, market share). Indeed, risk sharing may serve as an important signaling and screening mechanism, helping firms seeking to attract and retain "highly charged risk-takers" (Baron & Kreps, 1999).

However, such a risk-sharing solution is also not necessarily cost-free, because risk-averse agents may demand higher pay to make up for the risk that—due to contingencies beyond their control—increased effort may not necessarily yield the outcome on which their reward (or some portion of it) depends.

One way around this problem is to make the rewards contingent on *relative* (as opposed to absolute) performance, given that the performance of one's peers is also likely to be affected by such contingencies. However, by doing so, a kind of competitive or tournament dynamic is introduced that may be deleterious to an organization whose overall success is contingent on teamwork and interdepartmental cooperation. The adoption of a group-based agency framework (i.e., team- or departmental-based pay systems) may solve problems associated with a tournament dynamic but is likely to create a whole host of new concerns related to the problem of free riding. Specifically, under such a framework, because all team members benefit when a team-level outcome is achieved, individual team members have a natural incentive to let their peers do all the work. Although game theory (Axelrod, 1984; Dawes, 1980) suggests a number of factors that can ameliorate the free-rider problem inherent in group-based agency frameworks (e.g., small group size, group permanence), it may not always be possible to artificially impose these conditions on work groups for purposes of enhancing the effectiveness of the appraisal and reward system.

Agency-based contracts may be further complicated when employees are asked to delicately balance a number of less-than-complementary objectives. Principals may find that by making rewards contingent on the achievement of outcome "x" (say output), organizational outcome "y" (say quality) is sacrificed. Thus, many organizations seek to balance incentives across a number of critical outcomes by building into their incentive scheme a number of reward contingencies (e.g., meeting both short-term and long-term objectives). However, the more complex the agency contract becomes, the more blurry the instrumentalities and the weaker the incentive effect.

Thus, although an increasing number of organizations are adopting variable reward strategies grounded on the principles of agency theory, such systems of performance-based pay may not necessarily be the panacea they are often believed to be. In the next section, we will address some of the contingencies identified by strategy researchers that are likely to moderate the link between agency-type pay strategies and firm performance.

Contingencies and Choices in the Design of Appraisal and Reward Strategies

Although the theories reviewed above suggest that certain reward strategies (i.e., those offering high valence returns with clear instrumentalities) may be universally more effective than others in directing and encouraging desired employee behaviors and attitudes, on the whole, they suggest that such effectiveness is contingent on a wide variety of organizational, workforce, and contextual conditions. Several teams of researchers (see Flannery, Hofrichter, & Platten, 1996; Gomez-Mejia & Balkin, 1992a, 1992b; Milkovich & Newman, 1996) have attempted to identify the parameters by which appraisal and reward systems vary, as well as the factors that determine the appropriateness of one reward alternative over another. In this section, we group these parameters into five different categories of choices that managers typically need to make when designing a strategic appraisal and reward subsystem: basic choices, internal equity choices, external equity choices, employee equity choices, and appraisal choices.

Basic Choices

Milkovich and Newman (1996) identified a number of basic policy decisions that underlie all appraisal and reward subsystems and that shape subsequent system-related decisions. As they noted, "These policies form the building blocks, the foundation on which pay systems are built . . . [and] serve as the guidelines within which pay is managed to accomplish system objectives" (p. 13).

Among the most critical of these basic choices is the issue of which of two forms of equity (internal, external) to emphasize. As suggested above, it may be difficult (at best) for an employer to develop a pay strategy that places equal emphasis on the three forms of pay equity and still meets efficiency objectives (i.e., does not raise labor costs to the point that the firm can no longer compete effectively). Indeed, the choice often comes down to whether the firm should place an emphasis on ensuring consistency in the pay structure (i.e., internal equity) versus meeting market prices for labor (i.e., external equity). A focus on the latter can create a situation referred to as *pay compression* in which the differential between low- and high-level positions is narrowed as a result of the need to meet inflated market-level prices for highly-in-demand entry-level staff. Such a situation is not uncommon among high-technology firms constantly in search of fresh technical talent offering skills attuned to constantly changing business demands (Cascio, 1990). A focus on the former (i.e., internal equity) is most prevalent among firms that are highly dependent on retaining firm-specific knowledge and experience and that have less of a need for labor flexibility.

Put in other terms, firms placing an emphasis on internal labor markets (ILMs) are more likely to carefully guard internal consistency in their pay structure. For example, at the defense contractor MSI, a strong emphasis is placed on formal job evaluation to ensure that jobs are consistently and fairly valued across the organization. MSI's tall and rigid hierarchy allows it to ensure that jobs are more precisely placed in their appropriate grade along the pay structure. To provide room for continuous pay growth over time, MSI's pay structure incorporates far more grades or levels than might be found in other, less paternalistic high-technology companies.

Firms relying on external labor markets (ELMs) are more likely to emphasize the need to stay in line with ELM rates. For example, RLA Textiles' vice president for human resources dedicates a substantial portion of his time to collecting data on labor supply and comparative hourly wage rates for different types of workers in different geographic locations. The objective here is to ensure that RLA never pays more than its competitors but that it also never offers too little to be able to attract needed labor in real time.

In addition to such a labor market contingency, organizational structure is likely to play a role in determining the relative degree of emphasis placed on internal as opposed to external equity. Gomez-Mejia and Welbourne (1988) found that the degree of subunit autonomy (as opposed to interdependency) also affects the relative degree of emphasis placed on these two alternative forms of equity. Specifically, they suggested that the more autonomous the subunit, the greater the degree of emphasis on external equity, but that the more interdependency among a firm's business units, the more emphasis placed on internal equity.

Gomez-Mejia and Balkin (1992a) identified a number of additional basic choices that are made in the design of reward subsystems. First, they recognized that the organizational reward subsystem in most cases either implicitly encourages or discourages risk taking on the part of employees. Certain organizations have a need for stability and predictability. Perceiving the cost of multiple missed opportunities to be far less than that of one "disaster," such organizations are likely to use their compensation system as a way to both signal (to current employees) a preference for risk aversion and screen out risk takers from among job candidates. An "earnings-at-risk" program, such as that in place at GM's Saturn unit, is but one example of such an approach (Brown & Huber, 1992). Other typically innovation-driven organizations such as 3M offer internal venture capital, job security guarantees, and *supplementary* rewards tied to the profitability of the risky venture in order to encourage employee risk taking.

Second, and related to the risk aversion issue, is the question of "pay mix"—that is, the proportion of monetary compensation that is paid on a variable (as opposed to a fixed) basis. As we discussed in our review of agency theory, employers have a natural interest in sharing some of the risk inherent in compensation with their employees. The more they manage to do so, the more variable the compensation system and the more contingent employee pay on some individual or set of outcomes. Balkin and Gomez-Mejia (1984, 1986) tied this issue to firm life cycle and cash flow, arguing that younger, more cash-hungry firms are likely to rely more on variable pay as a means to enhance resource flexibility. For example, at Indigo Ltd., a developer of digital printing systems, on average, between 10% and 20% of employees' annual compensation was in the form of a performance-based bonus. However, it is likely that the degree to which firms increase pay variability is even more contingent on their ability to address those problems that we associated with agency-based contracts (e.g., blurred instrumentalities, tournament dynamic). Thus, according to Baron and Kreps (1999), greater reliance on fixed pay is more likely in those situations in which

- The production technology is complex (unclear means-ends linkage) and tasks are ambiguous
- The culture emphasizes cooperation
- Firm competitive advantage rides on hard-to-measure quality or innovation
- Large-sized and highly fluid work groups increase the risk of free riding

A third basic choice has to do with the degree of emphasis placed on monetary (tangible cash or benefit payments) as opposed to nonmonetary rewards such as recognition, career development, and job security. Simon (1991, 1993) suggested that economic returns alone are not sufficient to extract the unique value-adding assets controlled by employees. Expanding on Simon's argument, Bloom and Milkovich (1998a) noted that pay alone fails to create the organizational attachments necessary to achieve the "common mind-set" required for effective collective action. Simply put, economic returns structure a transactional relationship that must be easily expressed in pecuniary terms and that therefore can always be copied or purchased away by a competitor. However, Hambrick and Snow (1989) argued that it is much simpler for growing and dynamic firms than for mature firms using routine technologies and operating in stable contexts to provide nonmonetary rewards such as challenge, career development, and participation. The latter often need to make a concerted effort to provide such rewards by, for example, redesigning production processes and making greater use of ILMs. Such efforts can be costly, and a return on the investment can rarely be expected in the short term (Baron & Kreps, 1999).

Finally, in designing their appraisal and reward subsystem, Gomez-Mejia and Balkin (1992a) noted that firms must make a number of decisions regarding the way the system is to be administered. For example, to what degree are pay decisions to be tightly controlled by some central authority as opposed to being diffused to organizational subunits? And how flexible and responsive will the pay system be to the emergence of unpredictable and unique situations (e.g., the need to "break" a pay structure in order to recruit an engineer with "one-of-a-kind" skills and experience)? A firm's overall HR strategy is likely to determine both of these issues. For example, firms placing greater emphasis on the ELM are likely to decentralize specific compensation decisions in order to allow a closer tie to external market demands and are also more likely to adopt a flexible approach to the type of unique, market-driven situation described above.

To some extent, HR strategy may also determine whether a firm adopts a policy of open or secret pay. Although, according to several researchers (Baron & Kreps, 1999; Lawler, 1990), open pay is always preferable to secret pay, Balkin and Gomez-Mejia (1990) found that open-pay systems are more effective in organizations with cultures emphasizing involvement, commitment, trust, cooperation, and egalitarianism. Nevertheless, many firms characterized by precisely such cultural traits nevertheless attempt to ensure pay secrecy. For example, at Indigo, top management strongly emphasizes to its employees that, with the exception of their immediate family, they are forbidden to discuss their pay with anyone. Violations of this norm have been punished by dismissal. At Intel, however, although a policy of individual pay secrecy is in place, systemwide pay data is provided to all employees on request. As we will see in Chapter 6, these traits are characteristic of firms adopting a high-commitment HR strategy. Gomez-Mejia and Balkin (1992a) reported that in organizations lacking such cultural traits, open pay can "actually exacerbate hostilities and conflicts and add fuel to an already volatile situation" (p. 55).

Internal Equity Choices

As noted earlier, internal equity has to do with the degree to which organizational pay structures—"the array of pay rates for different work or skills within a single organization" (Milkovich & Newman, 1996, p. 45)—are internally consistent. Internal equity is greatest when, across jobs within the organization, this contribution/rewards ratio remains relatively stable: that is, when work of equal value is equally rewarded and when pay differentials accurately reflect work of unequal worth (Milkovich & Newman, 1996). Internal equity choices therefore concern the dimension(s) along which contributions are to be evaluated (i.e., job vs. skill/knowledge/competency) and the egalitarian nature of pay systems in terms of the size of pay differentials, eligibility for supplementary forms of pay, and the number of pay levels encompassed (broad vs. narrow bands).

Traditionally, to assess contribution, organizations assessed the value of the job performed by an employee. Assuming that work processes are stable and highly routinized and programmable and that employees are expected to perform one and only one job, the characteristics of the task rather than of the employee are likely to account for most of the variance in relative contribution. Consequently, fairness can best be ensured by evaluating the relative value of specific jobs on the basis of some comprehensive and valid evaluation framework (e.g., Hay Point System). Jaques (1990) argued that job-based systems reinforce notions of personal accountability and responsibility, something that skill- or competency-based systems cannot do. Becker and Huselid (1992) argued that the ranking framework and tournament dynamics inherent in most job-based systems may offer significant motivational potential, particularly if the spread between lower and higher positions is greater. As they noted, tournament theory suggests that "the appeal of successively higher salaries motivates employees to devote greater attention to organizational interests at all levels and discourages shirking" (p. 337). Indeed, their findings indicate substantial support for such a notion. Lawler (1990) noted that job-based internal equity facilitates staff movements, allows for centralized control of the pay system, is likely to yield a high "fairness" score on the part of employees, and may help managers avoid political conflicts stemming from particularism in pay. However, with regard to the latter two points, Ferris and Judge (1991) disagreed. They argued that political considerations enter into assessments of the relative contribution of jobs ("point grabbing") because job value can often be translated into managerial power. Consequently, employees may often have reason to doubt the validity and fairness in job valuations.

Moreover, with an increasing number of firms looking to enhance their operational flexibility by increasing the ability of employees to "multitask" or perform a *variety* of tasks (often in the context of work teams), the assumptions underlying the job-based approach may no longer hold. Job descriptions can no longer be considered stable, and employees can no longer be viewed as being assigned to any one particular job. Lawler (1986, 1990, 1994) claimed that for firms seeking operational agility, responsiveness, and flexibility, such a job-based approach may be highly dysfunctional. That is, in such a context, traditional systems of placing a value on the job may be less effective than systems based on placing a value on the multiple skills and/or competencies required for employees to be more versatile, take on multiple tasks, or work as "team players."

It has been argued that the appropriateness of these two alternative approaches to internal equity is to a great extent contingent on the existence of a high-commitment organizational culture (Ledford, 1991; Wallace, 1991). However, recent evidence (Murray & Gerhart, 1998) suggests that basing internal equity on employee skills may have less to do with organizational culture than with the existence of work processes that allow firms to take advantage of the enhanced skill base that they are now paying for. That is, a skill-based approach to internal equity may yield the greatest returns to firms whose HR strategies are grounded in the use of output as opposed to process controls (i.e., high-commitment, free-agent HR strategies).

Murray and Gerhart (1998) used time-series data from two facilities, one in which a skill-based pay program was implemented and one in which it was not, to assess the impact of skill-based pay on productivity, labor costs, and quality. The results indicate that the adoption of skill-based pay was associated with a 58% increase in the level of productivity (labor hours per part), a 15% decline in labor cost per part in the treatment facility, and an 82% lower level of scrap relative to the comparison facility. Though scrap rates increased in both plants over the 3 years studied, they did so at a much lower rate (12% vs. 66%) in the facility in which skill-based pay was adopted. The study suggests that although skill-based pay has the potential to raise employee earnings and generate substantial administrative costs, these outflows are likely to be offset by an increase in productivity, thus actually lowering total labor costs. Of course, this assumes that the organization restructures its work processes to take advantage of this enhanced skill base and generate such productivity improvements. As Murray and Gerhart (1998) concluded,

> To obtain such results, managers must realize that skill-based pay is a comprehensive human resource program. . . . A successful program also relies on committing adequate resources to training and certification appraisal and on ensuring timely and unbiased appraisals and complementary job design and production scheduling. (p. 77)

A second internal equity choice concerns the degree to which rewards in general and the pay structure in particular should be hierarchical as opposed to egalitarian. Although, in principle, the norm of internal equity suggests that the rewards/contribution ratio should remain constant, in practice this norm is not always followed. As Baron and Kreps (1999) noted, "If X contributes more than Y, X should be paid more than Y. But if X contributes twice as much as Y, it isn't necessarily required that X be paid twice what Y gets" (pp. 293). That is, in designing reward systems, organizations have the ability to build in as much dispersion or compression as the external labor market will permit. In certain nations (e.g., Japan), perhaps as a function of cultural values, only a relatively limited degree of dispersion is feasible. In the United States, however, it appears that labor market pressures act more to limit the degree of compression, with Ben and Jerry's Ice Cream as a classic example. Ben and Jerry's maintained a highly egalitarian pay structure in which the highest-paid employee could earn no more than seven times the pay of the lowest-paid employee. It was forced to drop this pay policy when it was unable to recruit an external CEO willing to accept a compensation package consistent with such a norm.

Egalitarian reward systems are characterized not only by flatter pay structures but also by the existence of fewer (but typically broader) pay grades or "bands" and the tendency to make a larger proportion of the workforce (and not just higher-level executives) eligible for special incentives such as bonuses and options. Hierarchical pay systems typically incorporate a greater number of more "narrow" pay grades and provide eligibility for special incentives only to higher levels. As noted by Milkovich and Newman (1996), underlying the adoption of egalitarian reward systems is the desire to expand the opportunities for, and meaningfulness of, promotion and thereby influence workforce stability. Baron and Kreps (1999) argued that egalitarian pay structures are more prevalent in organizations adopting a high-commitment HR strategy because it is highly supportive of the cooperative, status-free culture that such organizations seek to build and because such organizations (with their reliance on ILMs and intrinsic forms of motivation) are more insulated from external market pressures. The broad bands inherent in egalitarian structures may also allow for greater recognition of individual (as opposed to job-based) differences in performance. On the other hand, firms relying on an ELM may find that such egalitarian systems limit their ability to attract and retain talent that may be more highly valued on the outside unless they are willing to somehow expand the existing bands or create informal "sub-bands," a potentially costly proposition and one that, for the most part, is inconsistent with the very nature of an egalitarian reward system. Similarly, firms placing a high emphasis on workforce stability and process-based control (i.e., those with a paternalistic HR strategy) may find that such an egalitarian framework limits their ability to take advantage of a "tall" hierarchy as a means to minimize turnover and engender the desired "clan" culture (Hambrick & Snow, 1989).

External Equity Choices

A key decision in the design of any organizational reward system concerns the degree to which the firm's overall reward package matches or exceeds that of its competitors in the labor market. Gomez-Mejia and Balkin (1992a) identified three main reasons why external competitiveness is likely to be such a critical strategic issue for most organizations. First, it is a major influence on organizational recruitment success (Rynes, 1991). Second, compensation level is the major determinant of pay satisfaction and thus, in turn, of employee retention. Finally, particularly in labor-intensive firms, decisions regarding external equity can have a direct impact on the overall costs of production and thus on firm competitiveness. That is, firms in labor-intensive industries that pay above-market rates of compensation are also likely to have above-market production costs and thus to need to find an alternative to a cost-leader business strategy. This suggests that firm business strategy is likely to be a key contingency influencing external equity decisions, with firms that compete on the basis of cost leadership rarely paying above market levels of compensation for all employee groups. Organizational life cycle characteristics may also influence external equity decisions, as growing firms may seek to offset immediate fixed costs by offering greater incentives along with a relatively lower base salary. Finally, firms less concerned with internal equity (such as those adopting a free-agent or secondary HR strategy) are more likely to adopt a "lead-the-market" reward strategy with respect to highly valued employee groups or groups of employees on whom the organization's success is more dependent. In contrast, firms with a high-commitment or paternalistic HR strategy may attempt to leverage nontangible rewards (such as employment security or career growth) as a compensating differential to allow them to compete for and retain highly valued employees while still paying at or even below (rather than above) the market rate.

At MSI, for example, entry-level engineers tend to get compensated at below-market levels and advance at rates significantly slower than in other technology-based firms. One might therefore ask why young engineers continue to seek employment at MSI. The answer is twofold. First, MSI offers a high degree of job security, as well as a benefits package unmatched by its competitors in the labor market. Second, MSI is known to compensate its loyal and long-term employees at levels far above those prevailing in the labor market for similar medium- and high-level positions. Thus, in economic terms, for those remaining committed to the company and willing to "move up" over time, current pay may be viewed as actually incorporating a substantial supplement in the form of deferred compensation.

Employee Equity Choices

As noted earlier, employee equity concerns the way in which employees in the same organization, performing the same job, are differentially rewarded. Typically, organizations choose from one of four basic employee equity options or reward criteria: membership, tenure, skill, or performance. Organizations basing employee equity on membership simply reward all employees on an equivalent basis, assuming that at least a satisfactory level of performance is achieved. A limited degree of employee equity is achieved in that unsatisfactory employees are terminated, whereas satisfactory employees are retained, continue to receive compensation, and can hope to earn more by advancement from one pay grade to the next over time. Such systems, however, provide little or no material incentive for employees to perform above the minimal satisfactory level, and pay dissatisfaction can develop if employees perceive a lack of procedural justice in the manner in which they and their coworkers are moved from one pay grade to the next.

Not surprisingly, therefore, many organizations seek to rationalize the manner in which they differentially reward employees performing identical tasks by basing these rewards on objective criteria that, at least in principle, may have a positive impact on group, unit, or firm performance. These criteria typically include either tenure or skill/knowledge.

Underlying a tenure-based system of employee equity is the assumption that on-the-job experience increases the potential contribution of employees and that this increased contribution deserves an enhanced reward. Organizations adopting this framework either provide a direct and automatic pay increase for each year of service or base advancement (and hence earnings potential) on seniority criteria. A seniority-based system of employee equity may lower labor costs by promoting stability and may reduce transaction costs associated with recruitment, selection, and training. It may also enable the firm to retain proprietary knowledge and the synergies inherent in complex social networks.

Underlying a skill/knowledge-based system of employee equity is the assumption that although individual contribution is still basically contingent on the type of job performed, marginal enhancements in contribution can be generated on the basis of an expanded skill base. Organizations adopting this framework thus offer marginal, within-range pay enhancements to those employees meeting certain skill requirements or successfully completing specified training programs.

However, a large and increasing number of firms are using performance criteria as the primary means to ensure employee equity, providing marginal reward enhancements to those individual employees or groups of employees demonstrating above-average performance. As Baron and Kreps (1999) wrote, making pay partially or entirely contingent on performance is "a fairly delicate and potentially dangerous set of motivational tools, which should be used with circumspection" (p. 245). Although it may work well in some circumstances, depending on the parameters of the pay-for-performance system implemented and the nature of the organization and its work processes, it may not in others. As we reviewed in our discussion of agency theory, such systems may be risky, particularly in those contexts in which

- The organization emphasizes cooperation
- The focus is on hard-to-measure quality, innovation, or service for which clear indicators may not be available
- The work process is complex, involving ambiguous tasks and unclear cause-and-effect relations

Although, especially in these contexts, organizations may be best off opting for tenure- or skill-based systems of employee equity over performance-based systems, agency theory suggests that it is precisely when tasks are more nonprogrammable and when employees have greater discretionary responsibility and potential impact that principals will have the greatest interest in adopting performance-contingent pay systems. But does performance-based pay solve the agency problem inherent in nonprogrammable jobs when the inherent nature of these jobs makes them such poor candidates for agency-based contracts?

The case of executive pay may provide us with an answer. Clearly, for certain top-level organizational positions (e.g., CEO), though a tenure- or skill-based system of employee equity may resolve some internal equity concerns, it certainly provides no real solution to the agency issues critical at such organizational levels. Thus, executive pay is typically structured around some performance-based contingency. However, given the highly nonpreprogrammable nature of most executive positions and the highly charged political context within which most top managers operate, empirical evidence suggests that even contingent pay typically fails to solve the agency problem. Barkema and Gomez-Mejia (1998) concluded from their review of executive pay research that, in general, there exists an insignificant relationship between pay and performance and that only a very low portion (approximately 5%) of the variance in CEO pay is actually explained by performance (p. 135). Tosi, Werner, Katz, and Gomez-Mejia (1998) claimed that the supposed managerial risk sharing inherent in executive pay systems is greatly reduced when CEOs are given influence over the selection of performance criteria and appointments to corporate compensation committees. Thus, organizational power and politics also need to be taken into account when basing employee equity on performance criteria (Ferris & Judge, 1991).

Does this mean that organizations are less likely to use performance-based pay when tasks are nonprogrammable? Not at all. In fact, Gerhart and Milkovich (1992), in one of the first empirical studies of the link between compensation practices and firm performance, suggested that the use of contingent pay is in fact *greatest* when tasks are nonprogrammable and when incumbents are given greater discretionary responsibility and potential impact. Moreover, in a longitudinal study of over 300 business units, they found a strong, positive relationship between firm performance and the proportion of total pay based on performance-based incentives and bonuses. Specifically, they found that an increase in the "bonus-to-base" ratio of 10 percentage points (the mean was .20) was associated with a 0.48% increase in ROA. Given that this study was based on an analysis of compensation data for managerial (i.e., highly nonprogrammed) jobs only, it suggests that even where conditions for agency-type risk sharing are suboptimal, basing employee equity on performance contingencies may yield substantial benefits. Although some of these benefits may be a function of making labor into more of a variable (as opposed to fixed) cost, there is little doubt that the alignment of interests also plays a substantial role. Further, these results are consistent with several other studies suggesting a positive link between pay mix (i.e., higher proportion of variable performance-based pay to stable base pay) and firm performance (Abowd, 1990; Murphy, 1985).

However, a more recent study by Bloom and Milkovich (1998a) indicates that the positive link between pay mix and firm performance may in fact be contingent on the level of risk that agents are asked to share. These authors argued that in many cases in which tasks are nonprogrammable, the risks shifted onto the agent in the framework of a contingent pay system may be so high that the agent will either (a) demand a compensating differential in the form of increased base pay (as a kind of insurance policy), (b) leave, or (c) engage in practices designed to reduce pay variability (e.g., entrenchment and nonaction) that may coincidentally be detrimental to the firm. In such cases, they argued—and, more importantly, found—that increased use of contingent pay may in fact have an adverse impact on firm performance. Specifically, they found that higher-risk firms that relied more heavily on incentive pay tended to exhibit poorer performance than comparable high-risk firms that deemphasized incentive pay.

For organizations willing to swallow the risks noted above and implement some form of performance-based pay, additional choices must be made. First, at what level is performance to be measured—individual or aggregate? Assuming the latter, at what level should performance be aggregated—work group, unit, or corporate? Second, how frequently should performance be assessed and rewarded—semiannually, annually, or every 2 or 3 years? Third, should reward distributions be made immediately or deferred to some later point in time, and should they come in the form of a bonus or a merit increase? Fourth, which employee groups should be eligible for incentive pay, what percentage should actually meet minimal criteria for some payout, and what should the relative magnitude of the payout be? Although theories abound as to the contingencies governing the design of pay-for-performance programs, research examining the impact of such programs on firm performance is now in only the very early stages (Milkovich & Newman, 1996). Nevertheless, on the basis of theory and preliminary research, we may begin to cull some tentative answers to some of these questions.

Regarding the first issue—individual versus aggregate performance—individual-based systems such as merit pay and individual bonuses appear to be most effective only when

- There are minimal interdependencies among employees, or competition among employees is desired
- Specific, measurable outcomes are sought
- Delayed performance dysfunctions (i.e., those only appearing over time, such as poor product quality) can be traced back to an individual employee
- The employee, individually, has a relatively strong degree of control over these outcomes

Otherwise, aggregate frameworks tend to be more effective. Still, researchers (Baron & Kreps, 1999; Gomez-Mejia & Balkin, 1989) suggest that aggregate pay may be effective only when the organization is able to control incentives for free riding, when the overall HR strategy is structured around cooperation and teamwork, and when the organization can control the problems associated with "time-and-hurdle" and "ratchet" effects. Time-and-hurdle problems relate to the tendency of workers to "bank" expended effort from one assessment period to the next or to take dysfunctional action to just meet the period's specified quota or criterion. Ratchet effects have to do with the tendency of group incentives to lose their motivational effect as standards are shifted up over time and of group members to use peer pressure to avoid such upward shifts by punishing "rate busters."

Furthermore, the level of aggregation—work group, unit, or corporate—may have profound implications with respect to free riding because, as we already discussed, there is an inverse relationship between group size and the ability of group members to monitor and sanction free riding. Typically, therefore, organizations attempt to aggregate to the lowest possible level, depending on the type of work performed or position in the organizational hierarchy. For production workers, the most appropriate level may be the work group or department unless tight interdependencies with other work groups or departments reduce perceived instrumentalities to the point that group members sense that they lack the ability to control the variance in measured and compensatable outputs. For executives, however, this is likely to be the division or corporation as a whole, again depending somewhat on whether corporate units are tightly coupled (i.e., vertically integrated) or loosely coupled (horizontally integrated) and on the degree to which overall firm performance depends on developing an interdivisional synergy (Gomez-Mejia & Welbourne, 1988). Some organizations, such as AT&T, use a combination of aggregation levels—individual, team, business unit, and corporate—for different employee populations (Tully, 1993).

Two of the most popular forms of aggregate-level pay for performance programs are gain sharing (typically unitwide) and profit sharing (typically corporationwide). A number of studies suggest that despite the aggregation problem noted above, both programs may be associated with enhanced firm performance. Shuster (1983) studied six gain-sharing programs and (in four) found productivity improvements of approximately 30%, which could be, for the most part, attributed to the actual program. Other studies (Kaufman, 1992; McAdams & Hawk, 1994) suggest similar positive results, with net gains per employee estimated at between $1,300 and $3,700 per employee. Kruse's research (1983) suggests that profit sharing is associated with substantial enhancements in productivity and value added per employee. However, as Gerhart and Milkovich (1992) noted, because these studies are cross-sectional, it is impossible to determine the cause-and-effect relationship between profit sharing and firm performance (i.e., highly profitable firms may simply be more likely to adopt profit-sharing programs).

The timing of performance-based rewards with respect to both the length of time used to assess performance and the frequency of reward distributions is a critical issue as well. Reinforcement theory suggests that the motivational impact of a performance-based reward is greatest when the reward is granted on immediate completion of the desired behavior. Indeed, many piece rate and commission systems operate precisely in this manner, with the employee seeing his or her earnings rise in direct proportion to the actual units produced. Many nonincentive, variable-pay systems work in a similar fashion, with a bonus (i.e., a single lump sum payment that does not become part of the base salary) granted on the successful achievement of some specified objective or on the basis of a positive performance review.

However, certain long-linked work processes (such as those inherent in research and development) produce outcomes that are impossible to evaluate in the short run, and other tasks may require short-term performance plateaus or even declines (e.g., in revenues) to yield more significant long-term performance enhancements (e.g., enhanced market share). Furthermore, a focus on short-term performance could actually provide an incentive for employees to take actions yielding short-term benefits and then to leave the organization before the long-term implications of these actions become clear. Consequently, some organizations may prefer to provide smaller merit increases in base pay over time or at least to reward a portion of a large, one-time lump sum bonus in the form of some deferred payment (e.g., stock options) to discourage the development of a short-term orientation on the part of employees and/or employee attrition.

Despite the potential problems with performance-based pay in general and bonuses in particular, several studies (Dyer & Blancero, 1993; Tully, 1993) indicate a definite trend toward the wide-scale adoption of bonus-based variable pay. Whereas in the late 1980s just less than 50% of the 2,000 firms surveyed by Hewitt Associates reported a performance-based pay policy covering all exempt employees, in 1993 this number increased to 68%. Dyer and Blancero (1993), on the basis of their survey research, predicted that by the year 2000, over 33%, 23%, and 28% of executive, managerial, and professional compensation respectively will be in the form of variable pay. Moreover, by 1993, among these firms, the value of the mean bonus (5.9% of base pay) had surpassed that of the mean merit increase (4.3%). Baron and Kreps (1999) claimed that the movement toward bonuses and away from merit increases may be due to (a) the greater saliency of larger one-time bonus payments to employees (in line with reinforcement theory), (b) the heightened risk of perceived inequity as historical merit-based increases may no longer reflect current relative contributions, (c) the lower subjective expected utility of a merit increase if the employee is uncertain about his or her future in the organization, and (d) the long-term problems that merit increases can create with regard to pay structures and internal equity.

Finally, Flannery et al. (1996) saw the key choices with regard to employee equity as having to do with who is eligible to be compensated on the basis of performance, the percentage of those eligible actually receiving some reward, and the size of the reward received relative to base pay. These authors claimed that such choices are contingent on the HR strategy. Firms having more of a high-commitment strategy tend to offer such a scheme to between 80% and 100% of their employees and to ensure that of these, a similar proportion actually receive some reward. However, they also tend to limit the size of the incentive to between 10% and 25% of base pay. A recent study by Gerhart and Trevor (1996) suggested that firms adopting such an HR strategy may offer such broad eligibility as a means to ensure low employment variability. Critical to such firms is their ability to encourage employee trust and commitment. This becomes viable only when employees observe that the firm refrains from layoffs even during bad times. By applying contingent pay to a broader employee base, the organization increases its ability to refrain from layoffs because labor is no longer strictly a fixed cost. Furthermore, their results suggest that by more closely tying executive pay to long-term firm performance, firms effectively increase the personal risks for executives opting for a layoff as a "quick fix" to a temporary downturn.

In contrast, Flannery et al. find that firms adopting more of a secondary HR strategy tend to offer such performance-based incentives only to those 20% to 40% of employees considered to be "key" (i.e., those on whom the firm's future is highly contingent and whose skills are not easily replaceable), and that only some 20% to 40% of these will actually qualify for any performance-based reward. However, for those meeting performance criteria, payout levels are likely to be quite high—at a level equivalent to 60% or more of base pay.

Appraisal Choices

Organizations evaluate employee performance for a wide variety of purposes beyond those associated with rewards. For example, the performance appraisal system is often a core means of organizational communication because managers can highlight key organizational objectives, expectations, norms, and values by translating these into measurable performance criteria. Furthermore, performance appraisal data are used to guide decisions regarding employee training and development, internal career planning, and individual advancement, as well as to validate these and other (e.g., selection) HR decision-making processes. Indeed, as Baron and Kreps (1999) suggested, because appraisal systems are typically designed to serve so many different functions, they are often far from ideal with respect to any specific purpose. Key choices with respect to the design of these systems concern the degree to which appraisal data are to be (a) objective as opposed to judgmental, (b) relative versus absolute, (c) based on a forced or free distribution, and (d) based on narrow versus broad input.

Because performance appraisal data are used as a basis for numerous administrative decisions, employee procedural justice perceptions are critical. Procedural justice has to do with the perceived fairness of the process by which such administrative decisions (e.g., pay, advancement) are made (Greenberg, 1990). If employees feel that such decisions are based on inaccurate or unreliable data or on an inconsistent method of data analysis, the legitimacy of the entire decision-making framework may be questioned. In turn, there is a significantly lower probability that employees will accept the decision outcome and a greater probability that they will demonstrate that dissatisfaction by either voicing dissent or "voting with their feet" (Folger & Konovsky, 1989; Zenger, 1992).

One way to avoid such problems is to base performance appraisals on unambiguous, "objective" data. This is, however, more easily accomplished for some types of jobs than others because (a) a global performance "score" may have to take into account a variety of "objective" measures that may or may not be equally weighted, and (b) such objective data are simply hard to come by for some jobs. For example, whereas the performance of a typist might be appraised on the basis of the number of error-free characters typed per minute, such single-dimension, "objective" data might not accurately reflect performance for employees in other types of positions, such as sales or customer service. For the latter, multiple criteria (e.g., number of calls taken per hour, number of "bounce-ups" to a manager, number of customer complaints) may need to be considered, and this raises the question of how such criteria should be weighted if a global performance score needs to be calculated. To the degree that such weights are subjectively determined, procedural justice may suffer. Procedural justice may also suffer if the objective appraisal framework is so formulaic that performance-damaging conditions beyond the control of the employee (i.e., situational constraints; Bacharach & Bamberger, 1995) cannot be taken into account. In general, however, the more programmable the type of tasks performed, the more objective and formulaic the appraisal system is likely to be and the higher its "score" in terms of procedural justice.

More problematic are positions for which such objective data are either less available or not as clearly interpretable (e.g., research scientist, physician). For these types of positions, organizations typically have to rely on judgmental or "subjective" appraisals. Although these types of appraisal systems are more apt to take into consideration various situational constraints on performance that are unique to the position or individual employee (thus enhancing employee justice perceptions), they are also highly susceptible to evaluator bias (thus damaging justice perceptions).

In addition to the "objective versus subjective" choice, managers designing a strategic performance appraisal system need to determine the extent to which appraisal data will be interpreted on an absolute (e.g., number of calls handled per hour) versus relative (e.g., degree to which the number of calls handled is above the mean) basis. In general, the greater the number of (or potential for) job-related situational constraints, the greater the incentive to appraise performance on a relative basis. Assuming that others performing the same job face similar job-related uncertainties, a relative approach controls for such constraints and solves a problem common to most objective, formulaic appraisal systems. On the other hand, it creates a whole host of additional problems having to do with the selection of the referent group, collusion among those in the referent group (e.g., to keep standards low), and the creation of a zero-sum game (i.e., creation of a competitive climate among peers for whom overall performance is contingent on cooperation).

Two other choices need to be made if a more subjective appraisal system is to be put in place. First, a choice must be made between a forced and a free distribution of appraisal scores. Common to many subjective appraisal systems is the tendency of raters to score *all* ratees somewhere around the mean in order to avoid the "discomfort" of being challenged by a ratee or creating competition among interdependent peers. Forced-distribution systems eliminate this problem of a bias to the mean by requiring that raters distribute their scores along some predetermined distribution (e.g., no more than 10% of ratees can receive a rating of "outstanding"). Free-distribution systems have no such requirement. Although a forced-distribution approach solves the problem of a bias to the mean, it automatically creates a relative (as opposed to an absolute) appraisal system with all of the problems just noted.

Another way to deal with such biases and increase the overall validity of the appraisal system is to broaden the range of actors having input into the appraisal. Traditionally, appraisals were performed by that individual assumed to have the greatest understanding of and access to indicators of actual employee performance, namely the employees' supervisor. However, several studies indicate that to the extent that supervisors reflect only one type of employee client, supervisor-based appraisals may not capture the full range of employee performance (Murphy & Cleveland, 1995). Furthermore, given their ever-expanding span of control, supervisors may not always be available to observe and note critical performance incidents, whether positive or negative. Finally, broadening the base of raters can diminish the impact of personal bias on the part of any individual rater (Murphy & Cleveland, 1995). Thus, an increasing number of organizations are turning to peers, subordinates, and customers as additional sources of appraisal data. Appraisal systems structured around such multisource frameworks are commonly referred to as 360-degree feedback. Such systems, particularly the peer evaluation component, are most effective in tightly coupled organizations in which teamwork is key, in which the work process makes peers highly interdependent, and in which the work process is so complex and multidimensional as to make it difficult for any single evaluator to accurately and comprehensively assess. However, the inclusion of multiple raters may also increase the risk of political action (e.g., coalition behavior; Ferris & Judge, 1991) and tactical game playing (purposefully lowering a peer's rating to make oneself look better; Bamberger & Erev, 1999) in the appraisal process.

To illustrate the way in which different organizations might approach some of these choices, let us compare appraisal practices at MSI with those at Intel. At MSI, appraisal data are used primarily as a basis for making decisions regarding employee development and (to a far lesser degree) internal career advancement. Appraisal results have almost no direct impact on individual compensation because performance-based pay is for the most part nonexistent. Furthermore, MSI's appraisal system is based entirely on a unique form of peer assessment called *sociometry.* No supervisors are involved in the appraisal process, although they are responsible for providing the sociometry-based feedback (and may thus, informally, put their own "spin" on the results). Instead, peers are asked to assess, using a highly formalized appraisal instrument, (a) the degree to which their colleagues are cooperative and team oriented and (b) the quality of their colleagues' contribution and performance.

In contrast, given Intel's meritocracy-based culture, a strong emphasis is placed on the appraisal system as a basis for a wide variety of administrative decisions. Compensation, development, and advancement decisions are all very much based on the results of an extensive and rather complex and multidimensional system of performance appraisal. The appraisal process, though informal in the sense that no prespecified instrument is required, is nevertheless highly systematized, with all workers being appraised by a number of both supervisors and peers.

Linking Appraisal and Reward Strategies to HR Strategy

A common assumption implicit in much of the compensation strategy research is that to yield its desired effects, compensation strategy must offer a high degree of both "internal" and "external" fit (Milkovich & Newman, 1996). With regard to internal fit, researchers (Gomez-Mejia & Balkin, 1992a) tend to argue that the choices made with respect to the appraisal and reward system must be carefully aligned and not work in opposing directions. Regarding external fit, most scholars (Fay, 1987; Gomez-Mejia & Balkin, 1992a; Milkovich & Newman, 1996) tend to focus on the degree to which reward and appraisal practices as a whole are consistent with overall firm business strategy. Though we agree with the need for internal fit, the evidence with regard to external fit is less compelling (Delery & Doty, 1996), perhaps because the need is not so much to align compensation practices with firm business strategy as to align it with business unit HR strategy (Snell & Dean, 1994). Thus, although in this final section we begin with a review of the "ideal" compensation strategies suggested by various researchers for each type of generic business strategy, we conclude with an analysis of the types of internally consistent compensation choices offering the highest degree of fit with the dominant HR strategy.

However, before proceeding any further, it is important to note that in this section we will again be dealing with "ideal types"—that is, strategic profiles that most likely exist more in theory (or, one might say, in the minds of researchers) than in reality and that are used more as points of reference than as examples of how to "best" structure appraisal and reward systems. Clearly, most organizations are likely to fall somewhere in the gray area between different strategic profiles. As noted in Chapter 3, one reason this is likely to occur is that although there may exist a basic appraisal and reward subsystem architecture or framework, practices somewhat less consistent with the overall architecture may be adopted for particular employee groups at particular points in time and/or employed in different countries. Nevertheless, as we will discuss in greater detail in Chapter 7, there is some preliminary evidence that the more firms' actual practices are consistent with such ideal types of appraisal and reward subsystems, and the greater the degree of alignment between this subsystem and the firm's dominant HR strategy, the greater the effectiveness of the appraisal and reward subsystem and its contribution to firm performance (Delery & Doty, 1996; Gomez-Mejia & Balkin, 1992a).

The Link Between Compensation Strategy and Firm Business Strategy

Beginning in the late 1980s, HR theorists (see Broderick, 1986; Carroll, 1987; Fay, 1987) began to propose configurations of pay practices appropriate for particular types of organizational business strategies. For the most part, these frameworks adopted Miles and Snow's (1978, 1984) defender-prospector typology of business strategy and attempted to identify the pay practices most appropriate for each. For example, Carroll (1987) proposed that appraisal and reward practices in defender firms were characterized by frequent performance appraisals and extensive use of individual-level, variable pay and by only moderate use of group-based incentives (primarily gain sharing). In addition, according to Carroll, such firms place no more emphasis on external equity than on internal equity, offer only moderate-size bonuses, and make only moderate use of deferred compensation. In contrast, reward practices in prospector firms are characterized by a focus on sustained team effort and employee retention. Thus, according to Carroll, these firms conduct far less frequent performance appraisals and make almost no use of individual-based, variable pay. Instead, they rely on rewarding large bonuses (with a portion typically in a deferred form of payment) on the basis of team performance and place a greater emphasis on maintaining external over internal equity.

On the basis of an earlier factor analysis of compensation practices by Gomez-Mejia (1992), Gomez-Mejia and Balkin (1992a) identified two alternative compensation configurations, algorithmic and experiential. The former, for the most part, mirrors the compensation strategy posited by Carroll (1987) to be dominant in defender firms, whereas the latter, for the most part, mirrors that posited by Carroll to be dominant in prospector firms (see Table 5.1). For example, whereas the algorithmic configuration is grounded in a job-based pay system and emphasizes internal equity, the experiential configuration is grounded in a skill-based pay system and emphasizes external equity. Furthermore, to en-

Table 5.1 Key Appraisal and Reward Practices Associated With the Algorithmic and Experiential Configurations

Choice Domain	*Algorithmic*	*Experiential*
Job vs. skill basis of internal equity	Job	Skill
Internal vs. external equity orientation	Internal	External
Egalitarian vs. hierarchical	Hierarchical	Egalitarian
Base pay vs. incentives	Focus on base pay	Focus on incentives
Material vs. nonmaterial	Monetary rewards underemphasized	Stronger focus on monetary rewards
Administration	Centralized and bureaucratized	Decentralized and flexible
Risk sharing	Minimal	Emphasized
Basis of pay growth	Tenure and job	Demonstrated performance

SOURCE: Gomez-Mejia and Balkin (1992a).

hance organizational agility, pay decisions are highly decentralized in firms with experiential pay strategies, whereas they are highly centralized in organizations adopting more algorithmic pay strategies to maximize control over labor costs. However, Gomez-Mejia and Balkin's (1992a) model differs from that of Carroll in that they claimed that these two alternative configurations are "two poles on a continuum" (p. 67), with most organizations falling somewhere between them. Thus, they argued, depending on corporate or business unit strategy, a firm's compensation strategy may be more or less experiential relative to another firm's.

This perspective appears to have rather strong empirical support. Specifically, compensation strategies appear to vary along this continuum according to a variety of strategic taxonomies, including the defender/prospector and growth stage/mature stage dichotomies. For example, Balkin and Gomez-Mejia (1990) found that as corporate strategy moves toward a higher level of diversification, compensation systems become more bureaucratic and inflexible and increasingly exhibit the characteristics of an algorithmic configuration. Gomez-Mejia (1992) found that along the algorithmic-experiential continuum, business units characterized as prospectors scored nearly twice as high as defenders, with analyzers falling in the middle. Finally, rapid-growth firms and firms at the start of their life cycle scored higher on this continuum (i.e., tended to have more experiential pay systems) than stable, mature firms.

Even more significantly, Gomez-Mejia's (1992) findings, for the first time, provided support for the contingency notion that the relationship between the configuration of pay practices and firm performance (in this case, of some 243 manufacturing companies) may be contingent on corporate strategy. Specifically, Gomez-Mejia (1992) found that a more experiential compensation strategy was more strongly associated with enhanced firm performance for those firms having a single-product and unrelated-product corporate strategy and those business units characterized as prospectors. In contrast, a more algorithmic compensation strategy was more strongly associated with firm performance for those firms having a dominant- and related-product corporate strategy and those business units characterized as defenders. Prospectors with highly algorithmic compensation strategies were among the lower-performing firms, as were defenders with more experiential compensation strategies. Finally, on the basis of a comprehensive view of the literature, Gomez-Mejia and Balkin (1992a) concluded that the more individual pay practices deviate from the "ideal" strategy appropriate for the given organizational strategy, the lower their contribution to firm performance (p. 147). That is, in addition to finding support for the contingency theory requirement for external fit (i.e., between compensation strategy and organizational strategy), these authors suggested that internal consistency among the pay practices is required to maximize what they referred to as "pay effectiveness."

One limitation of these initial models may in fact be an over-reliance on the use of broad strategic typologies that fail to capture all of the contingencies that organizations hope to address in the design of their appraisal and reward subsystems. Indeed, Balkin and Gomez-Mejia (1990) found that although corporate and business unit strategies were significantly related to pay strategies, other factors accounted for the bulk of the variance in pay strategies. To get around this problem, Flannery et al. (1996) argued that rather than trying to "fit" appraisal and reward practices to one of two types of business strategies, it makes more sense to structure them around four alternative organizational "cultures," each of which may be more or less appropriate for a number of business strategies and each of which may be shaped by a number of environmental, strategic, and organizational factors. Flannery et al.'s (1996) "functional" culture is driven by the need to minimize uncertainty and unpredictability. To achieve these objectives, compensation practices must be consistent with uncertainty-reducing practices such as guaranteeing employment security, staffing by an internal labor market, and encouraging specializations. Thus, for example, firms characterized by a "functional" culture tend to place a heavy emphasis on internal equity. In contrast, organizations characterized by a "process" culture focus on quality and customer satisfaction and place a heavy emphasis on teams, learning, and skill development. Compensation practices in such firms tend to be supportive of such an orientation (e.g., team-based incentives) and to encourage a high level of organizational commitment. Flannery et al.'s (1996) "time-based" culture is adopted by firms seeking to reduce cycle times and capitalize on strategic opportunities by enhanced flexibility and agility. Because these organizations need to be able to attract the necessary talent in a short period of time and to motivate employees to work together as a team to meet project-specific objectives, their pay practices tend to reflect a focus on the external labor market and to reward team-based competencies and outcomes. Finally, the "networked" culture is adopted by firms focused on the completion of temporary projects on the basis of highly situational roles and contracted external human resources to maximize flexibility. Compensation practices consistent with these types of organizational cultures are similar to those found in the construction or film industries, namely a two-tiered pay structure and a heavy emphasis on external equity.

Snell and Dean (1994) offered yet another means to get around the limitations of a business strategy-based typology of appraisal and reward configurations. They argued that to be effective, compensation strategies might need to be aligned with the operational demands of the business unit. Although such operational demands are likely to be heavily influenced by business strategy, business strategy is not the only determinant of such demands. Thus, they contrasted two dominant operational designs in manufacturing business units—traditional or process controlled and integrated manufacturing or output controlled—and studied the degree to which each has alternative compensation profiles. Although their findings suggested that group incentives are more prevalent in integrated manufacturing contexts than in traditional manufacturing, they found little support for their other predicted differences (with regard to individual incentives, use of salary as opposed to hourly wage, and focus on skill as opposed to the job as a basis of internal equity). Indeed, what they discovered was that integrated manufacturing, when used as an opportunity to deskill the workforce and enhance employment variability, was associated with essentially the same compensation practices as the traditional manufacturing strategy. Only when a human resource strategy based on competency development and job redesign, as well as a focus on building employee commitment, was built into the integrated manufacturing strategy were significantly different reward practices in line with their predictions identified. Perhaps most importantly, the results of this study demonstrate that the focus in strategic compensation research may need to be more on the fit between appraisal and reward strategies and HR strategy at the business unit level than on the fit between appraisal and reward strategies and overall business or unit operational strategy.

Appraisal and Reward Subsystem Strategy and HR Strategy

In one of the few attempts to demonstrate the link between appraisal and reward practices and HR strategy, Dyer and Holder (1988) proposed that practices related to all five of the subsystem choices identified above would vary depending on four key HR strategy dimensions (contribution, composition, competence, and commitment). For example, firms adopting what they referred to as an "investment" HR strategy (having high expectations for employee initiative, a "comfortable" head count, very high competency requirements, and high employee commitment demands) could best achieve such strategic HR objectives by placing an emphasis on internal equity, building a "tall" hierarchical pay structure, using variable pay to only a limited extent, and basing this variable element on individual skill enhancements and aggregate performance. Although their framework provided the basic elements of a model of subsystem fit, it focused on a wide variety of HR subsystems and therefore provided only limited detail with regard to the nature of coherent appraisal and reward subsystems. Furthermore, it—like the strategic frameworks proposed by others (e.g., Arthur, 1992, 1994; Pfeffer, 1994)—assumed that, depending on the firm's strategic contingencies, there exists a single, optimal approach to compensation that is ideal for managing all employees. However, as noted earlier, Lepak and Snell (1999a, 1999b) questioned this assumption.

Nevertheless, it is still logical to assume that although different appraisal and reward practices may be in effect for different groups of employees in a single firm, there will be one dominant profile of appraisal and reward practices covering the majority of the business unit's nonexecutive employees. Indeed, as Gomez-Mejia and Balkin (1992a) noted, though

> specific conditions affecting the firm may call for algorithmic strategies in some cases and experiential strategies in others, . . . the failure of a firm's compensation strategies can often be attributed to the fact that its strategic pay choices work at cross-purposes, which neutralize their overall effectiveness. (p. 68)

The result is that most firms will, over time, attempt to identify some combination of pay practices that, although taking into account the value and uniqueness of different employee groups (Lepak & Snell, 1999b), still provides some degree of overall internal coherence and consistency (Gomez-Mejia & Balkin, 1992a).

Assuming, like Dyer and Holder (1988), that this cluster of compensation practices varies according to the firm's HR strategy, the literature reviewed above suggests the existence of four unique appraisal and reward subsystem profiles, one for each of the four ideal types of HR strategies discussed in Chapter 3. This framework, depicted in Table 5.2, applies the five choice domains discussed above to these four dominant HR strategies, namely the high-commitment, free-agent, paternalistic, and secondary strategies.

As can be seen in Table 5.2, the high-commitment strategy focuses on using the appraisal and reward system to enhance organizational agility, develop a cooperative and creative culture, and discourage employee attrition. Organizations typically adopting the high-commitment strategy, as we noted in Chapter 3, rely heavily on their employees to have the skills and flexibility needed to manage the uncertainties inherent in a complex and ambiguous transformation process, and they view such employees, as well as the complex social networks within which they are embedded, as more irreplaceable. However, rather than relying strictly on agency-type contracts, organizations adopting this strategy tend to adopt compensation and appraisal systems that develop a more normatively or affectively (as opposed to calculatively) based alignment of interest. Thus, they tend to focus on nonmaterial rewards designed to build organizational commitment and a greater sense of identity with the firm. Reward practices consistent with an internal labor market are critical in this respect, as are reward practices that encourage skill/competency development, flexibility, and a team orientation. Thus, for example, nonmaterial rewards are used to complement market-level monetary remuneration in order to attract only the highest-quality candidates for entry-level positions and to erect "barriers of entry" against competitors (Gomez-Mejia & Balkin, 1992a). Although variable pay may be used to further enhance an alignment of interest between employers and employees, it is rarely a significant element of the pay package, and—given the focus on cooperation—is typically based on some aggregate dimension of longer term performance (e.g., profit sharing). Furthermore, to reinforce a sense of community, cooperation, and lateral accountability, performance appraisals are often based on input provided by a variety of internal and external "clients," often in the form of 360-degree feedback.

Table 5.2 Appraisal and Reward Practices Associated With the
Four Generic HR Strategies

Choice Category	Choice	High Commitment	Free Agent	Paternalistic	Secondary
Basic	Internal vs. external	Mixed, but emphasis on internal	External	Internal	External
	Level of risk-sharing and risk-taking orientation	Some risk sharing; risk taking encouraged with moderate use of variable pay	Strong interest in risk sharing; risk taking encouraged; heavy use of variable pay	No risk sharing; risk aversion emphasized (moderate use of pay at risk); focus on fixed pay	Some risk sharing; risk aversion emphasized with moderate use of variable pay (i.e., pay at risk).
	Monetary vs. nonmonetary rewards	Emphasis on nonmonetary rewards	Mixed, with emphasis on monetary remuneration	Mixed, with emphasis on nonmonetary rewards	Emphasis on monetary remuneration
	Administration	Mixed, with tendency toward centralization and pay openness	Decentralized; pay secrecy	Highly centralized, tendency toward open pay	Decentralized; pay secrecy
Internal equity	Job vs. skill	Skill or competency	Skill or competency	Job	Mixed job and skill
	Hierarchical vs. egalitarian	Egalitarian	Mixed, with tendency toward hierarchical	Hierarchical	Hierarchical
External equity	Lag vs. market vs. lead	Market	Lead	Lag/market	Market
Employee equity	Membership vs. tenure vs. skill vs. performance	Mixed tenure, skill, and performance	Performance	Tenure, some skill, very limited performance	Membership, some performance
	Level of aggregation	Some individual, mostly group, unit, or corporate	Individual	No individual, some unit or corporate	Individual
	Timing	Long term	Short term	Long term	Mixed
	Bonus vs. merit increase	Mixed (some merit pay)	Bonus	Mixed (some deferred pay)	Bonus

Table 5.2 Continued

Choice Category	Choice	High Commitment	Free Agent	Paternalistic	Secondary
	Eligibility for, probability and level of payout	High eligibility and very high probability; very low payout	Moderate eligibility and probability; moderate payout	Low eligibility, high probability; low payout	Low eligibility ("stars" only), low probability; very high payout
Appraisal	Objective vs. judgmental	Judgmental	Mixed	Objective	Mixed
	Absolute vs. relative	Mixed, tendency toward absolute	Relative	Absolute	Mixed, tendency toward relative
	Forced vs. free distribution	Free	Forced	Not relevant	Free

At the opposite extreme, as noted in Chapter 3, is the secondary HR strategy, adopted by firms using a "technological fix" to handle the uncertainty inherent in the production process. Appraisal and reward systems for the largest proportion of employees in such organizations are grounded on the assumption that efficiency can be maximized by—for most jobs in the organization—focusing on the external labor market and maintaining a policy of employment at will to keep labor costs highly variable. Given the highly routinized nature of the work process and the temporary nature of the employment relationship, there is little choice but to emphasize monetary remuneration only and to keep the pay system as decentralized as possible so as to be able to take advantage of cost-saving opportunities presented by the external labor market. Internal equity is of concern only to the extent that a job- or skill-based rationale allows for the creation of a two-tier system, with a relatively small managerial and professional elite occupying the upper tier. The highly controlled nature of the work process makes risk sharing relatively unnecessary for the largest proportion of employees, but the existence of such an internal, dual labor market allows for a relatively large proportion of the total pay package for a relatively small number of key or "star" employees to be based on variable pay. Employee equity for the bulk of the workforce is based on membership. That is, although those with the highest level of short-term performance (typically assessed by the supervisor in terms of the employee's perceived level of compliance with employer demands) may not receive any variable-pay supplement, they tend to be those that are the last to be laid off. This can be a relatively powerful motivational force, particularly for a contingent workforce with limited alternative employment opportunities.

Appraisal and reward practices in firms adopting a free-agent HR strategy are also governed by an emphasis on the external labor market and a decentralized administrative framework (to take advantage of local or sector-specific opportunities presented by that labor market). Thus, although similar to firms adopting a high-commitment HR strategy in that they tend to place a heavy emphasis on flexibility and agility, they seek to *acquire* (rather than develop in house) candidates possessing a profile of skills and competencies applicable to a variety of relatively loosely defined "jobs." Pay structures are thus built around the relative contribution of skills and competencies as opposed to jobs. However, internal equity is often sacrificed to ensure the rapid acquisition of required skills and competencies. This, in turn, may necessitate a policy of pay secrecy to reduce the risk of problems associated with perceived internal inequity. Furthermore, given the assumption of employment at will and the temporary nature of employment relationships, as in the case of firms adopting a secondary strategy, an emphasis is placed on providing monetary remuneration and short-term, lump sum payouts, both at above-market rates. Given the highly nonpreprogrammed and variable nature of jobs in organizations adopting such strategies, as in firms with high-commitment HR strategies, appraisal practices tend to be based on judgmental input from a variety of sources. However, because the situational constraints relevant to such temporary positions may be less well understood, assessments may need to be based more on relative (as opposed to absolute) performance.

Finally, as noted in Chapter 3, organizations adopting a paternalistic HR strategy seek to achieve organizational predictability and stability by a preprogrammed transformation process and the development of a status-driven "clan" culture. The appraisal and reward subsystem supportive of such ends and means therefore must be driven by a focus on internal equity and the need to reinforce norms of loyalty and compliance. The preprogrammed nature of the transformation means that much of the variance in employee contribution will be a function of the job. Consequently, pay structures tend to be job based. These pay structures tend to be both hierarchical and "tall," reflecting the need to be able to provide for pay growth through internal advancement. The internalization of employment and the promise of such long-term nonmonetary rewards as employment stability allows such firms to pay less attention to external labor markets when setting pay levels and thus, in some cases, even to lag behind the market average, at least for some non-entry-level positions. Given the limited ability of employees to influence their relative rate of individual contribution and the importance of loyalty, employee equity at the individual level is typically based on seniority rather than performance. To the extent that pay is contingent on performance, the governing criterion is typically some objectively measured aggregate level of performance (e.g., corporate cost savings). As Gomez-Mejia and Welbourne (1991) suggested, individual-based criteria do not tend to sit well with the "family" atmosphere that such organizations often strive to construct.

It is important to note that although the typology described above assumes that the configuration of reward and appraisal practices is likely to be more heterogeneous across organizations than within them, hybrid profiles of reward and appraisal practices are not only possible but quite likely. Specifically, different reward and appraisal practices (each consistent with an alternative HR strategy) may be adopted for different employee groups within a single firm. For example, some firms may adopt compensation practices consistent with the high-commitment or free-agent strategy for their professional workforce but adopt practices more consistent with the secondary HR strategy for their unskilled production workforce. Firms adopting such a bilevel approach to compensation are essentially creating and maintaining a dual employment system, with employees in the first tier rewarded and appraised in one way and those in the second tier rewarded in another way. As noted above, several studies question the long-term efficacy of such an approach (Coombs & Gomez-Mejia, 1991; Gomez-Mejia, Balkin, & Milkovich, 1990), whereas others argue that it may offer firms the ability to maximize efficiency and flexibility (Lepak & Snell, 1999b).

Thus, although the framework presented above still describes only ideal types of reward and appraisal subsystems and is still somewhat based on a holistic assumption that a single set of practices is dominant across the *bulk* of employees in a firm, it does recognize the potential for significant *intra*-firm variation. Nevertheless, consistent with the findings of Gomez-Mejia and Balkin (1992a), it suggests that dominant reward and compensation practices in a firm will have the greatest positive impact on firm performance to the extent that they are internally consistent and to the extent that they are aligned with other HR subsystem practices.

Summary

In this chapter, we examined how the profile of various appraisal and reward practices may be used to direct and encourage desired employee attitudes and behaviors. After reviewing four main theories underlying the bulk of compensation research (i.e., expectancy, equity, human capital, and agency theories), we explored five groups of strategic factors—basic factors, internal equity factors, external equity factors, employee equity factors, and appraisal factors—that managers typically consider when designing the appraisal and reward subsystem. Although empirical research linking alternative reward and appraisal practices to firm performance is still in its early stages, it appears that the link between many reward and appraisal practices and firm performance is contingent on the degree to which the individual practice is consistent with other appraisal and reward practices, as well as on the degree of alignment between the configuration of reward and appraisal practices in use and the firm's broader strategic profile.

6

Employee Relations Subsystem

Whereas in the previous two chapters we focused on highly tangible strategic subsystems having to do with staffing and development and appraisal and rewards, in this chapter our focus is on a subsystem that revolves around such amorphous concepts as psychological contracts, voicing, justice, and social identity. More important, our focus is on a subsystem that, to a large extent, underlies many of the strategic options discussed in the previous two chapters. Specifically, our focus in this chapter is on the employee relations subsystem, a rather broad collection of frameworks, policies, and practices that together play a key role in the definition and maintenance of core organizational values and philosophies.

In the first part of this chapter, we begin by describing in more detail what we mean by the *employee relations subsystem* and why we believe that it is such a critical HR subsystem. We then review those subsystem parameters along which key decisions regarding the nature of employee relations are made, as well as some of the basic contingencies governing these choices. Then, in the second part of the chapter, we discuss how these choices with regard to the nature of employee relations tend to be made in a more or less predictable pattern depending on the overall nature of the dominant HR strategy.

Subsystem Domain and Significance

Most definitions of *employee relations* in the literature revolve around a particular set of HR activities (e.g., grievance handling, employee discipline) aimed at eliciting employee compliance with organizational policies and norms (see Milkovich & Boudreau, 1991, p. 568). However, we view the employee relations system as something much broader than simply a collection of HR functions. We define the employee relations subsystem as relating to those strategic managerial activities aimed at establishing, enforcing, and reinforcing the psychological contract between employer and employees and thus shaping both the tangible work environment and the less tangible normative base (i.e., culture) of the organization. In this sense, the employee relations subsystem encompasses a wide range of managerial choices having to do with (a) the nature of control and coordination in the workplace (Edwards, 1979), (b) the degree to which there is an interest in having employees internalize the organization as a core element of their identity (Bandura, 1986; Triandis, 1989), and (c) the way in which employee equity expectations are balanced with the organizational need for rule compliance (Bamberger & Donahue, in press; O'Reilly & Puffer, 1989). Such choices provide the foundation on which employees come to understand, interpret, and eventually internalize the terms of their employment relationship or work-related "psychological contract" (Rousseau, 1995).

Employee Relations Choices and the Psychological Contract

Rousseau and Wade-Benzoni (1994) defined work-related psychological contracts as "the beliefs people hold regarding the terms of their employment relationships . . . which affect employees' behavior toward . . . fellow employees and also affect their commitment to the organization" (p. 466). In this context, they identified three types of contracts, each of which they viewed as shaping and "signaling" the nature of the organizational culture (p. 472). The first type, the *transactional contract,* focuses on short-term, instrumental exchange. The obligations of the two parties engaging in such a contract are mutually perceived to be narrow in scope, based on a limited and specified degree of interdependence and requiring only a peripheral and temporary engagement. *Relational contracts,* on the other hand, focus on long-term, complex, and affective relationships (not unlike those in a family) that demand extensive emotional investments by both parties. That is, they demand the bilateral exchange of social and emotional resources such as loyalty, security, and trust. Both parties' expectations are for a deep, all-encompassing, and, most of all, long-term relationship. The third type of psychological contract is the *balanced contract.* Using the type of employment relationship existing at General Electric as an illustration, Rousseau and Wade-Benzoni described this contract as including both relational (e.g., shared values and mutual commitments) and transactional (mutual instrumental expectations) components.

Although work-based psychological contracts are clearly shaped by choices associated with the reward and people flow subsystems, choices regarding the three core issues noted above (i.e., nature of control and coordination, degree of internalization of an organization-based identity, the balancing of equity with rule compliance) also play a critical role in shaping the nature of an organization's psychological contract with its employees. For example, organizations investing in work-family programs may be viewed as making a concerted effort to shift the nature of their psychological contract with their employees toward the more relational end of the continuum (Osterman, 1995).

However, in addition to their contract- (and culture-) shaping role, choices regarding each of these three employee relations issues also play an important role in the maintenance of this contract and its often "taken-for-granted" nature. Specifically, choices regarding the nature of the workplace governance system and the relative importance placed on equity as opposed to compliance influence the degree to which such contracts are enforced, and thus psychologically reinforced. Unenforced contracts or contracts that are enforced inconsistently or inequitably are likely to result in a highly anomic (Durkheim, 1897/1951) and uncertain work context characterized by the effective breakdown in contracts. Rousseau and Wade-Benzoni (1994) referred to such a situation as one of "no guarantees," reflecting the absence of commitments and the deinstitutionalization of standards and taken-for-granted understandings. A number of studies (Bamberger & Donahue, in press; O'Reilly & Puffer, 1989; O'Reilly & Weitz, 1980) have found such situations to be associated with heightened levels of employee rule violation and lower levels of individual and group performance.

Subsystem Significance

Besides their impact on the shaping and maintenance of psychological contracts, choices affecting the core employee relations issues noted above are likely to have a variety of direct and critical organizational implications, many of which can be directly translated into dollars and cents. For example, as noted above, many organizations seek to enhance their employee relations by adopting programs designed to address the core work-family conflict problems experienced by at least some of their employees. Given that employees with children under the age of 13 tend to be absent far more frequently than other employees and to have higher-than-average rates of turnover (Miller, 1984), the adoption of some sort of work-family program can have a direct impact on a firm's labor costs and consequently its bottom line.

Choices regarding the nature of employee involvement and organizational rule compliance structures can have an impact on turnover-related costs. Freeman and Medoff (1984) argued that lacking an opportunity to "voice," the only alternative that dissatisfied employees may have when seeking to address their concerns is to "exit" the organization. Such "exit" behavior may take the form of quitting, thus increasing the costs associated with organizational staffing and training, not to mention those often associated with the destruction of critical intraorganizational networks and the loss of proprietary knowledge. Indeed, Rees (1991) found that in those districts in which teachers are afforded greater voicing opportunities through some form of grievance procedure, quit rates were significantly lower.

The lack of fairness in organizational governance processes, or what Greenberg (1990) referred to as procedural justice, may also serve as a prime motivator for employee unionization efforts. There is evidence that many nonunion employers, aware of this, attempt to maintain their nonunion status by adopting some form of alternative governance structure—one offering employees some framework through which to voice their concerns (Freeman, 1985; Freeman & Kleiner, 1990). Such employers tend to view the costs of unionization as far outweighing any of the possible disadvantages associated with some sort of internal system of employee voicing. However, other evidence suggests that such nonunion firms often reframe their governance structures not so much to avoid unionization as to avoid costly legal battles (Feuille & Hildebrand, 1995). One study (Dertouzos, Holland, & Ebener, 1988) found that employee-plaintiffs won 68% of the 120 wrongful discharge cases that were tried to a verdict in the California courts between 1980 and 1986, with an average penalty of over $400,000.

More important, however, employee relations choices made with the intent of shifting the psychological contract more toward the relational end (e.g., by adopting worker assistance programs such as in-plant child care) can have important commitment-related implications (Osterman, 1995). This is not a new concept. Already in the 1920s, with the adoption of the American Plan or welfare capitalism, firms attempted not only to avoid unionism (Brandes, 1970) but to "tie the employee to the firm and to create the illusion, if not the reality, of community" (Osterman, 1995, p. 697). Several researchers such as Edwards (1979), Kunda (1992), and MacDuffie (1995) have noted the economic advantages of the latter. With the "ostensible personal incorporation of organizational goals" (Kunda, 1992, p. 226), organizations may be able to reduce supervisory costs (because committed workers require less direct control), reduce absenteeism- and turnover-related costs (because committed workers are normatively and not just instrumentally motivated), and eliminate costly buffers previously built into the work process (e.g., inventories, backup systems) that were once required "as a safeguard against labor troubles" (MacDuffie, 1995, p. 201).

Key Subsystem Domains and Related HR Functions

As we noted above, the employee relations subsystem is shaped by the way an organization addresses questions relating to the nature of control and coordination, the degree to which employees are expected to internalize organizational goals, and the balancing of equity with rule compliance. Managerial decisions regarding these three issues are manifested across a number of subsystem domains. However, before discussing these subsystem domains and the way they reflect managerial decisions regarding these three core employee relations issues, we must first recognize that objectives of employee relations subsystems vary. Just how these objectives vary is important to understand because subsystem practices with regard to the three core employee relations issues depend, to a large extent, on subsystem objectives.

In some organizations, the overarching objective of the employee relations subsystem is to facilitate bureaucratic control and ensure employee rule compliance. Bennis (1985) illustrated this type of subsystem by referring to the philosophy of management once dominant in General Motors: "Don't think, dummy—do what you're told!" (p. v).

In others, the key subsystem goal is to eliminate barriers potentially inhibiting organizational effectiveness. In such organizations, although control and compliance remain important employee relations objectives, an emphasis is placed on harnessing employee knowledge (typically through some form of employee involvement program) to address key organizational problems. For example, employee-based task forces are a central element of Intel's problem-solving infrastructure. Such a task force framework was adopted several years ago by one of Intel's subsidiaries when that organization was making the transition to a compressed workweek. Employees were assigned to task forces dealing with such issues as production scheduling, operations and personnel support, compensation methods and overtime allocation, and employee shift scheduling.

Finally, in some organizations, the primary objective is to enhance individual attachment and commitment to the organization and its objectives and in this sense to achieve the two previous objectives (i.e., control and commitment, elimination of barriers to effectiveness) as well. That is, the objective of the employee relations system is to build on and complement a more utilitarian (Etzioni, 1961) control structure, thus allowing management to reduce its reliance on more traditional means of bureaucratic control (Kunda, 1992). As several authors (Edwards, 1979; Kunda, 1992) have noted, infusing organizational norms and values into workers' identity is perhaps the most sophisticated and effective (though complex and often costly) means to secure control, ensure compliance, and eliminate barriers to effectiveness.

These objectives are very much related to the two basic dimensions (i.e., nature of resource acquisition and nature of organizational control) underlying our typology of dominant HR strategies. That is, because organizations with HR strategies emphasizing internal over external acquisition place a premium on employee retention, they are more likely to shape their employee relations subsystem around more complex, commitment-related objectives. Similarly, given the high level of discretion granted to employees in organizations emphasizing output-based as opposed to process-based systems of control, these organizations are likely to shape their employee relations system around commitment objectives. As shown in Table 6.1, this logic suggests that a commitment-based HR strategy (output-based control with internal resource acquisition) is likely to be associated with an employee relations subsystem structured around the highest-level objectives noted above (i.e., enhancing individual attachment to the organization). A secondary HR strategy (process-based control with external resource acquisition) is likely to be associated with an employee relations subsystem structured around the lowest-level objective noted above (i.e., bureaucratic control and rule compliance). Finally, the paternalistic and free-agent HR strategies are likely to be associated with employee relations subsystems structured around a set of mixed objectives. In the case of the former, work sys-

Table 6.1 Dominant HR Strategies and Employee Relations Subsystem Objectives

Nature of Resource Acquisition and Retention	Nature of Organizational Control Processes	
	Process	Output
External	**Secondary HRS**	**Free-Agent HRS**
	ER objective: control and compliance; cost minimization and flexibility maximization	ER objective: bounded commitment
		ER focus: work systems emphasizing employee involvement and intensive collaboration within the context of a detailed employment contract; moderate to extensive governance system focus
	ER focus: fixed, compliance-based work systems; very limited (if any) governance system focus	
Internal	**Paternalistic HRS**	**Commitment HRS**
	ER objective: benevolent control and compliance; decreasing potential barriers to productivity	ER objective: creation of a "caring culture" and a sense of community to signal the expectation of volunteerism on the part of the employee
	ER focus: work systems incorporating limited employee involvement; employee assistance; moderate to extensive governance systems focus	ER focus: work systems emphasizing employee involvement; extensive governance systems focus; intensive focus on employee assistance and work-family benefits

tems based on strict control and compliance objectives are likely to be inconsistent with the clan culture and the focus on equity so dominant in such organizations (Baron & Kreps, 1999; Ouchi, 1980). In the case of the latter, work systems based strictly on commitment objectives are likely to be inconsistent with the temporary nature of employment relations dominant in firms adopting a free-agent HR strategy and the fact that the primary allegiance of most free agents is to their own craft or occupation, rather than to their employer (Gouldner, 1957).

Choices with regard to three key employee relations parameters tend to follow the subsystem objectives selected (Dyer & Holder, 1988). These employee relations parameters concern (a) the nature of the work system (i.e., having to do with control, coordination, and employee involvement objectives), (b) the degree to which the organization attempts to address employee concerns not directly related to the workplace (i.e., having to do with social identity and the internalization of the organization and its goals), and (c) the nature of the workplace system of governance (i.e., having to do with balancing equity and compliance objectives). Thus, if the primary objective is control and compliance, HR employee relations functions are likely to be limited to a focus on compliance-oriented (i.e., highly authoritarian) systems of governance and highly standardized and fixed work systems. If the goal is the elimination of barriers to enhanced organizational effectiveness, functions are likely to be expanded to include the development and administration of work systems based on some degree of employee involvement in, as well as the liberalization of, workplace governance systems (i.e., movement toward more integrative systems of governance; Bamberger & Donahue, in press). If commitment is the primary objective, then employee relations functions are likely to include a focus on alternative governance and work systems (particularly those emphasizing employee involvement), as well as the development and administration of assistance programs and culture-strengthening activities (such as those socialization-oriented development activities described toward the end of Chapter 4).

In the section below, we describe each of these subsystem domains in more detail and discuss how the nature of each of these subsystem domains is likely to vary across our four ideal types of HR strategies.

Strategic Choices and Employee Relations Domains

Work Systems Domain

Work systems have to do with the manner in which organizational inputs such as material, people, and data are transformed into some type of output (Bacharach & Bamberger, 1995; Perrow, 1979). In more operational terms, we view work systems as having to do with the way in which jobs are structured, discretion is allocated, and supervision is exercised. As Blau (1968) noted, "a fundamental issue" confronting executives of organizations is just how to manage, or, in other words, control and coordinate, such systems (p. 465). As Blau put it, such executives may "manage primarily by means of direct or indirect controls; the former entailing the maintenance of close contact with operations" and the "issuing of corrective orders whenever necessary" and the latter involving the use of "impersonal controls that constrain operations to follow automatically the policies and programs specified by top executives" (p. 465). However, sociologists such as Braverman (1974) and Edwards (1979) argue that in addition to these two alternative modes of structuring the work system, a third, even more indirect approach must be considered, one based on organizational norms and values.

Types of Work Systems

Direct administrative control through supervision involves the personal direction, evaluation, and disciplining of workers by management and the organization and control of work tasks by continuous and direct supervisory instruction (Edwards, 1979). In many skill- or craft-based occupations (construction trades), it is difficult if not impossible to routinize or standardize the transformation processes. That is, given the nature of the transformation process, jobs are inherently broad and complex, and the organization is dependent on the training of its members to handle the uncertainty embedded in its core tasks. In such organizations, direct and continuous supervisory involvement may offer those accountable for the organization's outputs the simplest means to ensure that these outputs meet basic quality and uniformity objectives. Thus, this rather traditional approach to work process design (grounded in the master-servant type of employment relationship predating the Industrial Revolution) calls for the retention of broad and complex jobs affording job incumbents a high degree of discretion when performing their tasks. In this sense, this type of work system is based on output rather than process control. However, because there is no guarantee that the interests of agents and principals are aligned, it also calls for a highly structured and status-oriented hierarchy providing supervisors with the authority needed to monitor and intervene so that organizational objectives (as opposed to the personal objectives of job incumbents) are attained.

The disadvantages of this traditional approach to the structuring of the work system stem from its reliance on output control in contexts in which there is no guaranteed alignment of interests on the part of agents and principals. Because there is no guarantee of goal consensus, such work systems demand close and relatively intensive monitoring and the creation of an extensive bureaucratic hierarchy designed to provide such monitoring in a highly "rational" and legitimate manner. For example, in most of RLA Textiles' plants, employees are subject to direct and continuous monitoring by a relatively large group of supervisors. Supervisors literally "look down the necks" of each of their subordinates (in some cases via ceiling-mounted video cameras) and attempt to control their workforce by threatening swift and severe punishment (i.e., dismissal) in those cases in which employees deviate from basic work rules and production norms. The ability of supervisors to fire their subordinates at will (and with minimal cost and hassle to the company and its management) provides supervisors with an effective fear-based mechanism to better align the interests of workers with those of management, at least for the short term.

However, over the long run, this can be costly to an organization, not only in terms of an expanded supervisory overhead (such direct and intense supervisory control may require the employment of a great many "chiefs" to monitor the work of relatively few "Indians") but in other ways as well. For example, particularly when these "Indians" are more skilled or professional workers, such systems of control may breed conflict, with administrators being viewed by workers as "organizational despots, encumbered by few restrictions on their power over workers" (Edwards, 1979, p. 33). And perhaps even more significantly, tight hierarchical structures and the strictly vertical and top-down flow of information may limit organizational agility and slow down organizational response time. This is precisely the case at MSI. A substantial portion of MSI's employees are highly trained and hard-to-replace scientists, engineers, and technicians. These professionals tend to resent any attempt to restrict their degree of autonomy. Indeed, there are frequent labor-management disputes over the boundaries of managerial versus professional control. Lacking the ability to align employee interests with those of management by means of reward practices, management has been forced to develop tight hierarchical structures and highly formalized control systems to ensure that objectives are met. The existence of these structures and rigid systems largely accounts for the longer product development cycles and slower market response time described earlier.

Taylorism, or indirect control through standardization and routinization, offers a solution to at least some of the disadvantages embedded in such traditional work systems.[1] It eliminates the paradox inherent in the approach described above by shifting the basis of managerial control from outputs to processes. That is, by separating the execution of work from its conceptualization and by deconstructing complex work processes into simple, routine steps requiring little if any prejob training—in other words, by controlling the actual task behaviors of workers—management can essentially guarantee the attainment of organizational goals in a far more streamlined fashion. Because workers have far less discretion and because most task-related decisions are preprogrammed into the work itself, there is a far more limited supervisory imperative. Furthermore, on the basis of such an approach, the nature of the dependence relationship between workers and their employers can be dramatically shifted in favor of the latter because it is easier to replace an unskilled worker than one with proprietary skills. Indeed, as we noted in Chapter 3, such an approach to work process design offers significant efficiency advantages to employers. Not surprisingly, therefore, by the 1920s indirect control through routinization and standardization had for the most part replaced direct supervisory control as the basis of work systems design (Perrow, 1979).

However, as has been well documented, Taylorism also has its disadvantages, most of which have to do with the alienating effects of such work systems (Blauner, 1964). That is, indirect control through routinization may engender a sense of meaninglessness, isolation, and self-estrangement on the part of workers. As Chinoy (1992) suggested in his classic analysis of automobile assembly-line workers, individuals experiencing such feelings of alienation on the job are likely to demand ever-increasing rates of pay to compensate for dissatisfaction on the job. Furthermore, as MacDuffie (1995) noted, the high levels of alienation inherent in such work systems tend to be accompanied by relatively high levels of turnover and absenteeism and low levels of worker motivation (p. 201). Consequently, organizations adopting such work processes have no choice but to develop buffers (e.g., inventories, substitute workforces, repair spaces) to protect against any type of disruption that might "prevent the realization of economies of scale" (p. 200). That is, rather than addressing the root cause of alienation, organizations adopting these types of work systems tend to invest in programs and structures designed to mitigate the severity of alienation's consequences. As MacDuffie wrote, such buffers may be seen as costly for several reasons:

> First, the buffers represent a commitment of resources not directly devoted to production. Inventory buffers in particular are costly to store and handle and can hinder the move from one product design to another. Most important, buffers can hide production problems. (p. 200)

A third type of work system incorporates output control with efforts aimed at ensuring that the interests of workers are aligned with those of their employers. Edwards (1979) maintained that "the most sophisticated level of control grows out of incentives to workers to identify themselves with the enterprise, to be loyal, committed and thus self-directed or self-controlled" (p. 150). These types of work systems are characterized by broad and flexible jobs, offering even those workers with limited skills greater responsibility and discretion. Employees are given extensive opportunities to participate in organizational decision making, are allowed a high degree of autonomy, and are encouraged to widen their skill base to increase the potential to optimize efficiencies in human resource mobilization. However, to ensure that such autonomy and discretion are exploited in a manner consistent with the organizational objectives determined by management, these work systems are also characterized by a high degree of normative control—"the desire to bind employees' hearts and minds to the corporate interest" (Kunda, 1992, p. 218). According to Kunda, norm-based control requires that management pay a great deal of attention to the development, articulation, and dissemination of an organizational ideology. As he noted, "Ideological principles are embodied in specific managerial policies governing the member's work life. These policies are designed to minimize the use and de-emphasize the significance of traditional bureaucratic control structures, and to elicit instead behavior consistent with cultural prescriptions" (p. 218). Thus, although an ideology of openness, flexibility, and tolerance is typically promoted, subtle forms of group pressure are used to "continually enforce in each other and in themselves an overt adherence to the (specified) member role" and to "silence any expression of deviance" (p. 219). Kunda acknowledged that such work systems may produce a highly motivated workforce and that the decreased reliance on inefficient bureaucratic systems of control may breed personal initiative and innovation. However, he and others (e.g., Covaleski, Dirsmith, Heian, & Samuel, 1998; Perlow, 1998) also noted that such systems have within them the roots of organizational tyranny, as the boundaries between work and nonwork lives become blurred and as organizations begin to question and redefine the boundaries of employee identity and privacy.

Work Systems, Employee Relations Objectives, and HR Strategies

A number of studies have attempted to identify the link between HR strategy and organizational work systems. The bulk of these studies are grounded in the assumption that work systems, like other elements of the employee relations subsystem, tend to be structured around the employee relations objectives embedded in the organization's dominant HR strategy. Furthermore, these studies suggest that organizations whose work systems are incongruent with their employee relations (ER) objectives tend to perform less effectively than organizations whose work systems and ER objectives are more closely aligned.

For the most part stemming from the early work of Walton (1985), these studies have focused on two alternative sets of ER objectives, namely control and compliance as opposed to commitment. Referring to the former, Walton noted that "at the heart of this traditional model is the wish to establish order, exercise control and achieve efficiency in the application of the work force"

(p. 78). According to Walton, organizations with HR strategies placing an emphasis on such ER objectives tend to adopt a combination of traditional work systems integrating elements of Taylorism (i.e., systems based on indirect control through routinization and standardization) with direct supervisory control. At their extreme, these systems rest on the notion that labor is a "variable cost," thus requiring that jobs be structured around the "lowest common denominator assumptions about workers' skill and motivation" (p. 78). This is necessary to ensure that workforce flexibility (the ability to staff jobs as needed) does not come at the cost of reduced performance standards.

In contrast, HR strategies calling for commitment-oriented employee relations objectives demand the adoption of work systems that promote the development of mutual trust, common interests, shared goals, and employee empowerment. As Walton (1985) noted, "In this new, commitment-based approach to the work force, jobs are designed to be broader than before, to combine planning and implementation, and to include efforts to upgrade operations, not just maintain them" (p. 79). With a focus on team-based work processes, the intent is to allocate much of the responsibility for performance monitoring to a set of peers, thus saving on the costs of supervision and, more important, eliminating the adversarial nature of labor-management relations dominant in control-based work systems.

In this sense, Walton described the ER objectives and associated work systems that one would expect to find in organizations adopting either secondary or commitment HR strategies. Although Walton did not directly address the kind of ER objectives sought by organizations adopting paternalistic HR strategies or the kind of work systems implemented by such organizations, he did suggest that many organizations have modified their control-oriented work systems to take into account many of the dysfunctional effects of direct supervisory control and Tayloristic work systems. Specifically, he suggested that, particularly in unionized firms such as GM, Ford, and AT&T, during the late 1970s and early 1980s, there was a move to modify work systems away from the classic Tayloristic model and toward a "transitional" model. Katz (1985) documented some of these modifications in the auto industry, noting a movement toward broader job classifications and the adoption of a variety of employee involvement and quality-of-work-life programs. Like Walton (1985), Katz noted that although there may be some broadening in the scope of individual responsibility on the job and thus some degree of employee empowerment, for the most part the traditional control- and compliance-oriented work system remains. What is different is the construction of a parallel administrative structure alongside it, one designed to correct, mitigate, or, in MacDuffie's terms, "buffer" some of the problems associated with traditional control-based work systems.

For the most part, empirical studies have demonstrated support for the types of work systems described by Walton (1985) and their tendency to cluster around organizations with different types of HR strategies (see Table 6.2). For example, Arthur (1992) used cluster analytical techniques to empirically identify "distinct patterns of employer choices" with regard to a variety of employee relations parameters, including work systems design (p. 489). Drawing on Galbraith (1977), Arthur argued that in organizations adopting HR strategies grounded in process or behavioral control, the key to ensuring efficiency and firm performance is to avoid any deviation from standard, routinized, and highly specified work processes, such as the introduction of employee involvement programs. Such deviations can cause "production bottlenecks" and increase the costs of production. Thus, Arthur's theory suggested that in organizations adopting secondary or paternalistic HR strategies, jobs will be more narrowly defined and work systems will be more constrained by formal and predetermined rules and standard operating procedures. In contrast, he suggested that ER objectives in organizations with free-agent or commitment HR strategies (i.e., strategies grounded in output-based control) will revolve around the alignment of employee-employer interest and the maximization of employee discretion. In this context, Arthur suggested that managers in such organizations will have an interest in broadly defining jobs so as to provide employees with the autonomy and discretion needed to deal with the uncertainty inherent in organizational transformation processes. Using a sample of American steel minimills, Arthur identified two main types of employee relations systems: a cost reduction system paralleling Walton's control framework and a "commitment" maximization system paralleling Walton's (1985) framework of the same name. Consistent with his predictions, Arthur found that, as compared to work systems in firms adopting a commitment model, cost reduction work systems are characterized by the presence of more simple and low-skilled jobs as well as by more limited opportunities for employee influence in decision making.

MacDuffie (1995) adopted a similar approach in his analysis of work systems and their link with HR strategy in his analysis of the auto industry. His empirical results provided empirical support for Walton's three-part typology of control-based, transitional, and commitment-based work systems and showed a link between the nature of work systems and organizational HR strategy. That is, his findings suggested that control-based work systems are most prevalent in

Table 6.2 Dominant HR Strategies and Employee Relations Choices by Subsystem Domain

ER Domain	Secondary	Paternalistic	Free Agent	Commitment
Work system	Control oriented: direct control through supervision, indirect control through routinization and standardization; no employee involvement in decision making	Transitional: benevolent Taylorism (job enrichment; limited employee involvement via establishment of a parallel hierarchy)	Bounded commitment: broadly defined jobs demanding cross-functional collaboration, team-based work; employee influence in decision making is extensive but limited to operational or project-related issues	Commitment oriented: flexible definition of job tasks; team-based work; peer pressure replaces supervisory control; extensive employee involvement in both operational and strategic decision making
Assistance	Not relevant	Limited primarily to EAP services	Not relevant; EAP services tend to be provided by union or professional organization	Extensive adoption of both EAPs and work-family programs
Workplace governance	Nonunion framework is dominant; few, if any, institutionalized mechanisms for dispute resolution	Union frameworks are widespread; in nonunion contexts, alternative dispute resolution mechanisms may be adopted for purposes of union avoidance and/or to reduce costs of litigation	Union and nonunion frameworks in effect; professional constraints on rule making and enforcement may also be in effect; alternative dispute resolution mechanisms used in nonunion contexts as specified in employment contract	Mostly nonunion governance frameworks with heavy emphasis on alternative dispute resolution; focus is on informal, peer-based dispute resolution, but formal, multistep grievance systems are relatively widespread

organizations having a "bundle" of practices and policies most characteristic of a secondary HR strategy, whereas transitional and commitment-based work systems are most prevalent in organizations having a "bundle" of practices and policies most characteristic of paternalistic and commitment HR strategies, respectively. Specifically, his findings suggested that, compared to organizations adopting secondary HR strategy, organizations adopting paternalistic HR strategies involve employees more in operational decision making and feature production jobs that tend to be more broadly defined, incorporating a higher degree of responsibility for quality-related tasks. Furthermore, compared to organizations adopting paternalistic HR strategies, organizations adopting commitment-oriented HR strategies involve employees even more in decision making and feature production jobs that tend to be even more broadly defined, incorporating an even higher degree of responsibility for quality-related tasks. Similarly, his findings suggested that the prevalence of job rotation is lowest in organizations adopting secondary HR strategies, higher in organizations adopting paternalistic HR strategies, and highest in firms adopting commitment-oriented HR strategies. This is consistent with the logic underlying commitment-oriented HR strategies, namely that to enhance organizational flexibility and learning capabilities, workers need to be exposed to as many aspects of the total production process as possible. Finally, the level of status differentiation (an important indicator of bureaucratic control) was found to be significantly higher in organizations with a secondary HR strategy than in organizations adopting a paternalistic HR strategy and significantly higher in firms adopting paternalistic HR strategies than in firms with a commitment-based HR strategy.

It should be rather obvious that none of the studies reviewed up to this point describe the nature of work systems in organizations in which the free-agent HR strategy is dominant. As we noted above, in such organizations, work systems based on compliance objectives are likely to be inconsistent with the output-based approach to the control of the work process. External experts are hired in such situations specifically because they have internalized the control of uncertain work processes that, although important to the organization, remain too peripheral to justify any attempt at preprogramming (Lepak & Snell, 1999b). It is critical for the organization to rapidly harness the knowledge and skills brought by these partners to the organization and to ensure maximum trust among as well as cooperation between these temporary "outsiders" and more permanent or core employees (Lepak & Snell, 1999b). Work systems based on process-based control operate against these objectives because they fail to provide these external experts with the autonomy needed to perform what is expected of them. Furthermore, such systems are likely to operate in a manner contrary to the occupational ethos and thus to raise suspicion rather than build trust (Bacharach, Bamberger, & Conely, 1991). Thus, the question remains: How do organizations shape work systems so as to be able to rapidly generate social cohesion in the context of an essentially transactional-based psychological contract?

The research of Lawler and Yoon (1995) may shed some light on this question. Their research suggests that organizations have two alternative strategies for stimulating the development of such cohesion. On the one hand, transactional relations can breed trust and cohesion if exchanges are repetitive and continue over a long enough period of time. The positive emotions generated by frequent and continuous exchanges over time tend to breed a sense of cohesion and trust, building bonds of emotional rather than strictly instrumental attachment. Alternatively, the construction of a common social identity can shorten the path to the development of such trust and cohesion. In the case of organizations with free-agent strategies, given the temporary nature of the employment relationship, work systems tend to be designed much more with the second process in mind. That is, to stimulate the rapid development of group cohesion and trust-based relations, such organizations tend to adopt commitment-oriented work systems closely paralleling those described by Arthur (1992, 1994) and Mac-Duffie (1995). Such systems include broadly defined jobs demanding intensive collaboration and cross-functional interdependence, a reliance on team-based work processes, and extensive employee involvement in decision making on operational, project-related issues (Matusik & Hill, 1998; Nonaka & Takeuchi, 1995).

However, because such external partners are likely to have a primary loyalty and attachment to their craft or profession and its traditions and ethos, and because the employment relationship is short term, such work systems are likely to be oriented toward more limited commitment objectives. Consequently, free-agent work systems are likely to differ from the commitment model described above in at least three important ways. First, given the short-term, transactional nature of the relationship, both employers and free agents have an interest in specifying expected outcomes (deliverables) and deadlines in the form of a detailed contract. Thus, unlike the model described above, norm-based managerial control in the case of free agents is bounded by contractual agreements. Second, although (as noted above) free agents' jobs tend to be broadly defined, occupational traditions and ethos tend to limit the employer's flexibility with regard to staffing and job design. That is, free-agent work systems tend to offer employers a more limited ability to add responsibilities or assign employees tasks not broadly covered by the contract (Bacharach et al., 1991; Sonnenstuhl & Trice, 1991). Finally, though free-agent work systems tend to encourage employee involvement in decision making, such involvement tends to be limited to matters related to the particular project to which the individual is assigned and even then to issues that are more operational (as opposed to strategic) (Bacharach et al., 1991).

Despite these limitations, to minimize agency problems, work systems in organizations in which the free-agent HR strategy is dominant are likely to be structured so as to maximize employees' commitment and contribution to the project or team to which they are assigned.

Assistance Domain

A second employee relations subsystem domain has to do with the noneconomic benefits provided by the organizations. Depending on the nature of the organization's ER objectives, such benefits may be used primarily to ameliorate personal problems that could pose a barrier to effective performance and/or to elicit desired employee attitudes and behaviors.

Forms of Assistance

Although there are numerous forms of noneconomic benefits that an organization can provide, two dominant forms are work-family programs and Employee Assistance Programs. As several researchers have noted (Brandes, 1970; Osterman, 1995; Roman & Blum, 1998), early forms of these programs had already become popular in the early part of the 20th century, primarily out of a desire to increase employees' commitment to the firm and/or to reduce their interest in unions.

Work-family programs include direct provision of day care on or off site, referrals for child care or elder care, and flexible work hours. Recent studies indicate that such benefits have become increasingly widespread over the past two decades. A Bureau of Labor Statistics survey of benefits in medium and large organizations found that the percentage of employees receiving child care support from their employers rose from 1% in 1985 to 5% in 1989 (Hyland, 1990). In a more recent study of a national probability sample of establishments with over 50 employees, Osterman found that over 40% of such firms currently offer flexible hours and that under 10% currently offer on- or offsite day care services to their employees. There is little doubt that underlying much of the growth of these programs is the increased labor force participation rate of women and, in particular, of women with children under the age of 3 (which rose from 28.3% in 1975 to 49% in 1993; Goodman, 1995, p. 6). As Osterman (1995) noted, "These demographic and labor-force participation patterns create pressure for the workplace to become more family friendly" (p. 683). Specifically, as a larger proportion of an organization's employees face child care or elder care problems, the risks of lateness, absenteeism, and distraction grow, as do the costs associated with them. Furthermore, the adoption of such programs may serve an important recruitment and retention function, signaling to potential recruits the existence of a "caring" or "family-oriented" organizational culture.

Employee Assistance Programs (EAPs) are "job-based programs operating within a work organization for the purpose of identifying "troubled employees," motivating them to resolve their troubles, and providing access to counseling or treatment for those employees who need these services (Sonnenstuhl & Trice, 1990). Early forms of employee assistance (such as R. H. Macy's workplace psychiatry program and Western Electric's counseling department) were grounded in the principles of welfare capitalism and the findings of early organizational researchers such as Elton Mayo (1945) and Roethlisberger and Dickson (1947) (of Hawthorne studies fame). On the basis of the human relations paradigm developed by these scholars (Perrow, 1979), organizations originally adopting such programs implicitly assumed that employees' potential maladjustment to their work can have an impact on their work performance. Consequently, they argued that it is in the employer's interest to assist the worker in addressing such problems. However, by the 1940s, organizations adopting employee welfare, social work, or counseling departments increasingly structured such activities around the assumption that employees' troubles stemmed primarily from off-job sources, such as alcoholism (Roman & Blum, 1998). Furthermore, by the 1950s, only a relatively small proportion of primarily larger firms were continuing to offer such services, and most of these programs focused strictly on employee drinking problems (Sonnenstuhl, 1996).

However, beginning in the 1970s, a combination of largely institutional and legal forces led to the rapid and widespread adoption of more broad-based programs aimed at preventing and treating a wide variety of employee behavioral-medical problems, including not only substance abuse but family disruptions, stress, and other psychiatric problems and work-based traumas (critical incident stress) as well (Sonnenstuhl, 1996). In their contemporary form, EAPs are designed to provide organizations with a mechanism to avoid costly disruptions, productivity losses, and increased turnover stemming from any of these primarily external sources. Supervisors refer employees to the EAP strictly on the basis of documented job performance problems before initiating disciplinary action. In a strictly confidential manner, the EAP provides an assessment of these problems and then refers the employee to the appropriate treatment provider. Follow-up occurs both during and after treatment in the hope that subsequent disciplinary action and eventual dismissal can be avoided altogether.

Like work-family programs, EAPs have become increasingly prevalent over the past two decades. Roman (1982) reported that by 1979, 57% of Fortune 1000 companies had some form of EAP, as compared to 25% just 7 years earlier. A more recent study (Hartwell et al., 1996) found that about 50% of the American workforce (employed in establishments with over 50 employees) have access to EAP services via their workplace. The majority of these programs (over 80%) are externally contracted, particularly in smaller organizations. Underlying the growth in EAPs, as noted above, are a variety of institutional and legal/regulatory forces, including the Drug-Free Workplace Act and the Americans with Disabilities Act (ADA). But undoubtedly, some of this growth is likely to be a function of the documented benefits provided by such programs to employers (Roman & Blum, 1998). These include (a) the increased ability of the organization to retain the services of employees in whom it has a substantial human capital investment; (b) reduced managerial involvement in counseling employees with behavioral disorders (thus freeing up managers for other, more central responsibilities); (c) greater control over employee health care costs; (d) reduced rates of absenteeism, lateness, and safety violations; and (e) improved compliance with the ADA's requirement for "reasonable accommodation."

Despite the increasing prevalence of such benefit programs, a substantial proportion of firms still fail to offer such services. This suggests that although such programs may offer a means to achieve important ER objectives for some firms, for others they do not. Indeed, there is evidence that the adoption of such programs is very much linked to the nature of a firm's overall HR strategy, and thus its ER objectives.

Assistance Programs, ER Objectives, and HR Strategy

Drawing on economics, it may be argued that employment benefits are likely to be more prevalent in internal labor market (ILM) firms (i.e., firms in which the paternalistic or commitment strategy is dominant) than in firms relying on external sources of labor (i.e., firms in which the secondary or free-agent HR strategy is dominant). Specifically, the economics literature (see Baron,

Davis-Blake, & Bielby, 1986; Doeringer & Piore, 1971) suggests that firms with ILMs are likely to make greater human capital investments in their workers than are other employers. Consequently, they have a greater interest in retaining employees, and, as noted above, benefits such as work-family programs and EAPs may be efficient in this regard. Indeed, Goodstein (1994) found support for such an argument with respect to work-family programs. His findings suggest that firms valuing employee loyalty are more likely to gear their ER subsystems to such programs.

However, Osterman (1995) argued that there is more to the link between HR strategy and at least work-family benefits than simple economics. He claimed that although such programs may be more prevalent in all ILM firms, they will be most prevalent in firms adopting commitment HR strategies—as he put it, "a distinctive subset of firms with ILMs" (p. 686). This, he argued, is because organizations in which the commitment HR strategy is dominant "depend on employee initiative and ideas" and the willingness of employees to "engage themselves and offer their ideas and knowledge with a degree of authenticity that, by its very nature, is not enforceable and which therefore requires a substantial element of volunteerism on the part of the workforce" (pp. 685-686). Such volunteerism may be stimulated by the adoption of work-family benefits in that the provision of such benefits signals caring on the part of the organization and—most importantly—the implicit expectation that such caring be reciprocated by the employee.

To gain a better understanding of which firms are more likely to adopt work-family programs and why, Osterman (1995) studied a random sample of 875 American for-profit establishments (i.e., a business address as distinct from a company per se) with 50 or more employees. After controlling for establishment size, proportion of the workforce that was female, and wage level, Osterman found that the ILM argument does little to explain the presence or absence of such programs. Specifically, such variables as the extent to which insiders were given a preference to fill job openings and the extent to which seniority was used as the criterion for determining which insider got promoted were not significantly related to the adoption of work-family programs. On the other hand, nearly all of the variables capturing the degree to which the firm's dominant HR strategy could be characterized as commitment oriented were significantly related to program adoption, and together these variables added significantly to the explanatory power of the equation.

Osterman's findings suggest that—as shown in Table 6.2—work-family programs are likely to be a key characteristic of the ER subsystem only in firms in which a commitment HR strategy is dominant. Although such programs may also ameliorate productivity problems (particularly for those workers faced with child care or elder care responsibilities), his findings suggest that the primary explanation for the adoption of such programs lies in the desire of organizations to create a community based on a culture of reciprocal caring. The same may not be true with respect to other forms of noneconomic benefits. That is, although other such programs may ultimately assist the organization in "winning the hearts and minds" of their employees, there is little empirical evidence that they were adopted with such goals in mind.

This may be particularly true with respect to EAPs (Sonnenstuhl, 1996). As noted earlier, early forms of EAPs and industrial welfare tended to be oriented toward the amelioration of productivity problems stemming from employee maladjustment, rather than toward producing a loyal employee. In this performance orientation, some employers may have even viewed the adoption of an EAP as an additional mechanism of benevolent control. That is, although such programs may have an underlying humanitarian purpose, they may also be a cost-effective and institutionally legitimate mechanism for dealing with employees who deviate from the organizational norm. Whereas firms relying on an external labor market (ELM) may find it far less costly to simply replace such employees, for ILM firms, there may be a substantial benefit for attempting to assist and/or rehabilitate such workers.

A study by Hartwell et al. (1996) provides empirical support to the notion that firms with dominant HR strategies based on an ELM orientation (i.e., secondary and free-agent HR strategies) are among the least likely to base their ER subsystems on the provision of such noneconomic benefits, whereas firms with ILM-based dominant HR strategies are among the most likely to adopt such programs. For example, EAP prevalence rates were the lowest (3%) in the construction industry as compared to 31% in the public utility and communications industries. As we noted earlier in this book, the construction industry is generally characterized by firms in which HR strategies based on an ELM orientation tend to dominate, whereas firms, at least in the public utility sector, are often pointed to as primary examples of organizations with paternalistic HR strategies. Indeed, many of the occupations and professions from which free agents are drawn (e.g., law, accounting, construction trades) tend to provide their own peer-based assistance programs (Bacharach, Bamberger, & Sonnenstuhl, 1996a). As Roman and Blum (1998) noted, members of such occupations are "not part of a typical employment relationship; they often have considerable autonomy in determining work hours, techniques and other aspects of work style" (p. 114). Furthermore, a strong sense of community and the lack of any long-term relationship with any given employer make a peer- or occupation-based assistance program much more feasible than an employer-based program (Bacharach, Bamberger, & Sonnenstuhl, 1994).

In principle, organizations in which a commitment-based strategy is dominant may be able to derive an additional benefit from the development of an EAP. Specifically, assistance programs may greatly reinforce the "caring" culture dominant in such firms (Roman & Blum, 1998, p. 102). Nevertheless, there does not appear to be any empirical evidence to suggest that such programs may be any more prevalent in such organizations than in organizations in which a paternalistic HR strategy is dominant. Consequently, as noted in Table 6.1 and 6.2, we conclude that a focus on employee assistance will be characteristic of ER subsystems in organizations in which either a paternalistic or a commitment HR strategy is dominant.

Governance Domain

A third, critical ER domain has to do with workplace governance, or, in other words, organizational rule-making and dispute resolution processes. Although such processes have, in the past, been most closely examined in the context of unionized firms and collective bargaining, researchers have recently begun to pay close attention to the small but increasing number of nonunion companies that have sought to offer their employees alternative mechanisms for dispute resolution and even a more extensive role in organizational rule making. Thus, to understand workforce governance systems, we need to examine ER choices having to do with (a) the nature of the employee role in organizational rule making and (b) the nature of workplace dispute resolution.

The core strategic choice regarding the nature of workforce governance has to do with whether such a system of governance will be based on the principle of independent and democratic employee representation. In most countries, this choice is left to the workers. It is they who are given the right to opt for union representation. Nevertheless, managers in many Western countries have used both legal and illegal means to try to influence the outcomes of such worker decisions. For employers, the stakes associated with such a decision can be rather high because the nature of both organizational rule making and dispute resolution is profoundly influenced by the presence of a union.

Union Versus Nonunion Governance Systems

The primary differences between union and nonunion governance systems have to do with (a) the degree to which employees are given an opportunity to independently select individuals from among their ranks to represent their interests and concerns before management and (b) the degree to which the resolution of disputes is based on a system of due process. Under a union-based governance system, management must negotiate work-related rules and systems of rule administration with the employees' representatives. These employment terms are specified in a contract that is subject to the interpretation of both sides. The need for a system of dispute resolution arises because the two sides often interpret contractual provisions on the basis of opposing logics or perspectives. As Feuille and Hildebrand (1995) noted, unions tend to interpret contract provisions on the basis of a "logic of employee rights," whereas management tends to base its interpretation on a "logic of efficiency" (p. 342). Typically, the provisions of most collective bargaining agreements specify an exchange between management and labor in which the former agrees to have its personnel decisions subject to challenge and possible reversal via some bilateral arbitration process and the latter agrees to forfeit the right to strike during the life of the contract (Feuille & Hildebrand, 1995). In general, disputes are not subject to immediate arbitration. Rather, disputes (or "grievances," as they are typically referred to) tend to follow a multistep prearbitration resolution process in which those unresolved at lower hierarchical levels are appealed to higher levels in both the company and the union.

Under a nonunion governance system, management is able to determine and administer work rules on a unilateral basis and can—also on a unilateral basis—determine whether and how it wants to resolve employee complaints. Nevertheless, as noted above, an increasing number of firms have attempted to provide employees with greater opportunities both to influence the shaping of work rules and to complain about current rules, practices, or decisions. For example, during the past two decades, employers have experimented with quality circles and semiautonomous work teams as means to provide employees with a greater sense of control over the determination and administration of work rules. In addition, employers have experimented with a wide range of alternative dispute resolution mechanisms, including multistep grievance systems, open door policies, the development of a position of "ombudsperson," and even peer review boards. However, in nearly all such cases, management reserves for itself the right to make the final decision. Intel, for example, uses a multistep disciplinary process in which employees are first given a warning and then put under a status of "corrective action." In the context of the latter, the employee and his or her supervisor jointly establish performance/behavioral goals for a defined period of time. At the end of this period, the employee's performance is evaluated against these preset objectives. Dismissal or other punitive action can be considered only after this assessment is made.

Indeed, many companies have adopted rather advanced nonunion governance frameworks precisely with the intent of eliminating any employee interest in seeking union representation. Such "union avoidance" ER strategies are grounded in the assumption that employees do not require "independent" representation to influence organizational rule making and receive due process in the handling of grievances. However, this assumption may be questioned because in many organizations lacking independent and collective representation, many employees may feel too much of a personal risk to individually "voice" concerns to their employer. Furthermore, this assumption may be questioned because most nonunion dispute resolution systems end with (at most) top-level managerial review (as opposed to external arbitration) as the final step (Chachere & Feuille, 1993).

ER Objectives and Workplace Governance

Why do some firms make union avoidance the cornerstone of their ER policy, whereas other firms (e.g., United Parcel) have a tradition of almost encouraging their workers to join a union? Furthermore, although collective bargaining pressures tend to force companies to provide employees or their representatives with a means to shape organizational rules and resolve disputes regarding the interpretation of these rules, why would a nonunionized firm seek to develop similar dispute resolution mechanisms? To answer such questions, a better understanding of the link between ER objectives and alternative workplace governance frameworks is required.

At the core of the union governance issue is the degree to which unionization is consistent or inconsistent with overall ER objectives. Although the "gut" response of most managers is that unionization is in no way in the employer's interest, the research of Freeman and Medoff (1984) and Mishel and Voos (1992) suggests otherwise. According to these researchers, employee turnover in union settings is lower than in nonunion settings, not only because of the existence of a union wage differential but also because unionized workers have the opportunity to express and enforce their opinions. That is, a union-based governance system provides individual workers with a formalized system of employee "voice" that, in the long run, can help eliminate inefficiencies in production. However, perhaps most important to managers, labor productivity tends to be higher in unionized firms than in nonunion firms, in part because owners have an incentive to utilize their available human capital more efficiently (Freeman & Medoff, 1984).

Consequently, for some firms, employee representation and the union-based governance system may in fact facilitate the achievement of key ER objectives. For example, unionization may provide such employers with an element of workforce stability and predictability. Providing employees with a sense of "voice" and control and providing a framework for real due process may help ameliorate employees' feelings of alienation and inequity and may thus, as discussed by Freeman and Medoff (1984), help in the elimination of productivity and efficiency barriers.

On the other hand, employee representation may certainly have important disadvantages to certain firms. For example, the imposition of a formal system of governance may greatly limit the employers' freedom of action with regard to resource deployment and work organization. Furthermore, to the extent that the union negotiates for work rules limiting the efficiency of various work processes, a union-based governance system may increase overall labor costs and slow the firm's reaction time to shifts in the market or technology. Finally, rather than developing a sense of commitment to their employer, employees may be more attached to their union (Bamberger, Kluger, & Suchard, 1999).

Thus, for other firms, the loss of managerial control and hence organizational flexibility may be associated with any formal workforce governance system, particularly a union-based system. For these employers, governance systems tend to be designed with only one ER objective in mind, namely regulatory compliance. That is, to the extent that employment-at-will policies must comply with employment laws (regarding, e.g., equal employment opportunity and the protection of those with recognized disabilities), governance systems are likely to be designed so as to minimize the risk of costly litigation while still providing managers with maximal flexibility.

Finally, ER objectives in still other firms may require the adoption of a nonunion workforce governance system closely mirroring those found in unionized firms. That is, to maximize employee commitment and attachment and to help internalize organizational norms, these firms may need to empower employees to contribute to the setting of work-related rules and policies and may need to adopt alternative dispute resolution mechanisms based on the principle of due process. Typically, such organizations attempt to empower employees by establishing formal plant-level groups, teams, or task forces mandated to address such issues as safety, quality, and employee development. A heavy emphasis on employee selection and socialization, as well as the shaping of the premises on which employee preferences are based, reduces the risk to the employer that employees' interests in the setting of work rules will greatly diverge from those of the employer. As discussed in earlier chapters, compensation and development practices play a critical role in the shaping of such employee decision premises.

The adoption of a due process-based dispute resolution framework is likely to further enhance employees' sense of procedural and distributive justice, further strengthening employees' perception of a caring culture and deepening bonds of attachment. Although nonunion employers are hesitant to offer outside arbitration as the final step in such a process, many do offer an adjudication panel composed (at least in part) of employees as the final step (Feuille & Hildebrand, 1995). In the United States, however, nonunion employers adopting such rule-making and dispute resolution frameworks need to be careful to avoid violating the Wagner Act's provision banning the establishment of employer-dominated labor organizations (Hogler, 1993).

HR Strategy and Workplace Governance Frameworks

Although there appears to be a link between ER objectives and workforce governance systems in theory, few empirical studies have focused on such relations. Nevertheless, the variance in governance frameworks across firms emphasizing alternative HR strategies has been examined in at least one study. Arthur (1992), in his study of American steel minimills, examined the link between HR strategy and due process—"the degree to which mills relied on formal procedures to resolve employment-related disputes" (p. 493). As expected, Arthur found formal grievance systems to exist in all 14 unionized plants. Of the nonunion minimills examined, 7 reported having no such formal grievance system whatsoever, and the remaining 9 plants reported having some sort of formal process for dealing with employee grievances. Most significantly, Arthur found a significant link between the dominant HR strategy and the nature of workplace governance. Specifically, he found that among the 12 firms in which a "pure-type cost-reducing" or "inducement" (i.e., secondary) HR strategy was dominant, the due process nature of workplace governance was significantly lower than the mean level for all of the minimills studied. In contrast, the level of due process was significantly higher than the mean in those firms in which a paternalistic HR strategy was dominant. The level of due process for those 14 firms (8 unionized and 6 nonunion) in which the commitment strategy was dominant was not found to be significantly different from the mean. Furthermore, the level of due process among specifically nonunion, commitment-oriented firms was found to be statistically identical to that of the mean for all union and nonunion steel minimills. Together, these findings suggest that, as proposed above, firms in which a commitment-oriented HR strategy is dominant attempt to closely mirror union-based governance practices even in those cases in which no union is present.

On the basis of these findings and the theory presented above, it is reasonable to assume that workplace governance practices will vary according to the dominant HR strategy in a firm. Such a pattern of variance is highlighted toward the bottom of Table 6.2. Specifically, as shown in Table 6.2, governance systems in firms in which the secondary HR strategy is dominant are likely to be characterized by a lack of formally constituted employee organizations. The temporary nature of employment relationships and the fact that many employees in such organizations may be employed by one firm and contracted to another make it difficult for employees to organize. These same conditions make it difficult for employers to justify the organization of nonunion frameworks (e.g., work teams, employee task forces) designed to provide employees with input into the setting of organizational rules and policies. Providing employees with such influence may slow down managerial decision-making processes and may be viewed as placing a constraint on managerial flexibility. Although the formation of such alternative employee representation frameworks may be an effective union avoidance tactic, as noted above, for such firms, the threat of unionization is limited to begin with due to the temporary and often contractual nature of the employment relationship.

Similarly, firms in which the secondary HR strategy is dominant are characterized by few if any institutionalized mechanisms for dispute resolution. As noted above, such firms tend to adopt the Tayloristic principle of separating the execution of work from its conceptualization and deconstructing complex work processes into simple, routine steps requiring little on-the-job training and even less prejob training. As a result, the firm's dependence on any particular worker or group of workers is limited. Consequently, such organizations tend to lack any incentive to provide employees with formal opportunities to "voice," preferring to let employees "vote with their feet." Instead, such firms tend to rely on informal voicing mechanisms based on the supervisor-employee relationship. To the extent that formal voicing or grievance mechanisms are provided, they tend to be limited to those issues (e.g., claims of age or gender discrimination) subject to strict government regulation. American courts have made it clear to employers that by adopting alternative dispute resolution frameworks for the resolution of employee claims of discrimination they can avoid the costs and risks of litigation (Feuille & Hildebrand, 1995).

In contrast, union-based workplace governance frameworks often characterize governance systems in firms in which the paternalistic HR strategy is dominant (Arthur, 1992; Dyer & Holder, 1988). As such, the collective bargaining process is likely to provide employees in such firms with at least a limited degree of control over work rules, and a formal grievance procedure ending in arbitration tends to provide employees with extensive due process rights. For employers operating in highly stable and less competitive product or service markets, such governance frameworks may offer a high degree of stability and predictability and thus enhanced organizational performance (Bacharach & Shedd, 1999).

However, because only 12% of the private sector workforce in the United States is unionized, it is obvious that many of the firms in which the paternalistic HR strategy is dominant operate under nonunion conditions. Governance systems in nonunionized paternalistic firms tend to differ from systems in unionized paternalistic firms in two respects. First, there is generally an absence of employee input into the setting of workplace rules. As in the case of the secondary HR strategy, the adoption of mechanisms designed to provide employees with input into the organization of work and the design of the work process would directly contradict many of the core Tayloristic assumptions on which this HR strategy is based. Furthermore, given the ILM grounding this strategy, such frameworks are typically not required to boost employee commitment to the firm. Stability, predictability, and employee commitment are typically provided by the presence of an ILM and a clan culture, which, in turn, make it costly to leave and which provide a strong incentive for loyalty.

Second, although formalized, multistep dispute resolution frameworks are prevalent in such systems, they tend to be characterized by strict limitations with regard to the employee's right to representation (i.e., the employee is typically forced to represent him- or herself). Furthermore, the final step tends to be an appeal to a senior line or staff manager or, at most, some sort of internal managerial panel (Chachere & Feuille, 1993). Firms in which the paternalistic HR strategy is dominant may be driven to adopt such dispute resolution frameworks by two factors. Given the stability of the workforce and the nature of work processes, such firms tend to be highly susceptible to union organization drives. Thus, the adoption of some form of remedial voicing system (Sheppard, Lewicki, & Minton, 1992) may play a key role in such firms' attempts to retain their nonunion status (Freeman & Kleiner, 1990). Second, as in firms in which the secondary HR strategy is dominant, such dispute resolution frameworks may be adopted out of an interest in reducing the risks of employee litigation.

In firms in which the free-agent system is dominant, both nonunion and union-based governance frameworks are likely to be in effect. In the case of firms hiring nonunionized free agents, although there may be no contractual requirement to provide employee input into the setting of work rules, institutionalized work practices and a professional ethos may nevertheless demand a certain degree of employee input. Indeed, the output-based system of control at the core of the free-agent strategy demands that employees be empowered to influence or even determine how to best structure the work process. Nevertheless, in such firms, formalized dispute resolution frameworks are unlikely to be prevalent unless they are specified in the particular free agent's employment contract. For example, to reduce the risks and costs of litigation, it may be to the advantage of both the employer and the free agent to specify that any unresolvable dispute be subject to third-party arbitration.

Collective bargaining provides many unionized free agents in the building trades and the arts with a more formal means of influencing the establishment of basic workplace rules and employment conditions. But for many professional free agents, professional associations may provide an alternative means by which employees can influence the setting of workplace rules. For example, though less directly, professional associations in such fields as law and accounting have succeeded in institutionalizing certain rules and work practices designed to protect the professional stature and labor market position of their nonunionized constituents (Abbott, 1993). In addition, both unions and professional associations (American Medical Association, state bar associations) have generally succeeded in institutionalizing formal dispute resolution systems, limiting the ability of the employer to unilaterally determine how to handle employee complaints or to implement sanctions against the employee. In the case of unionized free agents (i.e., members of craft unions), such dispute resolution mechanisms tend to be based on a multistep grievance process ending in arbitration. However, even in the case of nonunion, professional free agents, employers may be required to submit disputes to a professional (i.e., peer-based) review board.

Finally, as Arthur (1992) noted, although firms in which the commitment HR strategy is dominant are likely to be characterized by nonunion governance systems, this strategy in no way precludes the existence of union-based governance systems as well. Indeed, several authors (Arthur, 1992; Katz, 1985; Kochan et al., 1986) note that unionized firms in such industries as steel and automobile manufacturing have moved toward more of a commitment-based HR strategy, in part, by enhancing their union-based governance system. That is, while retaining a multistep grievance system ending in arbitration, they have attempted to expand the opportunities for employee involvement in the setting of work rules and the transformation of work processes. For example, in conjunction with the United Auto Workers, a number of automobile manufacturers have set up multiple frameworks for employee involvement (e.g., reorganizing of work around semiautonomous teams) and have given employee representatives extensive influence over such areas as safety, ergonomics, employee development, benefits, and employee assistance. Underlying such efforts is a desire not so much to reduce turnover (the existence of ILMs ensures a relatively low rate of turnover) as to more strongly align employee interests with those of the firm and enhance operational efficiencies.

Nevertheless, the bulk of those firms adopting the commitment strategy tend to be nonunionized. In these firms, as noted above, employers have attempted to use alternative employee representation and participation schemes to strengthen workers' sense of attachment to the organization. In some countries, such as Germany, this has been accomplished by the adoption of workers' councils or employee participation committees—representative bodies lacking the ability to strike or negotiate over economic issues. However, in the United States, such frameworks are currently precluded under the terms of the Wagner Act. Thus, in the United States, nonunion firms have had to "walk a tightrope" in finding alternative mechanisms to allow employee input into the setting of work rules and procedures. Semiautonomous work teams, quality circles, and labor-management task forces are among some of the most widely adopted mechanisms.

Similarly, governance systems in these firms are characterized by a focus on due process, though typically with management still retaining the right to make a final, unilateral decision. Feuille and Hildebrand (1995) noted that the most widely mentioned type of due process mechanism in such firms is the "open door" appeal to higher management, allowing the aggrieved employee to appeal an adverse decision up the organizational chain of command. As noted earlier, alternative mechanisms include mediation on the part of some organizational ombudsperson's office and/or settlement by a management or joint employee-management review panel. There is little robust evidence that such alternative dispute mechanisms have any positive impact on productivity in nonunion workplaces (Feuille & Hildebrand, 1995, p. 361). Nevertheless, by signaling their recognition of the importance of equity and procedural justice, the mere existence of such mechanisms may help organizational leaders achieve their key ER objective, namely the creation and strengthening of an organizational culture based on a sense of community, caring, and employee volunteerism.

Summary

We began this chapter by suggesting a need for a broader definition of the employee relations subsystem. Within this context, we defined this subsystem as relating to those strategic managerial activities aimed at establishing, enforcing, and reinforcing the psychological contract between employer and employees. On the basis of this definition, we suggested that the employee relations subsystem encompasses a wide range of managerial choices having to do with (a) the nature of control and coordination in the workplace, (b) the degree to which there is an interest in having employees internalize the organization as a core element of their identity, and (c) the way in which employee equity expectations are balanced with the organizational need for rule compliance. Thus, it should be clear that the ER subsystem is a core element of the HR system and that despite its industrial relations orientation, it often serves as the foundation on which other elements of the HR strategy are built (Ferris et al., 1998).

After explaining the significance of the employee relations subsystem and its potential impact on key organizational outcomes, we proposed that subsystem strategies tend to be based on ER objectives and that these ER objectives are themselves a function of the firm's dominant HR strategy. Specifically, we argued that the more ER objectives focus on simple employee rule compliance, the less sophisticated the ER subsystem. In contrast, the more firms place an emphasis on the enhancement of individual attachment and commitment to the firm, the more sophisticated and complex the ER subsystem is. Finally, in the second part of this chapter, we reviewed some of the literature describing how, across three critical subsystem domains—work systems, the provision of noneconomic benefits such as employee assistance, and the nature of the workplace system of governance—ER subsystems tend to vary in a fairly predictable manner depending on the nature of firms' dominant HR strategies.

Taken in combination with the previous two chapters, the material presented in this chapter suggests that HR subsystem practices tend to cluster into internally consistent packages or configurations. For example, as we noted in the current chapter, the adoption of formalized alternative dispute resolution systems is highly consistent with the staffing, training, and compensation practices typical of firms in which the commitment HR strategy is dominant. However, one question that remains to be examined is whether such consistency is really necessary to enhance firm performance. In the next and final chapter, we directly address this question in an attempt to gain a further understanding of the link between HR strategy in all of its respects and overall firm performance.

Note

1. In this chapter, we focus strictly on the work design elements of Taylorism. Taylor's scientific management approach also called for the adoption of more rational systems of selection and advancement—systems developed on the basis of scientific research. Taylor proposed more rational systems of compensation, placing an emphasis on performance-based incentives (i.e., piece rate). As Perrow (1979) wrote, the idea was to "take the eyes of labor and management off the division of the surplus (higher wages or higher profits) and instead turn them toward the problem of increasing the *size* of the surplus" (p. 64).

7

The Impact of Human Resource Strategy

Does HR strategy make a difference? That is, to what degree can managers expect to influence their "bottom line" by adopting one HR strategy over another? Given the centrality of such questions, it should come as no surprise that the bulk of strategic human resource management (SHRM) research in recent years has focused precisely on such issues. Indeed, if HR strategy is not associated with key organizational outcomes, then—aside from intellectual curiosity—researchers have little incentive for further inquiry. Over the past decade, dozens of studies have explored the association between HR strategy and a wide variety of organizational outcomes, including turnover, machine efficiency, employee productivity, innovativeness, financial performance, and firm survival. In this chapter, we review these studies, not only to assess the degree to which HR strategy may predict organizational outcomes but, perhaps more important, to gain a better understanding of the nature of such effects. In the first section of this chapter, we review several of the early, key studies suggestive of a link between HR strategy and firm performance. Next, we review the empirical research exploring alternative explanations for such a link and seeking to identify key moderators of the strategy-performance relationship. Finally, we discuss several of the key theoretical and operational challenges facing researchers in this area, as well as the implications of this research for practitioners.

Demonstrating the Link Between HR Strategy and Firm Performance

HR researchers have long had an interest in understanding the impact of specific HR practices on individual-level outcomes such as turnover and job satisfaction. For example, McEvoy and Cascio (1985) demonstrated that job enrichment and realistic job previews can be effective in reducing turnover, and Hackman and Oldham (1980) showed that job satisfaction and employee motivation may be enhanced by redesigned work systems. However, only in the past decade or so have scholars begun to investigate the impact of individual HR practices and systems of HR practices on organization-level outcomes such as productivity and financial performance (Dyer & Holder, 1988; Wright & McMahan, 1992). Initial studies in this genre aimed at establishing the nature and magnitude of the HR impact on such outcomes. For example, a number of studies suggest that productivity (i.e., lower labor costs and scrap rates) may be enhanced through the adoption of specific HR practices such as "transformational" labor relations (Cutcher-Gershenfeld, 1991), more intensive training and enriched work systems (Guzzo, Jette, & Katzell, 1985), and contingent pay systems (Weitzman & Kruse, 1990). Furthermore, work in the field of human resource accounting (Cascio, 1991; Flamholtz, 1985) suggests that substantial financial returns may be gleaned from HR practices designed to enhance a firm's human capital base, and utility analyses researchers (Boudreau, 1991; Schmidt, Hunter, MacKenzie, & Muldrow, 1979) suggest that HR practices yielding a one-standard-deviation increase in employee performance can produce a financial return equivalent to 40% of salary per employee.

Although these studies have consistently pointed to the positive impact of such HR policies and practices on a variety of organizational outcomes, because they all focus on individual HR policies or practices, the results need to be taken with some caution. As Huselid (1995) noted, firms adopting such practices in one area

> are likely to use them in other areas as well. Therefore, to the extent that any single example reflects a firm's wider propensity to invest in such practices, any estimates of the firm-level impact of the particular practice will be upwardly biased. (p. 641)

In simple terms, "The sum of these individual estimates may dramatically overstate their contribution to firm performance" (p. 641). Consequently, several more recent studies have examined the impact of such practices as manifested in terms of strategies or coherent bundles. Rather than focusing on the impact of specific HR practices, they examine the impact of coherent sets or systems of practice: that is, the impact of alternative HR strategies.

In some of the earliest studies examining the impact of HR strategy on organizational outcomes, Schuster (1986) and Kravetz (1988) examined the relationship between HR management "progressiveness" and firm profits. In both cases, a positive association was shown between strategy and performance, although in both cases the analyses were limited to simple bivariate correlations, thus making it impossible to control for the potential confounding effects of industry and firm size.

More recently, Arthur (1994) examined the impact of two alternative HR strategies (identified in his 1992 study) on firm performance. Specifically, he hypothesized that in manufacturing, plants adopting a commitment-based HR strategy would have better manufacturing performance than plants adopting a control-based HR strategy (p. 673). Drawing on both the resource/behavioral (Schuler & Jackson, 1987; Snell, 1992) and control (Eisenhardt, 1985; Ouchi, 1977, 1980) perspectives, Arthur (1994) justified this proposition by noting that

> by decentralizing managerial decision making, setting up formal participation mechanisms, and providing the proper training and rewards, a commitment system can lead to a highly motivated and empowered work force whose goals are closely aligned with those of management. Thus the resources required to monitor employee compliance, such as those needed to maintain supervision and work rules, can be reduced. In addition, employees under these conditions are thought to be more likely to engage in organizational citizenship behaviors; non-role, unrewarded behaviors that are believed to be, nonetheless, critical to organizational success. (p. 673)

Using a sample of 30 U.S. steel minimills, and controlling for the age, size, union status, and business strategy of the mills, Arthur (1994) found that plants adopting commitment HR strategies had a significantly lower number of labor hours per ton of output (an indicator of efficiency) and lower scrap rates (an indicator of production quality) (p. 679). Thus, on the basis of the strategic taxonomy developed in his earlier study (Arthur, 1992), Arthur concluded that HR strategy is associated with the variation in manufacturing performance. Moreover, Arthur's findings suggest that the commitment-based HR strategy may be composed of a set of "best practices" and may thus offer a universal source of competitive advantage. Nevertheless, in many ways, Arthur's study raised more questions than it answered. First, Arthur himself wondered how generalizable these findings would be with respect to manufacturers in other industries, not to mention organizations in entirely different fields (e.g., education, health). Second, though his findings suggest that the commitment-based HR strategy may be composed of a set of "best practices" and may thus offer a universal source of competitive advantage, Arthur acknowledged that the strategy-performance linkage may be contingent on other factors such as the nature of business strategy or the degree to which system practices are internally aligned. Given the small, single-industry sample, Arthur was unable to address either of these concerns. Finally, though demonstrating that HR strategy may indeed explain some of the variance in performance-related variables, Arthur was unable to place a precise figure on the magnitude of this effect.

Using a larger, multinational sample of automotive assembly plants, MacDuffie (1995) provided further support for a strategy-performance linkage, thus suggesting that Arthur's findings may indeed be generalizable (at least to firms in other heavy industries). More important, however, his study offered tentative answers to the two other questions raised by Arthur's study. First, MacDuffie's results suggest that although individual HR practices may be associated with enhanced firm performance, the greatest effects are manifested when these practices are grouped into internally consistent bundles. This finding suggests that the full positive impact of specific practices on performance may be contingent on the implementation of other, complementary practices. Second, MacDuffie's findings are supportive of the universalistic approach suggested by Arthur's findings. Specifically, although findings supportive of a contingency or "fit" perspective would have shown that both mass (i.e., control-based) and flexible (i.e., commitment-oriented in Arthur's framework) production plants with a good fit between their HR and production strategies outperform those with poor fit, MacDuffie's findings suggest that plants adopting the "innovative HR practices" typically associated with flexible production consistently outperform plants adopting alternative HR strategies, *regardless* of their production strategy.

Despite these important findings, MacDuffie's study was also somewhat limited by a small, single-industry sample. Furthermore, though suggesting that individual and systems of HR practices may have a substantial impact on a firm's "bottom line," MacDuffie's study (like Arthur's) focused on manufacturing outcomes such as productivity and quality. Consequently, like Arthur, MacDuffie was unable to quantify the magnitude of the impact of HR strategy on overall firm performance. Finally, like Arthur, MacDuffie was unable to control for two potential methodology-based biases. The first concerns the potential simultaneity between HR strategy and firm performance. In simple terms, using cross-sectional data, neither Arthur nor MacDuffie was able to take into account the possibility that more successful firms are systematically more likely to adopt more commitment-oriented dominant HR strategies. The second concerns the potential for selectivity or response bias because the probability of response may be greater for better performing firms and firms adopting "commitment" or "flexible" strategies.

Responding to these limitations, Huselid (1995) attempted to provide the first estimates of the magnitude of the HR strategy effect on a firm's bottom line while controlling for such potential biases (e.g., using outcome measures drawn from the year after that in which data on HR practices were collected). Drawing data from a national sample of nearly 1,000 firms, Huselid examined the impact of what he referred to as "high-performance work practices" on both intermediate employee outcomes (namely turnover and productivity) and short- and long-term measures of corporate financial performance. High-performance work practices include many of those same HR practices typically adopted in the context of a dominant HR strategy similar to that which both we and Arthur (1994) labeled "commitment" (e.g., extensive employee involvement and training, contingent pay, comprehensive and careful employee selection, extensive use of internal labor markets).

Rather than asking respondents to indicate the presence or absence of each of the high-performance HR practices, Huselid had respondents indicate the proportion of employees affected by each practice, thus providing a more sensitive estimate of the breadth and depth of practice implementation and providing an indication of the degree to which such practices could be deemed to be "dominant" in the firm. Furthermore, to avoid the biases inherent in the conceptual and empirical overlap among individual items, Huselid used factor analysis to identify the subsystems underlying these individual practices. Two such subsystems were identified: a motivation subsystem (similar to the reward subsystem discussed in Chapter 5, and including such items as the proportion of the workforce receiving formal performance appraisal and for whom such appraisals were used as the basis of compensation decisions) and an employee skills and organizational structures subsystem (similar to the people flow and employee relations subsystems discussed in Chapters 4 and 6, respectively, and including such items as the proportion of nonentry jobs that have been filled from within in recent years). Using such an approach, Huselid explored the degree to which subsystem practices associated with what we refer to as a commitment HR strategy had an impact on firm performance.

Huselid's (1995) findings suggest that the application of a commitment (or "high-performance") strategy with respect to the subsystems examined can yield substantial returns to a firm. For example, in practical terms, Huselid's findings indicate that each one-standard-deviation increase in each subsystem practice scale would reduce turnover by 7.05% or by 1.30 percentage points (from a mean of 21.48%), even after controlling for firm size, the impact of unions, and employee compensation. Similarly, under the same control conditions, a one-standard-deviation increase in each subsystem practice scale was found to raise net sales per employee (an indicator of productivity) in a single period by an average of $27,044, or nearly 16% of the mean sales per employee. Finally, with respect to firm financial performance, a one-standard-deviation increase in each subsystem practice scale was found to be associated with a per-employee gain in firm market value of $18,641 and a per-employee gain in annual accounting profits of $3,814.

Huselid's findings also provide some insight into the processes through which such practices influence firm financial performance. Specifically, Huselid's findings suggest that a significant proportion (i.e., approximately 75%) of the impact of the practices associated with the commitment strategy "is attributable to either lower turnover or higher employee productivity or both" (p. 663).

Finally, Huselid's analyses provided some initial insight into the role that internal and external fit (Baird & Meshoulam, 1988) might play in moderating the effects of HR strategy on firm financial performance. These findings suggest that although internal fit (i.e., the degree to which complementary practices are *not* implemented in isolation) does have a significant and positive impact on financial performance, external fit (i.e., the degree to which the HR strategy is aligned with firm business strategy) does not. Although, on the basis of these findings, one might be tempted to conclude that such practices are universally beneficial (i.e., will yield a significant positive impact on performance, regardless of the degree of internal consistency or external alignment), Huselid warned that "research based on refined theoretical and psychometric development of these constructs is clearly required before such a conclusion can be accepted with any confidence" (p. 668).

Explaining the Link Between HR Strategy and Firm Performance

How can this HR strategy effect on firm performance be explained? As we have suggested above and in earlier chapters, it is commonly assumed that the impact of HR strategy on firm performance is a function of three interrelated processes. First, HR strategy is likely to shape the human capital base of the firm by means of policies and practices having to do with recruitment and selection, as well as training and development. Second, HR strategy is likely to influence the degree to which the firm is able to exploit this human capital base in terms of employee motivation to stay with the firm and perform; this by means of policies and practices having to do with career development and advancement, compensation, and commitment-building benefits (e.g., employee assistance). Third, HR strategy can have an impact on firm performance by influencing the degree to which talented and motivated employees are provided with the job-related opportunities and discretion to contribute.

SHRM theorists have argued that underlying these assumed processes are a number of well-grounded organizational theories, several of which we discussed in Chapter 1. First, behavioral theory (Jackson et al., 1989; Schuler & Jackson, 1987; Wright & McMahan, 1992) explains the impact of HR strategy on human capital and motivation in that it argues that the human capital base of an organization may be enhanced to the degree that HR practices encourage employees to seek to develop desired organizational skills and competencies. Furthermore, it argues that certain HR activities can elicit and reinforce the kinds of behaviors and attitudes required by the firm. Second, agency theory (Eisenhardt, 1989) explains the impact of HR strategy on motivation in that it argues that HR practices may be used to better align the interests of workers with those of management. Finally, control theory (Ouchi, 1977; Snell, 1992; Thompson, 1967) explains the impact of HR strategy on the opportunities for employee contribution in that certain HR practices (particularly those regarding the nature of performance appraisal and the design of work systems) may provide for greater employee involvement and participation. These three assumptions and the theories underlying them are at the base of each of the studies reviewed above. Furthermore, Huselid's (1995) findings regarding the mediating role of turnover (i.e., loss of human capital) and productivity (i.e., level of motivation and opportunity structures) provide support for these assumptions.

The Search for Alternative Explanations

However, alternative explanations of the association between HR strategy and performance cannot be ruled out. For example, in a recent study, Welbourne and Andrews (1996) drew on population ecology theory (Hannan & Freeman, 1989) to argue that the positive impact of HR strategy on firm performance is explained by its impact on what they referred to as "structural cohesion, an employee-generated synergy that propels a company forward, allowing it to respond to its environment while still moving forward" (p. 896). That is, certain HR strategies may be more strongly associated with firm performance because they provide the stable infrastructure necessary for the organization to rapidly and effectively respond to change. Included as part of this stable infrastructure might be a highly cohesive workforce, an effective, highly cooperative network of teams, and a high level of goal consensus.

Focusing on start-up organizations, Welbourne and Andrews proposed that start-up organizations placing more value on employees at the time of their initial public offering (e.g., by citing employees as a source of competitive advantage in their mission statement) and having organization-based compensation programs such as stock options or profit sharing (to enhance goal consensus) increase their survival chances. Although the capital market tends to react negatively to firms using their capital for organizationally based employee reward programs, as predicted, their findings suggest that to the degree that start-up firms are able to use HR practices to enhance their structural cohesion, they may be able to enhance their long-term prospects for survival. Specifically, although the mean probability of survival was .70, firms with a high level of human resource value (i.e., one standard deviation above the mean) had a mean probability of survival of .79, and firms with a low level of human resource value (i.e., one standard deviation below the mean) had a mean probability of survival of .60. Firms adopting HR strategies structured around the use of organizational rewards (i.e., using organization-level rewards at a level one standard deviation above the mean) were able to increase their survival prospects to .87, whereas firms failing to do so (i.e., using organization-level rewards at a level one standard deviation below the mean) had survival prospects far below the mean (i.e., .45). Finally, survival prospects were nearly a third higher (.92) for firms placing a higher-than-average value on their employees and on the use of organizational rewards and were 50% lower (.34) for firms placing a low value on their employees *and* essentially failing to use organizational rewards as compared to the average firm. In sum, this study suggests that the nature of a start-up's HR strategy can affect its probability of survival by as much as 22%.

Underlying Welbourne and Andrews' findings is the notion that the link between HR strategy and firm performance may be explained or mediated by the level of organizational agility. That is, certain HR strategies may provide organizations with greater flexibility and responsiveness potential, and it is this agility that, in turn, yields enhanced performance. In start-up firms, Welbourne and Andrews argued that core elements of the commitment strategy provide the firm with the structural cohesion necessary for continuous and rapid shifts. However, the authors were careful to note that their findings might not be applicable to larger, more established firms for which increased inertia may only make it more difficult to respond to environmental shifts. In larger firms, such inertia may provide greater long-term agility but may also limit short-term responsiveness. Thus, the authors concluded by asking not whether inertia is good or bad for large firms but rather "where inertia should be enhanced (i.e., at the corporate or business level)" (p. 913).

However, with the exception of the Welbourne and Andrews study, researchers have, for the most part, failed to search for additional or alternative explanations of the HR strategy-performance link. Thus, for example, we know little about the potential role of social capital (Burt, 1992), organizational capital (Tomer, 1987), and organizational citizenship (Organ, 1988) as potential mediators of the strategy-performance relationship. As Becker and Gerhart (1996) noted, without elaborating on the "black box between a firm's HR system and the firm's bottom line . . . [that is] without intervening variables, one is hard pressed both to explain how HR influences firm performance and to rule out an alternative explanation for an observed HR-firm performance link such as reverse causation" (p. 793).

Instead, perhaps because of Huselid's (1995) intriguing findings with regard to the role of internal and external fit, most strategy researchers have in recent years focused their attention on the role of strategic complementarities and contingencies not as *mediators* of the strategy-performance link but rather as potential *moderating* constructs. That is, rather than identifying the particular processes underlying the link between HR strategy and firm performance, re-searchers have turned their attention to gaining an understanding of the mecha-nisms by which this relationship is weakened or intensified. At the core of this research are three alternative theoretical perspectives, commonly referred to as the universalistic, contingency, and configurational approaches.

Universalistic, Contingency, and Configurational Explanations

Although all three of these perspectives are grounded on the assumptions and theories specified above regarding the link between strategy and perfor-mance, they differ in terms of the degree to which the assumed HR strategy ef-fect is likely to be moderated by internal and external fit and the way in which such a moderation effect may operate. Researchers adopting a universalistic perspective (see Osterman, 1995; Pfeffer, 1994; Terpstra & Rozell, 1993) argue that many of the HR practices (e.g., participation, incentive pay) that we have associated with the commitment strategy and that Huselid referred to as "high-performance work practices" are, on an individual basis, always better than comparative practices that we have associated with the other HR strategies dis-cussed and that their effects on firm performance are additive. Consequently, they claimed that all organizations, regardless of size, industry, or business strategy, should adopt these so-called "best practices."

Researchers adopting a contingency perspective (Lengnick-Hall & Lengnick-Hall, 1988; Schuler & Jackson, 1987) posit that the assumptions un-derlying the strategy-performance link are applicable only under conditions of high external fit (Baird & Meshoulam, 1988). That is, they claim that to have a significant, positive impact on firm performance, HR practices must be aligned with the organization's overall business strategy.

Finally, underlying the configurational approach is the assumption of "equifinality" (Doty, Glick, & Huber, 1993; Meyer, Tsui, & Hinings, 1993) and a focus on the system or pattern of interrelated HR practices. Theorists adopting the configurational approach posit that internal coherence among individual HR practices is key and that, assuming that these practices are internally consis-tent, combinations of HRM practices are likely to have larger effects on organi-zational outcomes than the sum of the component effects due to individual prac-tices (Ichniowski, Shaw, & Prennushi, 1994). Resource-based theory (Barney, 1991) provides an explanation for such equifinality effects. When a complex pattern or system of interrelated HR practices are in place in an organization, these strategic capabilities become even more difficult to imitate. Lacking an understanding of just how these practices and policies interact, competitors are less likely to be able to reproduce such synergies. Furthermore, many of these policies and practices may be path dependent (Becker & Gerhart, 1996), requiring that competitors replicate "socially complex elements such as culture and interpersonal relationships" (p. 782) before being able to implement particular elements of the complex web of interrelated HR practices. MacDuffie's (1995) finding that "bundles" of internally aligned HR practices have a more powerful positive impact on manufacturing performance supports this perspective.

Several studies have attempted to test comparatively the alternative hypotheses implicit in each of these three perspectives. In one of the most comprehensive of these analyses, Delery and Doty (1996) examined seven key HR practices consistent with what we referred to as the commitment strategy (e.g., use of internal labor markets, training, profit sharing) and tested hypotheses consistent with all three perspectives. According to the universalistic perspective, they proposed a direct, positive link between these seven practices and financial performance. In line with the contingency perspective, they posited that the positive link between these practices and financial performance would be moderated by the degree to which the behaviors elicited or encouraged by these practices were consistent with the organization's strategy. The greater the degree of alignment between business strategy and individual HR practices, the better the financial performance. Finally, they argued that according to the configurational perspective, it is the synergistic effect of configurations of internally consistent HR practices that explains the link between HR strategy and firm performance. Thus, at the most basic level, they proposed that a firm's performance would improve as a function of the degree to which its HR practices, as a group, were internally consistent and most similar to an ideal-type strategy (e.g., commitment, secondary). However, because external fit was also viewed as a moderator of the strategy-performance link, they posited that a given system of aligned HR practices would enhance firm performance only when that strategy was appropriate for or consistent with the firm's business strategy. Thus, the strategy-performance link is moderated not only by the degree of internal consistency among HR practices but also by the degree to which this configuration of practices is aligned with the organization's strategy.

Using a stratified random sample of over 1,000 banks, their analyses yielded results that provided strong support for the universalistic perspective and some support for both the contingency and configurational perspectives. In line with the human capital, motivational, and work structure assumptions presented at the beginning of this section, three individual HR practices (i.e., employment security, profit sharing, and results-oriented appraisals) were all found to have a strong, positive association with financial performance, regardless of the other practices in place and regardless of organizational strategy. Financial performance was found to be some 30% higher for banks one standard deviation above the mean on each of these three practice scales than for those banks at the mean (p. 825).

In line with the contingency perspective, three HR practices—performance appraisal, participation, and internal career opportunities—were found to be associated with higher levels of financial performance only when these practices were aligned with organizational strategy. Specifically, as Delery and Doty wrote:

> Banks that implemented a prospector strategy involving high innovation reaped greater returns from more results-oriented appraisals and lower levels of employee participation than did banks that relied on a defender strategy. Banks implementing a defender strategy performed better if they relied less on results-oriented appraisals and gave their officers higher levels of participation in decision making. (p. 826)

Finally, Delery and Doty found that the more closely a bank's HR strategy resembled what they referred to as a "market-type" system, the higher its performance, whereas the more closely it resembled their "internal system" (similar to what we described as a paternalistic strategy), the worse its financial performance. Specifically, a decrease in distance from the market-type system of one standard deviation from the mean was estimated to result in a 13% increase in financial performance (p. 827). Taken as a whole, Delery and Doty's findings suggest that although the behavioral-, agency-, and control-based assumptions underlying the link between HR strategy and firm performance may explain part of the strategy effect, a more complete understanding is not possible without taking contingency and configurational factors into account. Specifically, as Delery and Doty concluded, "Some HR practices are more appropriate under certain strategic conditions and less appropriate under others" (p. 829).

Consistent with Delery and Doty's conclusions, Youndt, Snell, Dean, and Lepak (1996) argued that the universalistic and contingency perspectives may not be mutually exclusive and may in fact be more complementary than competitive. Their study focused on the continuing debate over the value of "deskilling" as opposed to "upskilling" as a core element of a firm's HR strategy. Although the universalistic perspective suggests that HR strategies focused on "upskilling" will, regardless of an organization's strategic posture, produce significant returns for the firm, such a notion may be applicable only if we assume that all firms have an inherent interest in providing their employees with greater opportunities to contribute. Youndt et al. (1996) argued that this may be the case only for firms adopting a quality or flexibility-based manufacturing strategy. However, for organizations adopting a cost-based manufacturing strategy, such an assumption may not hold. Instead, such organizations may seek to reduce their labor force and lower wage levels by adopting mechanized production systems requiring lower skill levels and decision-making capabilities on the part of their remaining employees. Thus, they posited that the value of these two alternative strategies—an administrative strategy (similar to our secondary HR strategy) and a human capital-enhancing strategy (similar to our commitment strategy)—"ultimately rides on the particular manufacturing strategy a firm adopts" (p. 837). Therefore, in keeping with the universalistic perspective, they posited a main effect between HR strategy and firm performance in line with the universalistic perspective *as well as* a conditional effect on the part of manufacturing strategy as it relates to the link between HR strategy and firm performance, in keeping with the contingency perspective.

Using a sample of 97 industrial plants in Pennsylvania surveyed at two points in time, the researchers found support for both perspectives. Specifically, in line with the predictions of the universalistic perspective, a measure tapping the extent to which a plant's HR practices were consistent with a human capital enhancement (i.e., commitment) strategy was significantly associated with firm performance (e.g., productivity) and uniquely accounted for up to 14% of the variance in various performance measures. However, the conditional effects of manufacturing strategy on the HR strategy-performance link explained an additional 14% of the variance in these performance measures. Specifically, in the context of a cost-based manufacturing strategy, an administrative (i.e., secondary) HR strategy had a significant, positive association with firm performance, whereas, in the context of a quality-based manufacturing strategy, a human capital-enhancing (i.e., commitment) HR strategy had a significant positive association with firm performance. As the authors concluded, "Maximizing performance appears to depend on properly aligning HR systems with manufacturing strategy" (p. 853).

Finally, a recent study by Wright, McCormick, Sherman, and MacMahan (1998) provides some of the strongest support to date for the configurational perspective. Their study of HR practices in petrochemical refineries suggests that internal fit among these practices is crucial and that "HR practices derive their effectiveness from existing as a coherent and internally consistent system of practices" (p. 4). Specifically, they found that commitment-oriented selection, compensation, and appraisal practices were positively related to refinery financial performance only in those cases in which a highly participative work system was in place. These practices were inversely related to refinery performance when no such system was in place and employee participation was low. Moreover, refineries allowing employees to exercise discretionary behavior (e.g., activities, decision making) directed toward the achievement of organizationally relevant goals were found to exhibit superior performance only when a bundle of HR practices consistent with a commitment HR strategy (e.g., selective staffing, emphasis on training and development, contingent compensation) were implemented. Such findings are consistent with the control theory proposition that enhanced human capital and employee motivation are effective in boosting firm performance only when organizational work systems provide opportunities and mechanisms for employee contribution. Moreover, consistent with the configurational perspective, they point to the moderating role of internal consistency in explaining the link between HR strategy and firm performance.

Becker and Gerhart (1996) attempted to resolve this debate regarding the explanatory potential of these three main perspectives by arguing that it all depends on the level of analysis. They posited that to the extent that the universalistic notion of best practice is valid, it is likely to be so only at the highest level of the HR system. That is, as a set of guiding principles, there may be a set of universal or best HR practices—for example, valuing employee performance. However, how this universal principle is implemented is likely to be contingent on "appropriate firm-specific alignments" (p. 786). That is, practices designed to effect such a universal guiding principle are likely to vary at the operational or business level from firm to firm and will yield high performance at this level only to the extent to which they are aligned with one another and are consistent with the business unit's overall strategic profile. Thus, one explanation for the inconsistent findings with regard to the configurational perspective may have to do with the different levels of analysis (i.e., corporate vs. business level) at which such studies have been conducted. The authors explained inconsistent findings with regard to the configurational perspective by suggesting that strategic configurations may provide explanatory value only in terms of potentially complex, nonlinear, and often idiosyncratic interactions. This being the case, researchers using factor analysis to empirically identify strategic configurations may fail to capture the situational specificity of such configurations and end up mis-specifying key configurational components.

However, elsewhere, Gerhart, Trevor, and Graham (1996) provided an alternative explanation for these inconsistent findings and a strong resolution for the universalistic/contingency/configurational debate. They noted that although individual best practices may add basic value to the firm, they provide only a limited source of sustained competitive advantage because such practices are less difficult to imitate. Greater value may be created to the extent that firms are able to generate a complex system of integrated best practices that meet the unique business needs of the firm: that is, that offer a high degree of internal and external fit. A study by Huselid and Becker (1995) provides some basic inferential support for this notion, but as Becker and Gerhart (1996) suggested, research that more directly measures this best-practice-contingency continuum and its effects on firm performance "should be an important priority for future work" (p. 788).

One final explanation for the relatively weak findings regarding the contingency and configurational approaches may be that the benefits of external and internal strategic fit may be offset by reduced organizational flexibility. Wright and Snell (1998) argued that given managers' cognitive limitations as processors of information and decision makers, it cannot be assumed that managers will be able to match their HR strategies to actual (as opposed to perceived) organizational conditions, even if that is what they desire to do. Even if managers *are* able to correctly interpret weak signals regarding critical contextual conditions and even if they *do* have perfect knowledge regarding the cause-effect linkages between HR practices and the firm's ability to respond to such conditions, there is no guarantee that they will be able to design and implement the necessary changes in HR, let alone to do so in a timely manner. Consequently, Wright and Snell (1998) suggested that when HR strategies are so internally consistent that it is impossible to change one practice without threatening the entire web of interrelated practices, the organization's ability to respond to environmental shifts may be further constrained. If, as a result, the HR practices in use become increasingly misaligned with organizational demands, any positive impact of internal consistency on the HR strategy-performance relationship may be effectively negated.

The Challenges Ahead

In the discussion above, we have suggested that SHRM research needs to pay greater attention to the "black box" between HR strategy and firm performance. Specifically, researchers need to test more directly some of the assumptions underlying the strategy-performance link. Critical in this regard is the need to ascertain the causal relationship between HR strategy and firm performance. However, researchers also need to identify additional and alternative theories that might explain the strategy-performance relationship and test these theories against those discussed in our analysis in a competitive framework (Boxall, 1998). In addition, drawing from Becker and Gerhart (1996), we have suggested the need for multilevel analyses and alternative configurational frameworks designed to ascertain the degree to which the universal, contingency, and configurational approaches are competing as opposed to complementary. However, before SHRM researchers can turn to these important issues, a number of methodological and practical issues remain to be resolved.

Measurement Challenges

First, researchers need to better tailor their measures of effectiveness and HR practices to the particular context (Rogers & Wright, 1998). As Becker and Gerhart (1996) noted, metrics appropriate at the corporate level (e.g., market value) fail to provide an adequate standard for studies at the business unit level. Furthermore, the standard metrics of capital market value and profit fail to reflect organizational performance among firms striving to meet alternative objectives, such as increased market share, revenue growth, or technological innovation. HR strategies designed to meet profit goals, for example, may have an adverse impact on growth or market share objectives. The measurement of organizational effectiveness has long been debated in organizational theory (Perrow, 1961; Seashore & Yuchtman, 1967), and to assume that a given set of financial indicators reflects a consensus among all organizational constituencies regarding organizational goals is, to put it bluntly, somewhat naive.

However, measurement problems affect not only the dependent (or outcome) variables in the HR strategy-performance equation but also the independent (or predictor) variables. Different researchers not only focus on different practices (Becker & Gerhart, 1996; Dyer & Reeves, 1995) but also measure the implementation of these practices in different ways. For example, whereas

Huselid (1995) assessed the proportion of employees affected by a given practice (breadth of practice), Welbourne and Andrews (1996) used a Guttman-scale approach and focused on the degree to which certain practices were adopted (depth of practice). The fact that different researchers measure strategic HR practices in different ways makes it difficult to cumulate findings. This is only more the case in studies in which researchers identify some bundle, system, or strategic configuration of HR practices. Although these systems or strategies are, as noted in Chapter 3, comparable, they are far from identical. Even those strategic profiles or configurations identified empirically appear to vary from industry to industry and may in fact exist more in the minds or interpretations of the researchers than in reality. For example, incentive bonus plans were viewed by Arthur (1994) as a core component of the control strategy, whereas MacDuffie (1995) viewed this practice as characteristic of the "flexible" HR strategy. Until researchers come to some consensus as to the theoretical nature of ideal types of strategic configurations, it will be impossible to generate the standard metrics by which to capture empirically the relationship between such systems of practices and performance.

Third, affecting the measurement of both the independent and dependent variables in the strategy-performance equation is the relatively high potential for unreliability. Such random measurement error could significantly bias regression coefficients. As Becker and Gerhart (1996) noted, particularly where subjectivity or judgmental assessments are required, "future research would benefit from the use of multiple raters from each organization" (p. 795) and, we might add, the use of interrater reliability estimates as opposed to internal consistency-based estimates of reliability (i.e., Cronbach's alpha). The use of multiple raters would also reduce the risk of method bias when the same respondent was asked to provide data on both independent and dependent variables (particularly because there is often a strong social desirability incentive for a given respondent to report both the adoption of best practices and superior firm performance and because a respondent's affective state may influence his or her description of both practices and performance). In addition, effect estimates would most probably become more stable across studies if researchers replaced standard regression-based analytical approaches with LISREL-type models (which take random measurement error into account) (Gerhart, 1997).

Finally, researchers must take into account that measures taken at different levels of analysis (work group, plant, division, corporation) are likely to yield different results (Lepak & Snell, 1999a, 1999b). As Delery (1998) noted, "The key issue is that the constructs of interest must be measured at the appropriate level" (p. 295). As he pointed out, implicit in the research decision to average the use of practices across the organization is the possibly false assumption that all employee groups are equally important. Our argument, that there tends to exist a dominant HR strategy in most organizations, assumes that core strategic practices are applied across most of an organization's employees. Yet in any individual firm, such an approach should be viewed as being based on a working assumption requiring empirical validation.

Model Specification Problems

A second challenge facing researchers has to do with the enhancement of model specification. Specifically, three main specification errors remain to be addressed by researchers. The first and most critical specification error has already been discussed and has to do with the absence of critical mediating variables in models of HR strategy and firm performance. Structural equation models would facilitate the estimation of such mediational effects and would go a long way in helping researchers gain an understanding of the manner in which individual HR practices and systems or strategic configurations of such practices add value to the firm.

The second, as identified by Becker and Gerhart (1996) has to do with the inclusion of variables likely to co-vary with the HR system in models of the HR strategy-performance linkage. Such variables include the quality of management in parallel organizational systems, such as marketing and finance, and organizational capital structure. As Huselid and Becker (1996) noted, "There is considerable evidence that firm reputations for a wide range of management practices are highly correlated" (p. 403). Although many researchers successfully control for some of these exogenous variables, most fail to control for the bulk of them because such data are not always available (Becker & Gerhart, 1996, p. 795). Huselid and Becker (1996) claimed that an alternative means by which to account for the potential simultaneous occurrence of these other management practices is to use longitudinal data because such data provide an opportunity for a "cleaner" estimate of the true effects of HR strategies (p. 404). However, the advantages of longitudinal data in this case may be offset by an increased risk of measurement error, and Huselid and Becker (1996) concluded that the value of panel data sets to assess the HR strategy-performance link "can be legitimately questioned" (p. 420).

The third specification error has to do with the incorporation of temporal effects. Relatively few studies of the strategy-performance relationship are based on longitudinal data. Those that are still tend to include data on HR practices from only one point in time. This makes it impossible to ascertain the degree to which any shift in HR strategy or the adoption of new strategic practices over time may have a subsequent impact on firm performance. Indeed, until such longitudinal data are collected, it will be nearly impossible to determine which effect is stronger: HR strategy on performance or performance on HR strategy. Gerhart (1997) viewed this issue of causality as central to future SHRM research because "perceptions of HRM practices may be distorted (or influenced) by financial performance" (p. 17).

Similarly, by collecting longitudinal data on strategic HR practices, researchers will be able to uncover the potential feedback effects of one practice or system of practices on another. Knowledge of such feedback effects will provide important insights into the potentially path-dependent nature of HR strategy. In addition, longitudinal research designs will allow us to gain a better understanding of how the HRS-performance relationship may vary over the course of the organizational life cycle. Boxall (1998), for example, suggested that different "styles" of HR management are required as organizations move from the establishment phase to more mature and then decline and renewal contexts.

Finally, by collecting such longitudinal data, researchers will be able to more accurately estimate the potential implementation-to-benefit lag in the return stemming from shifts in HR strategy. For example, on the basis of such longitudinal data, Welbourne and Wright (1997) found that although managerial perceptions of human capital resources were inversely related to initial public offering price, within 3 years perceived human capital resources became the most powerful predictor of stock price. In an indirect "modest" test of this lag, Huselid and Becker (1996) found that high-performance work systems "begin to provide returns that are reflected in firm profitability and market value one to two years after implementation" (pp. 418-419). However, the degree to which this lag may be contingent on contextual conditions remains unknown, as does the magnitude of the impact over longer periods of time. The authors noted (p. 421) that panels 4 to 5 years old may be required "to fully specify this relationship."

Practical Challenges

Finally, HR researchers and practitioners alike must confront what Becker and Gerhart (1996) called a "major 'disconnect' " between what the research literature suggests and what firms should and actually do (p. 796). That is, a major challenge facing SHRM researchers is to make their research results meaningful to practitioners in the field. Although the results of the studies discussed above suggest that firms should have a significant incentive to adopt, at the very least, key strategic HR practices, such program adoption may be more complex than commonly assumed. First, the incentive to adopt such practices may be greatest among those having the most to gain and the least to lose, namely those firms exhibiting poor performance relative to their competitors (Bamberger & Fiegenbaum, 1996; Pil & MacDuffie, 1996). However, such firms are also likely to lack the necessary resources and complementarities (i.e., flexible production systems, highly developed management) required to implement such practices in an effective manner. Second, even among firms having the necessary resources and complementarities, organizational inertia (Hannan & Freeman, 1989; Snell & Dean, 1994), institutional (DiMaggio & Powell, 1983) and political (Bamberger & Fiegenbaum, 1996; Johns, 1993) pressures, and difficult-to-change managerial mental models or logics (Bacharach, Bamberger, & Sonnenstuhl, 1996; Pil & MacDuffie, 1996) may make it impossible for many firms to effectively manipulate individual HR practices, let alone entire HR systems. Indeed, in a recent study of HR practices, Huselid et al. (1997) found that U.S. firms are far more proficient in technical HR activities (such as monitoring employee safety and health and administering compensation and benefit systems) than in strategic HR practices such as developing employee empowerment and development programs and work systems restructuring (e.g., adoption of team-based approaches). Even more significantly, these researchers found the level of proficiency in strategic HR activities to be only modestly correlated with firm performance. If this is the case, simply increasing the proficiency of the HR function in strategic HR practices may be insufficient to create the effects identified by the studies reviewed above.

References

Abbott, A. (1993). The sociology of work and occupations. *Annual Review of Sociology, 19,* 187-209.

Abowd, J. M. (1990). Does performance based managerial compensation affect corporate performance? *Industrial and Labor Relations Review, 43,* 52S-73S.

Abrahamson, E. (1991). Managerial fads and fashions: The diffusion and rejection of innovations. *Academy of Management Review, 16,* 586-612.

Ackermann, K. F. (1986). *A contingency model of HRM strategy: Empirical research findings reconsidered.* Paper presented at the European Institute for Advanced Studies in Management Workshop on Strategic Human Resources Management, Brussels.

Adams, J. S. (1963). Toward an understanding of inequity. *Journal of Abnormal and Social Psychology, 67,* 442-436.

Analog Devices, Inc. (1993). *Corporate objectives* (Case Nos. 9-181-001/002 and 9-183-019). Norwood, MA: Harvard Business School.

Armstrong, S. M. (1994). Coping with transition: A study of layoff survivors. *Journal of Organizational Behavior, 15,* 597-621.

Arthur, J. B. (1992). The link between business strategy and industrial relations systems in American steel minimills. *Industrial and Labor Relations Review, 45,* 488-506.

Arthur, J. (1994). Effects of human resource systems on manufacturing performance and turnover. *Academy of Management Journal, 37,* 670-687.

Axelrod, R. (1984). *The evolution of cooperation.* New York: Basic Books.

Bacharach, S. B., & Bamberger, P. (1995). When working smarter isn't enough: Job resources inadequacy and individual performance at work. *Human Resource Management Review, 5*(2), 79-102.

Bacharach, S. B., Bamberger, P., & Conley, S. (1991). Negotiating the see-saw of managerial strategy: A resurrection of the study of professionals in organizational theory. *Research in the Sociology of Organizations, 8,* 217-240.

186

Bacharach, S. B., Bamberger, P. A., & Sonnenstuhl, W. J. (1994). *Member assistance programs: The role of labor in the prevention and treatment of substance abuse.* Ithaca, NY: ILR Press.

Bacharach, S. B., Bamberger, P., & Sonnenstuhl, W. J. (1996a). Member assistance programs: An emergent phenomenon in industrial relations. *Industrial Relations, 35,* 261-275.

Bacharach, S. B., Bamberger, P., & Sonnenstuhl, W. J. (1996b). The organizational transformation process: Dissonance reduction and logic of action. *Administrative Science Quarterly, 41,* 477-506.

Bacharach, S. B., & Lawler, E. J. (1980). *Power and politics in organizations.* San Francisco: Jossey-Bass.

Bacharach, S. B., & Shedd, J. (1999). *Institutional change in exchange relations* (Working Paper). Ithaca, NY: Cornell University, Department of Organizational Behavior.

Baird, L., & Meshoulam, I. (1988). Managing two fits of strategic human resources management, *Academy of Management Review, 13*(1), 116-128.

Baird, L. L., Meshoulam, I., & DeGive, G. (1983). Meshing human resources planning with strategic business planning: A model approach. *Personnel, 60*(5), 14-25.

Balkin, D. B., & Gomez-Mejia, L. R. (1984). Determinants of R&D compensation strategies in the high tech industry. *Personnel Psychology, 37,* 635-650.

Balkin, D. B., & Gomez-Mejia, L. R. (1986). A contingency theory of compensation. In S. Rynes & G. T. Milkovich (Eds.), *Current issues in human resource management.* Plano, TX: Business Publications.

Balkin, D. B., & Gomez-Mejia, R. L. (1990). Matching compensation and organizational strategies. *Strategic Management Journal, 11,* 153-169.

Bamberger, P. (1991). Re-inventing innovation theory: Critical issues in the conceptualization, measurement, and analysis of technological innovation. *Research in the Sociology of Organizations, 9,* 265-294.

Bamberger, P. A., Bacharach, S. B., & Dyer, L. (1989). HR management and organizational effectiveness: High technology entrepreneurial startup firms in Israel. *Human Resource Management, 28,* 349-366.

Bamberger, P., & Donahue, L. (In press). Employee discharge and reinstatement: Using moral hazard and reintegrative shaming theories to help explain the mixed consequences of last chance agreements. *Industrial and Labor Relations Review, 53.*

Bamberger, P., & Erev, I. (1999). *The social consequences of peer evaluation* (Working Paper). Haifa, Israel: Technion, Faculty of Industrial Engineering and Management.

Bamberger, P. A., & Fiegenbaum, F. A. (1996). The role of strategic reference points in explaining the nature and consequences of human resources strategy, *Academy of Management Review, 21,* 926-958.

Bamberger, P., Kluger, A., & Suchard, R. (1999). The antecedents and consequences of union commitment: A meta-analysis. *Academy of Management Journal, 42,* 304-318.

Bamberger, P. A., & Phillips, B. (1991). Organizational environment versus business strategy: Parallel versus conflicting influences on HR strategy. *Human Resources Management, 30,* 153-182.

Bandura, A. (1986). *Social foundations of thoughts and actions: A social cognitive theory.* Englewood Cliffs, NJ: Prentice Hall.

Barkema, H. G., & Gomez-Mejia, L. R. (1998). Managerial compensation and firm performance: A general research framework. *Academy of Management Journal, 41,* 135-145.

Barley, S. R., & Kunda, G. (1992). Design and devotion: Surges of rational and normative ideologies of control in managerial discourse. *Administrative Science Quarterly, 37,* 363-399.

Barney, J. B. (1986). Organizational culture: Can it be a source of sustained competitive advantage? *Academy of Management Review, 11,* 656-665.

Barney, J. B. (1991). Firm resources and sustained competitive advantage. *Journal of Management, 17,* 99-120.

Barney, O., & Smith, S. (1989). *Flexible workplace.* New York, NY: Amacom.

Baron, J. N., Davis-Blake, A., & Bielby, W. (1986). The structure of opportunity: How promotion ladders vary within and among organizations. *Administrative Science Quarterly, 31,* 248-273.

Baron, J. N., & Kreps, D. M. (1999). *Strategic human resources: Frameworks for general managers.* New York: John Wiley.

Barrick, M. R., & Mount, M. K. (1991). The big five-personality dimensions and job performance: A meta-analysis. *Personnel Psychology, 44,* 1-26.

Becker, B., & Gerhart, B. (1996). The impact of HRM on organizational performance: Progress and prospects. *Academy of Management Journal, 39,* 779-801.

Becker, B., & Huselid, M. (1992). The incentive effects of tournament compensation schemes. *Administrative Science Quarterly, 37,* 336-350.

Becker, S. G. (1964). *Human capital.* New York: Columbia University Press.

Becker, S. G. (1975). *Human capital.* Chicago: University of Chicago Press.

Beer, M., Spector, B., Lawrence, P. R., Mills, D. Q., & Walton, R. E. (1984). *Managing human assets: The groundbreaking Harvard Business School program.* New York: Free Press.

Beer, M., Spector, B., Lawrence, P. R., Mills, D. Q., & Walton, R. E. (1985). *Human resource management.* New York: Free Press.

Bennis, W. (1985). Foreword. In D. McGregor (Ed.), *The human side of enterprise* (pp. iv-viii). New York: McGraw-Hill.

Bernardin, H. J., & Klatt, L. A. (1986, November). Managerial appraisal systems: Has practice caught up to the state of the art. *Personnel Administrator,* pp. 79-86.

Blalock, H. M. (1969). *Theory construction: From verbal to mathematical formulation.* Englewood Cliffs, NJ: Prentice Hall.

Blau, P. M. (1968). The hierarchy of authority in organizations. *American Journal of Sociology, 73,* 453-467.

Blauner, R. (1964). Alienation and freedom. Chicago: University of Chicago Press.

Bloom, M., & Milkovich, G. T. (1998a). Relationships among risk, incentive pay, and organizational performance. *Academy of Management Journal, 41,* 283-297.

Bloom, M., & Milkovich, G. T. (1998b, January-February). Rethinking international compensation. *Compensation and Benefits Review, 30,* 15-23.

Borman, W. C., & Motowidlo, S. J. (1992). Expanding the criterion domain to include elements of contextual performance. In N. Schmitt & W. C. Borman (Eds.), *Personnel selection* (Vol. 4). San Francisco: Jossey-Bass.

Boudreau, J. W. (1991). Utility analysis in human resource management decisions. In M. D. Dunnette & L. M. Hought (Eds.), *Handbook of industrial and organizational psychology* (2nd ed., Vol. 2, pp. 621-745). Palo Alto, CA: Consulting Psychologists Press.

Boxall, P. (1998). Achieving competitive advantage through human resource strategy: Toward a theory of industry dynamics. *Human Resource Management Review, 8,* 265-288.

Brandes, S. (1970). *American welfare capitalism.* Chicago: University of Chicago Press.

Braverman, H. (1974). *Labor and monopoly capitalism: The degradation of work in the twentieth century.* New York: Monthly Review Press.

Breaugh, J. A. (1981). Relationships between recruiting sources and employee performance, absenteeism, and work attitudes. *Academy of Management Journal, 24,* 142-147.

Broderick, R. F. (1986). *Pay policy and business strategy: Toward a measure of fit.* Unpublished doctoral dissertation, Cornell University.

Brown, K., & Huber, V. (1992). Lowering floors and raising ceilings: A longitudinal assessment of the effects of an earning-at-risk plan on pay satisfaction. *Personnel Psychology, 45,* 279-311.

Burack, E. (1986, Summer). Corporate business and human resource planning practices: Strategic issues and concerns. *Organizational Dynamics, 15,* 73-78.

Burt, R. S. (1992). *Structural holes: The social structure of competition.* Cambridge, MA: Harvard University Press.

Caldwell, D. F., & Spivey, W. A. (1983). The relationship between the recruiting source and employee success: An analysis by race. *Personnel Psychology, 36,* 67-72.

Cappelli, P., & Sherer, P. D. (1991). Managerial promotion: The effect of socialization, specialization and gender. *Industrial and Labor Relations Review, 42,* 77-88.

Cappelli, P., & Singh, H. (1992). Integrating strategic human resources and strategic management. In D. Lewin, O. S. Mitchell, & P. Sherer (Eds.), *Research frontiers in IR and HR* (pp. 165-192). Madison, WI: Industrial Relations Research Association.

Carroll, S. J. (1987). Business strategies and compensation systems. In D. B. Balkin & L. R. Gomez-Mejia (Eds.), *New perspectives on compensation.* Englewood Cliffs, NJ: Prentice Hall.

Cascio, W. F. (1990). Human resources management in high technology industry. In L. R. Gomez-Mejia & M. W. Lawless (Eds.), *Organizational issues in high technology management* (Vol. 11, pp. 179-198). Greenwich, CT: JAI.

Cascio, W. F. (1991). *Costing human resources: The financial impact of behavior in organizations,* Boston: PWS-Kent.

Chachere, D. R., & Feuille, P. (1993). Grievance procedures and due process in nonunion workplaces. In J. F. Burton (Ed.), *Proceedings of the forty-fifth annual meeting of the Industrial Relations Research Association* (pp. 446-455). Madison, WI: Industrial Relations Research Association.

Chakravarthy, B. S., & Doz, Y. (1992). Strategy process research: Focusing on corporate self-renewal. *Strategic Management Journal, 13,* 5-14.

Chandler, A. (1962). *Strategy and structure.* Cambridge, MA: Harvard University Press.

Chinoy, E. (1992). *Automobile workers and the American dream* (2nd ed.). Urbana: University of Illinois Press.

Cohen, Y., & Pfeffer, J. (1986). Organizational hiring standards. *Administrative Science Quarterly, 31*(3), 1-24.

Conyon, M. J., & Peck, S. I. (1998). Board control, remuneration committees, and top management compensation. *Academy of Management Journal, 41,* 146-157.

Coombs, G., Jr., & Gomez-Mejia, L. G. (1991). Cross functional compensation strategies in high technology firms. *Compensation Review, 23,* 40-49.

Cooper, W. H., Graham, W. J., & Dyke, L. S. (1993). Tournament players. In G. R. Ferris (Ed.), *Research in personnel and human resource management* (Vol. 2, pp. 83-132). Greenwich, CT: JAI.

Covaleski, M. A., Dirsmith, M. W., Heian, J. B., & Samuel, S. (1998). The calculated and the avowed: Techniques of discipline and struggles over identity in six big public accounting firms. *Administrative Science Quarterly, 43,* 293-327.

Cutcher-Gershenfeld, J. (1991). The impact on economic performance of a transformation in industrial relations. *Industrial and Labor Relations Review, 44,* 241-260.

Davis-Blake, A., & Uzzi, B. (1993). Determinants of employment externalization: A study of temporary workers and independent contractors. *Administrative Science Quarterly, 38,* 195-223.

Dawes, R. (1980). Social dilemmas. *Annual Review of Psychology, 31,* 161-193.

Deal, T. E., & Kennedy, A. A. (1982). *Corporate culture: The rites and rituals of corporate life.* Reading, MA: Addison Wesley.

Delery, J. E. (1998). Issues of fit in SHRM: Implications for research. *Human Resource Management Review, 8,* 289-309.

Delery, J. E., & Doty, H. D. (1996). Modes of theorizing in strategic human resources management: Tests of universalistic, contingency, and configurational performance predictions. *Academy of Management Journal, 39,* 802-835.

Demanpour, F. (1991). Organizational innovation: A meta-analysis of effects of determinants and moderators. *Academy of Management Review, 34,* 555-590.

Dertouzos, J. N., Holland, E., & Ebener, P. (1988. *The legal and economic consequences of wrongful termination.* Santa Monica, CA: Rand Corporation.

DiMaggio, P. J., & Powell, W. W. (1983). The iron cage revisited: Institutional isomorphism and collective rationality in organizational fields. *American Sociological Review, 35,* 147-160.

Dobbin, F. R., Edeman, L., Meyer, J. W., Scott, W. R., & Swidler, A. (1988). The expansion of due process in organizations. In L. G. Zucker (Ed.), *Institutional patterns and organizations: Culture and environment* (pp. 71-98). Cambridge, MA: Ballinger.

Doeringer, P. B., & Piore, M. J. (1971). *Internal labor markets and manpower analysis.* Lexington, MA: Heath Lexington.

Doty, D. H., & Glick, W. H. (1994). Typologies as a unique form of theory building: Toward improved understanding and modeling. *Academy of Management Review, 19,* 230-251.

Doty, D. H., Glick, W. H., & Huber, G. P. (1993). Fit, equifinality and organizational effectiveness: A test of two configurational theories. *Academy of Management Journal, 36,* 1196-1250.

Dreher, G. F., & Kendall, D. W. (1995). Organizational staffing. In G. R. Ferris, S. D. Rosen, & D. T. Barnum (Eds.), *Handbook of human resource management* (pp. 446-461). Cambridge, MA: Blackwell.

Durkheim, E. (1951). *Suicide.* Glencoe, IL: Free Press. (Original work published 1897)

Dyer, L. (1983). Bringing human resources into the strategy formulation process. *Human Resources Management, 22,* 257-271.

Dyer, L. (1984). Studying human resource strategy: An approach and an agenda. *Industrial Relations, 23,* 153-169.

Dyer, L. (1985). Strategic human resources management and planning. In K. Rowland & G. Ferris (Eds.), *Research in personnel and human resources management* (Vol. 3, pp. 1-30). Greenwich, CT: JAI.

Dyer, L., & Blancero, D. (1993). *Workplace 2000: A delphi study* (Working Paper). Ithaca, NY: Cornell University, Center for Advanced Human Resource Studies.

Dyer, L., & Holder, G. W. (1988). A strategic perspective of human resources management. In L. Dyer & G. W. Holder (Eds.), *Human resources management: Evolving roles and responsibilities* (pp. 1-45). Washington, DC: American Society for Personnel Administration.

Dyer, L., & Reeves, T. (1995). HR strategies and firm performance: What do we know and where do we need to go? *International Journal of Human Resource Management, 6,* 656-670.

Edwards, R. (1979). *Contested terrain: The transformation of the workplace in the twentieth century.* New York: Basic Books.

Eisenhardt, K. M. (1985). Control: Organizational and economic approaches. *Management Science, 31,* 134-149.

Eisenhardt, K. M. (1989). Agency theory: An assessment and review. *Academy of Management Review, 14,* 57-74.

Ellis, R. J. (1982). Improving management response in turbulent times. *Sloan Management Review, 23*(2), 3-12.

Etzioni, A. (1961). *A comparative analysis of complex organizations.* New York: Free Press.

Fama, E. F., & Jensen, M. C. (1983). Agency problems and residual claims. *Journal of Law and Economics, 26,* 327-349.

Faulkner, D., & Johnson, G. (1992). *The challenge of strategic management.* London: Kegan Paul.

Fay, C. H. (1987). Using the strategic planning process to develop a compensation strategy. *Topics in Total Compensation, 2,* 117-128.

Fennel, M. L. (1984). Synergy, influence and information in the adoption of administrative innovations. *Academy of Management Journal, 27,* 113-129.

Ferris, G. R., Arthur, M. M., Berkson, H. M., Kaplan, D. M., Harrell-Cook, G., & Fink, G. (1998). Toward a social context theory of the human resource management-organizational effectiveness relationship. *Human Resource Management Review, 8,* 235-264.

Ferris, G. R., & Judge, T. A. (1991). Personnel/human resource management: A political influence perspective. *Journal of Management, 17,* 1-42.

Ferris, G. R., Schellenberg, D. A., & Zammuto, R. F. (1984). Human resource management strategies in declining industries. *Human Resources Management, 23,* 381-394.

Feuille, P., & Hildebrand, R. L. (1995). Grievance procedures and dispute resolution. In G. R. Ferris, S. D. Rosen, & D. T. Barnum (Eds.), *Handbook of human resource management* (pp. 340-369). Cambridge, MA: Blackwell.

Flamholtz, E. G. (1985). *Human resource accounting* (2nd ed.). San Francisco: Jossey-Bass.

Flamholtz, E., & Lacey, J. (1981). *Personnel management: Human capital theory and human resource accounting.* Los Angeles: University of California at Los Angeles, Institute of Industrial Relations.

Flannery, T. P., Hofrichter, D. A., & Platten, P. E. (1996). *People, performance and pay.* New York: Free Press.

Folger, R., & Konovsky, M. (1989). Effects of procedural and distributive justice on reaction to pay raise decisions. *Academy of Management Journal, 32,* 115-130.

Fombrun, C. (1982). Conversation with Reginald H. Jones and Frank Doyle. *Organizational Dynamics, 10,* 42-63.

Fombrun, C., Tichy, N. M., & Devanna, M. A. (1984). *Strategic human resources management.* New York: John Wiley.

Forbes, J. B., & Wertheim, S. E. (1995). Promotion, succession and career planning systems. In G. R. Ferris, S. D. Rosen, & D. T. Barnum (Eds.), *Handbook of human resource management* (pp. 494-510). Cambridge, MA: Blackwell.

Foulkes, F. K. (1980). *Personnel policies in large nonunion companies.* Englewood Cliffs, NJ: Prentice Hall.

Freeman, R. B. (1985). *The new look in wage policy and industrial relations* (Conference Board Research Rep. No. 865). New York: Conference Board.

Freeman, R. B., & Kleiner, M. M. (1990). The impact of new unionization on wages and working conditions. *Journal of Labor Economics, 8,* S8-S25.

Freeman, R. B., & Medoff, J. L. (1984). *What do unions do?* New York: Basic Books.

Galbraith, J. (1977). *Organizational design.* Reading, MA: Addison-Wesley.

Galbraith, J., & Nathanson, D. (1978). *Strategy implementation: The role of structure and process.* St. Paul, MN: West.

Gerhart, B. (1990). Gender differences in current and starting salaries: The role of performance, college major and job title. *Industrial and Labor Relations Review, 43,* 418-433.

Gerhart, B. (1997, October). *Human resource management and firm performance: Challenges in making causal inferences.* Paper presented at the Conference on Research and Theory in Strategic Human Resource Management: An Agenda for the 21st Century, Ithaca, NY.

Gerhart, B., & Milkovich, G. T. (1992). Employee compensation: Research and practice. In H. C. Triandis, M. D. Dunnette, & L. M. Hough (Eds.), *Handbook of industrial and organizational psychology* (Vol. 3, pp. 481-569). Palo Alto, CA: Consulting Psychologists Press.

Gerhart, B., & Trevor, O. (1996). Employment variability under different managerial compensation systems *Academy of Management Journal, 39,* 1692-1709.

Gerhart, B., Trevor, O., & Graham, M. (1996). New directions in employee compensation research. *Research in Personnel and Human Resource Management, 14,* 143-203.

Gerstein, M., & Reisman, H. (1983). Strategic selection: Matching executive to business conditions. *Sloan Management Review, 24,* 33-49.

Gibbons, R., & Katz, L. F. (1991). Layoffs and lemons. *Journal of Labor Economics, 9,* 351-380.

Gomez-Mejia, L. R. (1992). Structure and process of diversification, compensation strategy, and firm performance. *Strategic Management Journal, 13,* 381-398.

Gomez-Mejia, L. R., & Balkin, D. B. (1989). Effectiveness of individual and aggregate compensation strategies. *Industrial Relations, 28,* 431-445.

Gomez-Mejia, L. R., & Balkin, D. B. (1992a). *Compensation, organization strategy and firm performance.* Cincinnati, OH: Southwestern.

Gomez-Mejia, L. R., & Balkin, D. B. (1992b). Determinations of faculty pay: An agency theory perspective theory. *Academy of Management Journal, 35,* 921-955.

Gomez-Mejia, L. R., Balkin, D. B., & Milkovich, G. T. (1990). Rethinking your rewards for technical employees. *Organizational Dynamics, 18*(4), 62-75.

Gomez-Mejia, L. R., & Welbourne, T. (1988). Compensation strategy: An overview and future step. *Human Resources Planning, 11,* 173-189.

Gomez-Mejia, L. R., & Welbourne, T. (1991). Compensation strategies in global context. *Human Resource Planning, 14,* 29-41.

Goodman, W. (1995). Boom in day care industry the result of many social changes. *Monthly Labor Review, 118,* 3-12.

Goodmeasure, Inc. (1985). *The changing American workplace: Work alternatives in the '80s.* New York: American Management Association

Goodstein, J. (1994). Institutional pressures and strategic responsiveness: Employer involvement in work-family issues. *Academy of Management Journal, 37,* 350-382.

Gouldner, A. (1957). Cosmopolitans and locals: Toward an analysis of latent social roles. I. *Administrative Science Quarterly, 2,* 281-306.

Greenberg, J. (1990). Looking fair versus being fair: Management of impressions of organizational justice. *Research in Organizational Behavior, 12,* 111-157.

Greer, C. R., & Stedham, Y. (1989). Counter-cyclical hiring as a staffing strategy for managerial and professional personnel: An empirical investigation. *Journal of Management, 15,* 425-440.

Guthrie, J. P., Grimm, C. M., & Smith, G. K. (1991). Environmental changes and management staffing: An empirical study. *Journal of Management, 17,* 735-748.

Guzzo, R. A., Jette, R. D., & Katzell, R. A. (1985). The effect of psychologically based intervention programs in worker productivity: A meta analysis. *Personnel Psychology, 38,* 275-291.

Hackman, J. R., & Oldham, G. R. (1980). *Work redesign.* Reading, MA: Addison-Wesley.

Hambrick, D. C., & Snow, C. C. (1989). Strategic reward system. In C. C. Snow (Ed.), *Strategy, organization design and human resource management.* Greenwich, CT: JAI.

Hannan, M. T., & Freeman, J. (1989). *Organizational ecology.* Cambridge, MA: Harvard University Press.

Hannon, J. M., Huang, I. C., & Jaw, B. S. (1995). International human resource strategy and its determinants in Taiwan. *Journal of International Business Studies, 26,* 531-554.

Hartwell, T. D., Steele, P., French, M. T., Potter, F. J., Rodman, N., & Zarkin, G. A. (1996). Aiding the troubled employees: The prevalence, cost and characteristics of employee assistance programs in the United States. *American Journal of Public Health, 85,* 83-106.

Hogler, R. L. (1993). Employee involvement and Electromation, Inc.: An analysis and a proposal for statutory change. *Labor Law Journal, 44,* 261-274.

Huselid, M. A. (1995). The impact of human resource management practices on turnover, productivity and corporate financial performance. *Academy of Management Journal, 38,* 635-672.

Huselid, M. A., & Becker, B. (1995, August). *High performance work systems and organizational performance.* Paper presented at the annual meeting of the Academy of Management, Vancouver, British Columbia.

Huselid, M. A., & Becker, B. E. (1996). Methodological issues in cross-sectional and panel estimates of the human resource-firm performance link. *Industrial Relations, 35,* 400-422.

Huselid, M. A., & Becker, B. (1997, August). *The impact of high performance work system implementation effectiveness and alignment with strategy on shareholder wealth.* Paper presented at the annual meeting of the Academy of Management, Boston.

Huselid, M. A., Jackson, S. E., & Schuler, R. S. (1997). Technical and strategic human resource management effectiveness as determinates of firm performance. *Academy of Management Journal, 40,* 171-188.

Hyland, S. (1990). Helping employees with family care. *Monthly Labor Review, 117,* 37-39.

Ichniowski, C., Shaw, K., & Prennushi, G. (1994). *The impact of human resource management practices on productivity* (Working Paper 15). New York: Columbia University, Columbia Business School.

Jackson, S. E., & Schuler, R. S. (1995). The need for understanding human resources management in the context of organizations and their environment. *Annual Review of Psychology, 46,* 237-264.

Jackson, S. E., Schuler, R. S., & Rivero, J. C. (1989). Organizational characteristics as predictors of personnel practices. *Personnel Psychology, 42,* 727-786.

Jacoby, S. M. (1985). *Employing bureaucracy: Managers, unions and the transformation of work in American industry, 1900-1945.* New York: Columbia University Press.

Jaques, E. (1990). In praise of hierarchies. *Harvard Business Review, 68,* 127-133.

Jarrell, D. W. (1993). *Human resources planning: A business planning approach.* Englewood Cliffs, NJ: Prentice Hall.

Johns, G. (1993). Constraints on the adaptation of psychology-based personnel practices: Lessons from organizational innovation. *Personnel Psychology, 46,* 569-592.

Kahneman, D., & Tversky, A. (1979). Prospects theory: An analysis of decisions under risk. *Econometrica, 47,* 262-291.

Kanter, R. M. (1984). Variation in managerial career structures in high technology firms: The impact of organization characteristics on internal labor market patterns. In P. Osterman (Ed.), *Internal labor markets* (pp. 109-131). Cambridge: MIT Press.

Katz, D., & Kahn, R. (1978). *The social psychology of organizations.* New York: John Wiley.

Katz, H. C. (1985). *Shifting gears.* Cambridge: MIT Press.

Kaufman, R. T. (1992). The effects of improshare on productivity. *Industrial and Labor Relations Review, 45,* 311-322.

Kerr, J. (1982). Assigning managers on the basis of life cycle. *Journal of Business Strategy, 2*(4), 58-65.

Kerr, J. L., & Jackofsky, E. F. (1989). Aligning managers with strategies: Management development versus selection. *Strategic Management Journal, 10,* 157-190.

Kerr, J. L., & Slocum, J. W., Jr. (1987). Managing corporate culture through reward systems. *Academy of Management Executive, 1,* 99-108.

Ketchen, D. J., Thomas, J. B., & Snow, C. C. (1993). Organizational configurations and performance: A comparison of theoretical approaches. *Academy of Management Journal, 36,* 1278-1313.

Kirman, J. P., Farley, J. A., & Geisinger, K. F. (1989). The relationship between recruiting source, applicant quality, and hire performance: An analysis by sex, ethnicity, and age. *Personnel Psychology, 42,* 293-308.

Koch, M. J., & McGrath, R. G. (1996). Improving labor productivity: Human resource management policies do matter. *Strategic Management Journal, 17,* 335-354.

Kochan, T. A. (1997, October). *Human resources and the changing social contract.* Paper presented at the Conference on Research and Theory in Strategic Human Resources Management: An Agenda for the 21st Century, Ithaca, NY.

Kochan, T. A., Katz, H. C., & McKersie, R. B. (1986). *The transformation of American industrial relations.* New York: Basic Books.

Kogut, B., & Zander, U. (1992). Knowledge of the firm, combinative capabilities, and the replication of technology. *Organization Science, 3,* 383-397.

Kossek, E. E. (1987). Human resource management innovation. *Human Resource Management, 26*(1), 71-92.

Kravetz, D. J. (1988). *The human resource revolution: Implementing progressive management practices for bottom-line success.* San Francisco: Jossey-Bass.

Kruse, D. L. (1983). *Profit sharing: Does it make a difference?* Kalamazoo, MI: Upjohn Institute.

Kunda, G. (1992). *Engineering culture: Control and commitment in a high technology corporation.* Philadelphia: Temple University Press.

LaBelle, C. M. (1983). *Human resources strategic decisions as responses to environmental challenges.* Unpublished master's thesis, Cornell University.

Lado, A. A., & Wilson, M. (1994). HR systems and sustained competitive advantage: A competency-based perspective. *Academy of Management Review, 19,* 699-727.

Lawler, E. E., III. (1986). What's wrong with point factor job evaluation. *Compensation and Benefits Review, 19,* 20-28.

Lawler, E. E., III. (1990). *Strategic pay.* San Francisco: Jossey-Bass.

Lawler, E. E., III. (1994). From job-based to competency-based organizations. *Journal of Organizational Behavior, 15,* 3-15.

Lawler, E. E., III, Mohrman, S., & Ledford, G. E., Jr. (1992, September). The Fortune 1000 and total quality. *Journal for Quality and Participation.*

Lawler, E. J., & Yoon, J. (1995). Network structure and emotion in exchange relations. *American Sociological Review, 63,* 871-894.

Ledford, G. E. (1991, March-April). The case studies of skill based pay: An overview. *Compensation and Benefits Review, 23,* 11-23.

Lengnick-Hall, C. A., & Lengnick-Hall, M. L. (1988). Strategic human resources management: A review of the literature and a proposed typology. *Academy of Management Review, 12,* 454-470.

Leontiades, M. (1982). Choosing the right manager to fit the strategy. *Journal of Business Strategy, 2,* 58-69.

Leontiades, M. (1983). A diagnostic framework for planning. *Strategic Management Journal, 4*(1), 11-26.

Lepak, D. P., & Snell, S. A. (1999a, August). *Examining the human resource architecture: The moderating effects of strategic orientation.* Paper presented at the annual meeting of the Academy of Management, Chicago.

Lepak, D. P., & Snell, S. A. (1999b). The strategic management of human capital: Determinants and implications of different relationships. *Academy of Management Review, 24*(1), 1-18.

Lundy, O., & Cowling, M. (1996). *Strategic human resource management.* London: Routledge.

MacDuffie, J. P. (1995). Human resource bundles and manufacturing performance: Organizational logic and flexible production systems in the world of auto industry. *Industrial and Labor Relations Review, 48,* 197-221.

Mahoney, J. (1992). The choice of organizational form: Vertical financial ownership versus other methods of vertical integration. *Strategic Management Journal, 13,* 559-584.

Maier, H. (1982). Innovation, efficiency and the quantitative and qualitative demand for human resources. *Technological Forecasting and Social Change, 21,* 15-31.

March, J., & Simon, H. (1958). *Organizations.* New York: John Wiley.

Mason, N. A., & Belt, J. A. (1985, August). *Effectiveness of specificity in recruitment advertising.* Paper presented at the 45th annual meeting of the Academy of Management, San Diego, CA.

Matusik, S. F., & Hill, C. W. L. (1998). The utilization of contingent work, knowledge creation and competitive advantage. *Academy of Management Review, 23,* 680-697.

Mayo, E. (1945). *The social problems of an industrial civilization.* Cambridge, MA: Harvard Business School.

McAdams, J. L., & Hawk, E. J. (1994). *Organizational performance and rewards.* Phoenix, AZ: American Compensation Association.

McEvoy, G. M., & Cascio, W. F. (1985). Strategies for reducing employee turnover: A meta-analysis. *Journal of Applied Psychology, 70,* 342-353.

Meyer, A. D., Tsui, A. S., & Hinings, C. B. (1993). Configurational approaches to organizational analysis. *Academy of Management Journal, 36,* 1175-1195.

Meyer, J. W., & Rowan, B. (1977). Institutionalized organizations: Formal structure and myth and ceremony. *American Journal of Sociology, 83,* 340-363.

Miles, E. R., & Snow, C. C. (1978). Designing strategic human resources systems. In R. Miles & C. Snow (Eds.), *Organization strategy, structure and process.* New York: McGraw-Hill.

Miles, E. R., & Snow, C. C. (1984). Designing strategic human resources systems. *Organizational Dynamics, 16,* 36-52.

Milkovich, G. T., & Boudreau, J. W. (1991). *Human resource management* (6th ed.). Homewood, IL: D. Irwin.

Milkovich, G. T., & Newman, J. M. (1996). *Compensation.* Chicago: D. Irwin.

Miller, T. I. (1984). The effects of employer-sponsored child care on employee absenteeism, turnover, productivity, recruitment or job satisfaction: What is claimed and what is known. *Personnel Psychology, 37,* 277-289.

Mintzberg, H. (1978). Patterns of strategy formation. *Management Science, 24,* 934-948.

Mintzberg, H. (1979). *The structure of management.* Englewood Cliffs, NJ: Prentice Hall.

Mintzberg, H. (1987, July-August). Crafting strategy. *Harvard Business Review, 65,* 66-75.

Mintzberg, H. (1990). The design school: Reconsidering the basic premises of strategic management. *Strategic Management Journal, 11,* 171-195.

Mintzberg, H., & Waters, A. (1982). Tracking strategy in an entrepreneurial firm. *Academy of Management Journal, 25,* 465-499.

Mishel, L., & Voos, P. B. (1992). Unions and American economic competitiveness. In L. Mishel & P. B. Voos (Eds.), *Unions and economic competitiveness* (pp. 1-12). Armonk, NY: M. E. Sharpe.

Murphy, K. J. (1985). Corporate performance and managerial remuneration: An empirical analysis. *Journal of Accounting and Economics, 7,* 11-42.

Murphy, K., & Cleveland, J. (1995). *Understanding performance appraisal: Social, organizational and goal-based perspectives.* Thousand Oaks, CA: Sage.

Murray, B., & Gerhart, B. (1998). An empirical analysis of a skill-based pay program and plant performance outcomes. *Academy of Management Journal, 41*(1), 68-78.

Nahapiet, J., & Ghoshal, S. (1998). Social capital, intellectual capital and the organizational advantage. *Academy of Management Review, 23,* 242-266.

Nkomo, S. (1986). The theory and practice of HR planning: The gap still remains. *Personnel Administrator, 31*(8), 71-84.

Nonaka, I., & Takeuchi, H. (1995). *The knowledge creating company: How Japanese companies create the dynamics of innovation.* New York: Oxford University Press.

Olian, J. D., & Rynes, S. L. (1984). Organizational staffing: Integrating practice with strategy. *Industrial Relations, 23,* 170-183.

O'Reilly, C. A., & Puffer, S. M. (1989). The impact of rewards and punishments in a social context: A laboratory and field experiment. *Journal of Occupational Psychology, 62,* 41-53.

O'Reilly, C. A., & Weitz, B. A. (1980). Managing marginal employees: The use of warnings and dismissals. *Administrative Science Quarterly, 25,* 467-484.

Organ, D. (1988). *Organizational citizenship behavior.* Lexington, MA: D. C. Heath.

Osterman, P. (1987). Choice of employment systems in internal labor markets. *Industrial Relations, 26*(1), 48-63.

Osterman, P. (1995). Work/family programs and the employment relationship. *Administrative Science Quarterly, 40,* 681-700.

Ouchi, W. (1977). The relationship between organizational structure and organizational control. *Administrative Science Quarterly, 22,* 95-113.

Ouchi, W. (1980). Markets, hierarchies, and clans. *Administrative Science Quarterly, 20,* 129-141.

Ouchi, W. (1981). *Theory Z: How American companies can meet the Japanese challenge.* Reading, MA: Addison-Wesley.

Ouchi, W., & Maguire, M. A. (1975). Organizational control: Two functions. *Administrative Science Quarterly, 20,* 559-569.

Perlow, L. A. (1998). Boundary control: The social ordering of work and family time in high technology corporations. *Administrative Science Quarterly, 43,* 328-357.

Perrow, C. (1961). The analysis of goals in complex organizations. *American Sociological Review, 26,* 688-699.

Perrow, C. (1979). *Complex organizations: A critical essay* (2nd ed.). Glenview, IL: Scott, Foresman.

Peters, T., & Waterman, R. (1982). *In search of excellence.* New York: Harper & Row.

Pfeffer, J. (1994). *Competitive advantage through people: Unleashing the power of the workforce.* Boston: Harvard Business School Press.

Pfeffer, J., & Baron, J. (1988). Taking the workers back out: Recent trends in the structuring of employment. *Research in Organizational Behavior, 10,* 257-303.

Pfeffer, J., & Salancik, G. R. (1977). Organizational context and the characteristics and tenure of hospital administrators. *Academy of Management Journal, 20,* 74-88.

Pfeffer, J., & Salancik, G. R. (1978). *The external control of organizations.* New York: Harper & Row.

Pil, F. K., & MacDuffie, J. P. (1996). The adoption of high-involvement work practices. *Industrial Relations, 35,* 423-455.

Pinfield, L. T., & Berner, M. F. (1994). Employment systems: Toward coherent conceptualization of internal labor market. *Research in Personnel and Human Resource Management, 12,* 41-78.

Piore, M., & Sable, C. (1984). Why companies might be moving steadily towards specialization and flexibility. *International Management, 39*(10), 97-100.

Porter, M. E. (1980). *Competitive strategy.* New York: Free Press.

Porter, M. E. (1985). *Competitive advantage: Creating and sustaining superior performance.* New York: Free Press.

Powell, W., & DiMaggio, P. J. (Eds.). (1991). *The new institutionalism in organizational analysis.* Chicago: University of Chicago Press.

Prahalad, C. K., & Hamel, G. (1990, May-June). The core competence of the corporation. *Harvard Business Review, 68,* 79-91.

Premack, S. L., & Wanous, J. P. (1985). A meta-analysis of realistic job preview experiments. *Journal of Psychology, 70,* 706-719.

Quinn, J. B (1978, Fall). Strategic change: The logic of incrementalism. *Sloan Management Review, 28,* 7-21.

Quinn, J. B. (1980). *Strategies for change: Logical incrementalism.* Homewood, IL: D. Irwin.

Quinn, J. B. (1988). Strategies for change. In J. B. Quinn, H. Mintzberg, & R. M. James (Eds.), *The strategy process: Concepts, contexts and cases.* Englewood Cliffs, NJ: Prentice Hall.

Rees, D. L. (1991). Grievance procedure strength and teachers' quits. *Industrial and Labor Relations Review, 45,* 31-45.

Reilly, R. R., Brown, B., Blood, M. R., & Malatesta, C. Z. (1981). The effects of realistic previews: A study and discussion of the literature. *Personnel Psychology, 34,* 823-834.

Richey, M. W. (1992). The impact of corporate downsizing on employees. *Business Forum, 17,* 9-13.

Roethlisberger, F. J., & Dickson, W. J. (1947). *Management and the worker.* Cambridge, MA: Harvard University Press.

Rogers, E. W., & Wright, P. M. (1998). Measuring organizational performance in SHRM: Problems, prospects and performance information markets. *Human Resource Management Review, 8,* 311-331.

Roman, P. M. (1982). Employee programs in major corporations in 1979: Scope, change and receptivity. In J. Deluca (Ed.), *Prevention, intervention and treatment: Concerns and models* (Alcohol and Health, Monograph 3, pp. 177-200). Washington, DC: Government Printing Office.

Roman, P. M., & Blum, T. C. (1998). The prevention of behavioral disabilities from nonwork sources: Employee assistance programs and related strategies. In T. Thompson, J. F. Burton, & D. E. Hyatt (Eds.), *New approaches to disability in the workplace* (pp. 87-120). Madison, WI: Industrial Relations Research Association.

Rousseau, D. M., & Wade-Benzoni, K. A. (1994). Linking strategy and human resource practices: How employee and customer contracts are created. *Human Resource Management, 33,* 463-489.

Rousseau, M. (1995). *Psychological contracts in organizations: Understanding written and unwritten agreements.* Thousand Oaks, CA: Sage.

Rynes, S. L. (1991). Recruitment, organizational entry, and early work adjustment: A call for new research directions. In M. D. Dunnette & L. M. Hough (Eds.), *Handbook of industrial and organizational psychology* (2nd ed., Vol. 2, pp. 399-444). Palo Alto, CA: Consulting Psychologists Press.

198 HUMAN RESOURCE STRATEGY

Schmidt, F. L., Hunter, J. E., MacKenzie, R. C., & Muldrow, T. W. (1979). Impact of valid selection procedures on workforce productivity. *Journal of Applied Psychology, 64,* 609-626.

Schneider, B., & Konz, A. M. (1989). Strategic job analysis. *Human Resource Management, 28*(1), 51-63.

Schuler, R. S. (1987). Personnel and human resource management: Choices and corporate strategy. In R. S. Schuler & S. A. Youngblood (Eds.), *Readings in personnel and human resources management* (3rd ed.). St. Paul, MN: West.

Schuler, R. S. (1992, Summer). Strategic human resources management: Linking the people with the strategic needs of the business. *Organizational Dynamics, 21,* 18-31.

Schuler, R. S., & Jackson, S. E. (1987a). Linking competitive strategies with the human resources practices. *Academy of Management Executive, 1,* 207-219.

Schuler, R. S., & Jackson, S. E. (1987b). Organization strategy and organizational level as determinants of human resources management practices. *Human Resources Planning, 10,* 125-141.

Schuster, F. E. (1986). *The Schuster report: The proven connection between people and profits.* New York: John Wiley.

Schwab, D. P. (1982). Recruiting and organizational participation. In K. M Rowland & G. R. Ferris (Eds.), *Personnel management* (pp. 103-128). Boston: Allyn & Bacon.

Seashore, S. E., & Yuchtman, E. (1967). Factorial analysis of organizational performance. *Administrative Science Quarterly, 12,* 377-395.

Senge, P. M. (1990). *The fifth discipline.* New York: Doubleday.

Sheppard, B. H., Lewicki, R., & Minton, J. (1992). *Organizational justice.* Lexington, MA: Lexington.

Shuster, M. (1983). The impact of union-management cooperation on productivity and employment. *Industrial and Labor Relations Review, 36,* 415-430.

Simon, H. A. (1947). *Administrative behavior.* New York: Macmillan.

Simon, H. A. (1991). Organizations and markets. *Journal of Economic Perspectives, 5,* 25-44.

Simon, H. A. (1993). Strategy and organizational evolution. *Strategic Management Journal, 14,* 131-142.

Smith, E. C. (1982a). Strategic business and human resources: Part I. *Personnel Journal, 61,* 606-610.

Smith, E. C. (1982b). Strategic business and human resources: Part II. *Personnel Journal, 61,* 680-683.

Snell, S. A. (1992). Control theory in strategic human resource management: The mediating effect of administrative information. *Academy of Management Journal, 35,* 292-327.

Snell, S. A., & Dean, J. W. (1992). Integrating manufacturing and human resource management: A human capital perspective. *Academy of Management Journal, 35,* 467-504.

Snell, S. A., & Dean, J. W. (1994). Strategic compensation for integrated manufacturing: The moderating effects of jobs and organizational inertia. *Academy of Management Journal, 37,* 1109-1140.

Snell, S. A., Youndt, M. A., & Wright, P. M. (1996). Establishing a framework for research in strategic human resource management: Merging source theory and organizational learning. *Research in Personnel and Human Resources Management, 14,* 61-90.

Snow, C. C., & Snell, S. A. (1993). Staffing as strategy. In N. Schmitt & W. C. Borman & Assocs. (Eds.), *Personnel selection in organizations* (pp. 448-474). San Francisco: Jossey-Bass.

Sonnenfeld, J. A., & Peiperl, M. A. (1988). Staffing policy as a strategic response: A topology of career systems. *Academy of Management Review, 13,* 588-600.

Sonnenstuhl, W. J. (1996). *Working sober.* Ithaca, NY: ILR Press.

Sonnenstuhl, W. J., & Trice, H. M. (1990). *Strategies for Employee Assistance Programs: The crucial balance.* Ithaca, NY: ILR Press.

Sonnenstuhl, W. J., & Trice, H. M. (1991). Organizations and types of occupational communities: Grid-group analysis and the linkage of organizational and occupational theory. *Research in the Sociology of Organizations, 9,* 295-318.

Stark, D. (1986). Rethinking internal labor markets: New insights from a cooperative perspective. *American Sociological Review, 51,* 492-504.

Strauss, A., Schatzman, L., Ehrlich, D., Bucher, R., & Sabshin, M. (1963). The hospital and its negotiated order. In E. Friedson (Ed.), *The hospital in modern society* (pp. 147-169). Glencoe, IL: Free Press.

Swiercz, P. M. (1995). Research update: Strategic HRM. *Human Resource Planning, 18*(3), 53-62.

Taylor, S., Beechler, S., & Napier, N. (1996). Toward an integrative model of strategic international human resource management. *Academy of Management Review, 21,* 959-985.

Teece, D. J. (1984). Economic analysis and strategic management. *California Management Review, 26*(3), 87-110.

Terpstra, D. E., & Rozell, E. J. (1993). The relationship of staffing practices to organizational level measures of performance. *Personnel Psychology, 46,* 27-48.

Thompson, J. D. (1967). *Organizations in action.* New York: McGraw-Hill.

Tomer, J. F. (1987). *Organizational capital: The path to higher productivity and well-being.* New York: Praeger.

Tosi, H. L., Werner, S., Katz, J., & Gomez-Mejia, L. R. (1998). *A meta-analysis of executive compensation studies.* Unpublished manuscript, University of Florida at Gainesville.

Triandis, H. C. (1989). The self and social behavior in differing cultural contexts. *Psychological Review, 96,* 506-520.

Truss, C., & Gratton, L. (1994). Strategic human resources management: A conceptual approach. *International Journal of Human Resources Management, 5,* 663-720.

Tully, S. (1993, September 20). The real key to creating wealth. *Fortune,* pp. 38-50.

Tyson, S. (1987). The management of the personnel function. *Journal of Management Studies, 24,* 523-532.

Ulrich, D. (1997). *Human resources champions.* Boston: Harvard Business School Press.

Vroom, V. H. (1964). *Work and motivation.* New York: John Wiley.

Walker, J. W. (1980). *Human resources planning.* New York: McGraw-Hill.

Wallace, M. J. (1991). Sustaining success with alternative rewards. In M. L. Rock & L. A. Berger (Eds.), *The compensation handbook.* New York: McGraw-Hill.

Walton, R. E. (1985). From control to commitment in the workplace. *Harvard Business Review, 63*(2), 77-84.

Weber, M. (1904). *Max Weber on the methodology of the social sciences* (E. A. Shills & H. A. Finch, Eds. & Trans.). Glencoe, IL: Free Press.

Weitzman, M. L., & Kruse, D. L. (1990). Profit sharing and productivity. In A. S. Blinder (Ed.), *Paying for productivity: A look at the evidence.* Washington, DC: Brookings Institute.

Welbourne, T. M., & Andrews, A. O. (1996). Predicting the performance of initial public offerings: Should human resource management be in the equation? *Academy of Management Journal, 39,* 891-919.

Welbourne, T. M., & Wright, P. M. (1997). *Which resources matter?* (Cornell University Working Paper 97-02). Ithaca, NY: Cornell University.

Whetten, D. A., Keiser, J. D., & Urban, T. (1995). Implications of organizational downsizing for the human resource management function. In G. R. Ferris, S. D. Rosen, & D. T. Barnum

(Eds.), *Handbook of human resource management* (pp. 282-296). Cambridge, MA: Blackwell.

Williamson, O. E. (1975). *Markets and hierarchies: Analysis and antitrust implications.* New York: Free Press.

Williamson, O. E. (1981). The economics of organization: The transaction cost approach. *American Journal of Sociology, 87,* 548-577.

Wils, T., & Dyer, L. (1984, August). *Relating business strategy to human resource strategy: Some preliminary evidence.* Paper presented at the annual meeting of the Academy of Management, Boston.

Wright, P. M., & McMahan, C. G. (1992). Theoretical perspectives for strategic human resources management. *Journal of Management, 18,* 295-319.

Wright, P. M., McMahan, G. C., McCormick, B., & Sherman, W. S. (1998). Strategy core competence and HR involvement as determinants of HR effectiveness and refinery performance. *Human Resources Management, 37,* 17-29.

Wright, P. M., & Snell, S. A. (1991). Toward an integrative view of strategic HRM. *Human Resource Management Review, 1,* 203-235.

Wright, P. M., & Snell, S. A. (1998). Toward a unifying framework for exploring fit and flexibility in strategic human resource management. *Academy of Management Review, 23,* 756-772.

Youndt, M. A., Snell, S. A., Dean, J. W., Jr., & Lepak, D. P. (1996). Human resource management, manufacturing strategy and firm performance. *Academy of Management Journal, 39,* 836-866.

Zaltman, G., Duncan, R., & Holbeck, J. (1973). *Innovations and organizations.* New York: John Wiley.

Zammuto, R. F. (1988). Organizational adaptation: Some implications of organizational ecology for strategic choice. *Journal of Management Studies, 25,* 105-120.

Zenger, T. R. (1992). Why do employers only reward extreme performance? Examining the relationships among performance, pay, and turnover. *Administrative Science Quarterly, 37,* 198-219.

Author Index

Subject Index

Agency theory, 8, 101-102, 172
Agility, 62-63
Alignment, 63
American Plan, 137
Americans with Disabilities Act (ADA), 152
Analysis, cluster/factor, 54-58
Appraisal/reward subsystem, 2, 5, 98-99, 132
  administration of, 106
  agency theory, 101-102
  appraisal choices, 117-121
  compensation-performance link, 99-102
  design of, 102-121
  egalitarianism in, 109-110
  employee equity choices, 111-117
  expectancy/equity theories, 99-100
  external equity choices, 110-111
  human capital theory and, 100-101
  human resource strategy link, 121-131
  internal equity choices, 106-110
  monetary/nonmonetary rewards, 105-106
  pay compression, 103
  pay mix, 105
  performance criteria, 112-117
  policy decisions in, 103-106
  reinforcement theory, 116
Architect management model, 3

Assistance domain, 139 (table), 147 (table), 150-155

Behavioral role theory, 7, 172
Biographical information banks (BIBs), 87
Bonus-based variable pay, 112-117
Buffering, organizational logic of, 56-57
Business strategy, 3, 4-5
  compensation systems and, 122-126, 123 (table)
  cost leadership, 40, 52
  employee role performance, 48-49, 58-59, 60-61
  employment relationship rules, 43-44
  external/internal factors in, 23, 58
  goals/logics in, 50, 51 (table), 52-54
  innovation, 52, 104
  life-cycle, 30, 31
  organizational, 23-26
  typologies of, 40-41, 48
  See also Human resource strategy formulation; Human resource strategy models
Buy option, 75-80, 86-87

Collective bargaining, 2, 156, 162

About the Authors

Peter Bamberger (PhD, 1990, Cornell University) is Senior Lecturer in human resource management and industrial relations at the Davidson Graduate School of Business Administration, Technion—Israel Institute of Management. He is also a Senior Research Associate at the Smithers Institute of the New York State School of Industrial and Labor Relations, Cornell University. Bamberger is co-editor of *Research in the Sociology of Organizations,* and his research has been published in such journals as *Administrative Science Quarterly, Industrial and Labor Relations Review, Academy of Management Journal,* and *Academy of Management Review.* His current research focuses on the formulation and impact of human resource strategy, union commitment, and peer relations in the workplace.

Ilan Meshoulam has BAs in accounting and finance from Haifa University and American University, respectively, an MB in personnel management from American University, and an MBA and DBA in behavioral sciences from Boston University. He recently joined the Faculty of Management at Haifa University. He spent over 25 years as Vice President and has held other executive positions in large high-technology firms in both Israel and the United States, such as Control Data, Digital Equipment, Intel, Elbit, and Indigo. He has served as a board member in several organizations. He also acts as consultant to large firms in Israel. He is a member of the Israeli Industrial Engineering and Management Association, the Human Resources Management Society, the World Future Society, and the Academy of Management.